Raspberry Pi for Absolute Beginners: A Step-by-Step Guide to Mastering the Basics

First Edition
Sarful Hassan

Preface

Welcome to "Raspberry Pi for Absolute Beginners". This book is designed to guide you through the exciting world of Raspberry Pi, from the very basics to advanced hands-on projects. Whether you're new to programming or looking to explore the endless possibilities of this tiny computer, this book will take you step-by-step through everything you need to know.

Who This Book Is For

This book is aimed at absolute beginners who have little or no experience with Raspberry Pi or programming. Whether you're a hobbyist, student, or someone who wants to explore the potential of the Raspberry Pi, you'll find simple explanations, helpful illustrations, and practical examples to kickstart your journey.

How This Book Is Organized

This book is divided into clear, manageable chapters, starting with an introduction to Raspberry Pi, how to set it up, and gradually moving into programming, controlling hardware, and building projects. Each chapter builds upon the last, allowing you to grow your knowledge step by step.

1. Getting Started: Setting up and configuring Raspberry Pi.
2. Networking: Connecting to the internet and sharing files.
3. Using the Operating System: Navigating the operating system and using the terminal.
4. Python Programming: Learning the basics of Python and writing your first programs.
5. Hardware Basics: Using GPIO pins, sensors, and controlling devices.
6. Motor and Sensor Control: Working with motors and sensors for various projects.
7. Displays: Connecting and using different display types with your Raspberry Pi.

What Was Left Out

To keep this book beginner-friendly, we have left out some advanced topics such as machine learning, deep integration with IoT devices, and complex robotics projects. However, you will gain enough foundational knowledge to explore those areas later.

Code Style (About the Code)

The code examples provided in this book follow clear and beginner-friendly coding standards. Each example is explained in detail, with annotations to help you understand how the code works and how to modify it for your own projects.

Release Notes
First Edition

This is the first edition of this book, developed with the intent to introduce newcomers to the world of Raspberry Pi in the simplest possible way. Future editions may include advanced topics based on reader feedback.

Conventions Used in This Book

- Bold text for important concepts and definitions.
- Code snippets in monospace font to highlight programming examples.
- Step-by-step instructions to guide you through practical exercises.

Using Code Examples

You are welcome to use the code examples provided in this book for personal or educational projects. If you're using the code in any commercial project, a simple credit to the author would be appreciated.

MechatronicsLAB.net Online Learning

We also offer additional learning resources, tutorials, and project ideas at MechatronicsLAB.net. Explore a wider range of topics and enhance your Raspberry Pi journey by visiting our website.

For any further questions, feel free to reach out to us at MechatronicsLAB.net@gmail.com.

Acknowledgments for the First Edition

This book would not have been possible without the support of many people. Special thanks go to my family and friends for their encouragement. I would also like to extend my gratitude to the Raspberry Pi community for creating such a vibrant space for innovation and learning.

Copyright

Disclaimer

Dedication

To my mother, whose unwavering support and love made all of this possible.

Table of Contents

Chapter 1: Introduction to Raspberry Pi and Setup

1.0. Introduction

This section is designed to guide you through setting up and managing your Raspberry Pi from the ground up. Whether you have no experience with computers or are completely new to the Raspberry Pi, the goal is to make the process simple and enjoyable. You'll learn about the components, how to choose the right model for your needs, how to set up your system, and much more.

What to Expect from This Section

- A step-by-step, beginner-friendly approach to setting up and using your Raspberry Pi.
- Clear explanations of technical terms and hardware components.
- Hands-on tips for getting your Raspberry Pi up and running quickly.
- Guidance on selecting the right accessories and operating system to maximize your experience.

Why Raspberry Pi Is Perfect for Beginners

- **Affordable and Accessible:** Raspberry Pi is a cost-effective way to dive into computing, and its wide availability makes it easy to get started.
- **Versatile and Compact:** Despite its small size, the Raspberry Pi is incredibly powerful and can be used for a variety of projects, from simple tasks like browsing the web to more complex tasks like building a home automation system.
- **Large Support Community:** With many resources available online, including forums, tutorials, and guides, Raspberry Pi is supported by a vast community that's always ready to help beginners.

- **Learn While Doing:** Raspberry Pi encourages hands-on learning, which makes it ideal for beginners to explore coding, electronics, and project-building.

1.1. What is a Raspberry Pi?

A **Raspberry Pi** is a small, affordable computer that you can use to learn programming, build projects, and experiment with different technologies. It's about the size of a credit card, but it can do many of the things that a regular desktop computer can do, like browsing the internet, playing videos, and even coding. Raspberry Pi is ideal for beginners because it's inexpensive, easy to set up, and versatile for different projects.

Brief History of the Raspberry Pi

The **Raspberry Pi Foundation** created the first Raspberry Pi in 2012 with the goal of making computing and programming more accessible to students and hobbyists. The idea came from a need for an affordable computer to teach coding, especially for young people. Since its release, the Raspberry Pi has evolved through several versions, each adding more power and capabilities, but keeping the low-cost, beginner-friendly approach. Today, it's used worldwide not just in education but also in industries, hobbyist projects, and even research.

Understanding What It Can Do

A Raspberry Pi can do an incredible variety of things, from basic tasks like:

- **Browsing the web**
- **Watching videos**
- **Word processing**
- **Programming in languages like Python and Scratch**

It can also handle more advanced projects like:

- **Building a home media centre**
- **Creating a personal web server**
- **Building a robot**

- **Automating tasks in your home (like controlling lights or appliances)**

It's often used in DIY electronics, thanks to its GPIO pins, which allow you to connect it to sensors, LEDs, motors, and other components. You can control these parts through coding, making it a powerful tool for learning about electronics and coding at the same time.

1.2. Understanding the Components

When starting with a Raspberry Pi, it's important to familiarise yourself with its components, such as the different models, ports, and connectors, which will help you understand how to use accessories and set up various projects. Let's break down each part in a beginner-friendly way.

Overview of Raspberry Pi Models

Raspberry Pi comes in several versions, each with different features and price points. Here's a basic breakdown of the most common models:

- **Raspberry Pi 4**: The most powerful and latest full-size model, available with 2GB, 4GB, or 8GB of RAM. Ideal for tasks like programming, media centres, and even light desktop use.
- **Raspberry Pi 3**: A step down in power, but still very capable for projects like home automation or robotics.
- **Raspberry Pi Zero**: A smaller, more affordable version meant for simpler tasks or when space is limited. Great for embedded projects like digital picture frames.

Each model varies in processing power, RAM, and the number of ports available, so the choice depends on the type of project you want to work on.

Explaining Ports and Connectors (USB, HDMI, GPIO, etc.)

Each Raspberry Pi model comes with different **ports and connectors** to attach accessories like keyboards, monitors, or external sensors. Here's a breakdown of the most common ones:

- **USB Ports**: Used to connect peripherals like a keyboard, mouse, or external storage. Some models come with multiple USB ports, including both USB 2.0 and faster USB 3.0 options (Pi 4).
- **HDMI Port**: Allows you to connect a monitor or TV to display the output. Some Raspberry Pi models, like the Pi 4, have two micro-HDMI ports for dual displays, while others, like the Pi Zero, have a mini-HDMI.
- **Ethernet Port**: For wired internet connection. This is available on models like the Pi 4 and Pi 3. For models without this, like the Pi Zero, you can use a USB-to-Ethernet adapter.
- **GPIO Pins (General Purpose Input/Output)**: A set of pins that allow you to connect various electronic components like LEDs, sensors, motors, etc., directly to your Pi. These pins are crucial for building DIY projects and interacting with external hardware.
- **MicroSD Slot**: This is where you insert the microSD card, which serves as the storage for the operating system and data.
- **Audio Jack**: On models like the Pi 4, this allows you to connect speakers or headphones.

What Is a GPIO Pin and How Does It Work?

GPIO (General Purpose Input/Output) pins are one of the Raspberry Pi's most exciting features for beginners. These pins allow your Pi to interact with the world by controlling hardware like sensors, motors, and LEDs. Here's how they work in simple terms:

- The GPIO pins can either **send** or **receive** electrical signals.
    - When **sending**, you can control devices like lights or motors (e.g., turning an LED on or off).
    - When **receiving**, they can detect signals from other hardware like sensors (e.g., when a button is pressed).

You can control these pins using code (Python is the most common language for this), allowing you to build projects like simple home automation systems, robots, or weather stations.

Why It's Important:

Understanding the GPIO pins unlocks the potential of the Raspberry Pi for building interactive projects. Knowing how to use them allows you to go beyond using the Pi as a simple computer and start creating custom hardware setups.

What Are Heat Sinks and Do You Need Them?

A **heat sink** is a small metal device that you attach to components like the processor to help dissipate heat. Heat sinks are essential for keeping your Raspberry Pi cool, especially when you are running demanding applications like gaming or continuous processing (e.g., using it as a server).

- **Do You Need Them?** If you plan on using your Raspberry Pi for lightweight tasks like learning to code or simple web browsing, you likely won't need heat sinks. However, if you're going to be running more resource-intensive projects, such as overclocking the CPU (making it run faster than normal), using heat sinks can help prevent overheating and maintain performance.

Use if Needed:

- **When to Install Heat Sinks**: If your Raspberry Pi is running hot, especially during gaming, 3D rendering, or server tasks, adding heat sinks (and possibly a fan) will help keep the temperature in check, preventing system slowdowns or crashes.

1.3. Selecting a Model of Raspberry Pi

Choosing the right **Raspberry Pi model** is crucial for ensuring that your project runs smoothly, fits within your budget, and meets your performance needs. In this section, we'll help beginners understand how to pick the best Raspberry Pi model for their project.

Raspberry Pi Model Comparison for Beginners

Raspberry Pi comes in several models, each with different specifications and uses. Here's a quick comparison of the most common models:

- **Raspberry Pi 4 Model B**: The most powerful model available, with options for 2GB, 4GB, or 8GB of RAM. This is ideal for high-performance projects such as using it as a desktop computer, media center, or running multiple services simultaneously.
- **Raspberry Pi 3 Model B+**: A less powerful but still highly capable model. It's perfect for projects like robotics, simple servers, or learning to code. It also comes with built-in Wi-Fi and Bluetooth.
- **Raspberry Pi Zero 2 W**: A smaller and more affordable version, ideal for simple projects that don't require as much processing power. It's great for low-cost DIY projects like IoT devices or small robots.
- **Raspberry Pi Pico**: This is a microcontroller, not a full computer like the other models. It's best for projects where you want to control specific hardware (like sensors or motors), and it's extremely low-cost, but it can't run an operating system.

Which Model Suits Your Project or Needs?

Here's a guide to help you choose the best Raspberry Pi model based on what you want to achieve:

- **General Computing and Learning to Code**: The **Raspberry Pi 4 Model B** is your best choice. Its increased RAM and processing power mean it can handle web browsing, running programming environments, and even media streaming.
- **Simple Robotics or Electronics Projects**: The **Raspberry Pi 3 Model B+** or **Raspberry Pi Zero 2 W** are great choices for lightweight projects like controlling lights, sensors, or small motors. They have enough processing power for basic tasks and are more budget-friendly.
- **IoT or Embedded Systems**: If you want to build a smart home device or sensor system, the **Raspberry Pi Zero 2 W** is ideal. It's small, affordable, and has built-in wireless connectivity.
- **Advanced Desktop or Media Center**: The **Raspberry Pi 4 Model B** with 4GB or 8GB RAM is your go-to model. It's powerful enough to function as a mini desktop or a media center that can stream HD videos.

Budget-Friendly Models for Beginners

If you're just starting out and want to experiment without spending much, here are the most budget-friendly options:

- **Raspberry Pi Zero 2 W**: It's incredibly affordable (usually around $10-$15) and perfect for simple DIY projects or learning to code. However, keep in mind that its performance is lower than the full-sized models.
- **Raspberry Pi 3 Model B+**: Though not as powerful as the Pi 4, it's more than sufficient for most beginners, and it's cheaper than the Pi 4. If you're on a budget and need something more versatile, this is a great option.
- **Raspberry Pi Pico**: At around $4, the Pico is perfect if you want to start small with microcontroller-based projects. It

won't run a full operating system, but it's excellent for controlling hardware.

Which Raspberry Pi Model Should You Start With?

For most beginners, the **Raspberry Pi 4 Model B** (with 2GB or 4GB RAM) is a great starting point. It's powerful, flexible, and can handle a wide variety of projects, from learning to code to creating more advanced systems like media centers or small servers.

However, if your budget is tight or your project doesn't require as much power, the **Raspberry Pi 3 Model B+** or **Raspberry Pi Zero 2 W** are also great choices. Both models are beginner-friendly and can be used for basic electronics, learning programming, and simple robotics.

Why It's Important:

Choosing the right Raspberry Pi model affects your project's success and your budget. If you pick a model that's too underpowered, you might struggle to complete your project, while an overpowered model could waste money on unnecessary performance. By selecting the model that matches your needs, you can ensure your project runs smoothly and efficiently without overspending.

1.4. What You'll Need to Get Started (Kit Essentials)

Getting started with a Raspberry Pi is simple, but having the right components and accessories will make the process smoother and help you avoid issues. Let's go over the essential items you need and some optional accessories that can improve your experience.

Basic Kit Components (Pi, microSD, power supply, etc.)

At a minimum, you'll need the following **basic components** to get your Raspberry Pi up and running:

- **Raspberry Pi Board**: This is the main component. Depending on your project, choose a model that fits your needs (e.g., Pi 4 for general use, Pi Zero 2 W for smaller projects).

- **microSD Card**: This acts as your Raspberry Pi's storage and is where the operating system will be installed. A 16GB or 32GB card is a good starting point, but for larger projects, you might want more capacity.
- **Power Supply**: Each Raspberry Pi model requires a specific power supply. For example, the Pi 4 needs a 5V/3A USB-C power supply, while the Pi 3 uses a 5V/2.5A micro-USB power supply.
- **HDMI Cable**: This connects your Raspberry Pi to a monitor or TV. For the Pi 4, you'll need a micro-HDMI to HDMI cable; older models use a standard HDMI cable.
- **Keyboard and Mouse**: These are required for interacting with the Pi unless you're running it headless (without a display). Any USB keyboard and mouse will work.
- **Monitor**: Any monitor or TV with an HDMI input will work. This is optional if you're planning to run your Raspberry Pi without a display (e.g., accessing it remotely).

Optional Accessories (Case, camera, heatsink, etc.)

While not strictly necessary, **optional accessories** can enhance your Raspberry Pi's capabilities:

- **Case**: Protects your Pi from dust and physical damage. Essential if you're placing your Pi in a rough environment or plan on moving it around.
- **Heat Sinks**: Helps cool your Raspberry Pi during intensive tasks, like gaming or running a server. These are small metal pieces that attach to the processor and other heat-generating components.
- **Camera Module**: The official Raspberry Pi camera module is great for photography, video projects, and even computer vision applications.
- **USB Hub**: If you need more USB ports, especially on models like the Pi Zero, a powered USB hub can be very useful.

- **Touchscreen Display**: If you want to make a portable project, a touchscreen can eliminate the need for an external monitor.
- **GPIO Header Kit**: If you're working with electronics, a GPIO kit will make it easier to connect sensors, LEDs, and other components.

Do You Need a Case for Your Pi?

A **case** is not always required, but it is highly recommended for several reasons:

- **Protection**: It protects the board from physical damage, dust, and spills. If your Raspberry Pi is going to be used in a harsh environment, a case is essential.
- **Aesthetics**: A case makes your Raspberry Pi look more polished, especially for projects like media centers.
- **Cooling**: Some cases come with built-in ventilation or space for adding heat sinks and fans, which can help keep your Pi cool during heavy use.

Use if Needed:

- If you're using the Pi in a **permanent setup** (e.g., a desktop replacement or a media center), a case is a good idea. If you're working on **short-term projects** or **experiments**, you might not need one.

How to Choose a Suitable Case for Your Raspberry Pi

Choosing the right case depends on your project and needs. Here are some factors to consider:

- **Model Compatibility**: Make sure the case is designed for your specific Raspberry Pi model (e.g., Pi 4, Pi Zero, etc.). Different models have different port placements, so not all cases will fit.
- **Material**: Cases come in plastic, metal, or even wood. Plastic cases are affordable and lightweight, while metal cases offer better durability and cooling.

- **Cooling**: If your Raspberry Pi will be running resource-heavy tasks, consider a case that has space for heat sinks or fans to keep the system cool.
- **Design**: Some cases offer easy access to GPIO pins and other connectors, while others provide a sleek, fully enclosed design.

Can You Use Any Keyboard and Mouse with Raspberry Pi?

Yes, you can use **any standard USB keyboard and mouse** with the Raspberry Pi. Wireless USB keyboards and mice also work, but here are a few things to consider:

- **Wired vs. Wireless**: A wired USB keyboard and mouse work straight out of the box. If you use a wireless set, make sure the USB receiver is compatible, as some models may require special drivers.
- **Bluetooth Keyboards and Mice**: The Raspberry Pi 4 and Pi 3 come with built-in Bluetooth, so you can also connect Bluetooth peripherals. However, initial setup might require a wired keyboard and mouse to configure Bluetooth.

Why It's Important:

Choosing compatible peripherals, like the right keyboard, mouse, or case, helps avoid setup issues and ensures smooth operation. This is particularly important for beginners who want to get their Raspberry Pi running without troubleshooting hardware compatibility problems.

1.5. Selecting a Power Supply

Selecting the correct power supply is crucial for the safe and efficient operation of your Raspberry Pi. Using the wrong power supply can result in poor performance or even damage to your Pi. Let's walk through the basics of choosing the right one.

How to Choose the Right Power Supply for Your Pi Model

Each Raspberry Pi model has specific power requirements, and it's important to match the correct power supply to ensure it works properly. Here's a simple guide:

- **Raspberry Pi 4 (Model B)**: Requires a **5V/3A USB-C** power supply. The Pi 4 uses more power than previous models due to its increased performance.
- **Raspberry Pi 3 (Model B/B+)**: Requires a **5V/2.5A micro-USB** power supply. It uses less power than the Pi 4 but more than the Pi Zero.
- **Raspberry Pi Zero (Model W/2 W)**: Requires a **5V/1.2A micro-USB** power supply. This is a low-power device, so it doesn't need as much current as the full-sized Pi models.
- **Raspberry Pi Pico**: As a microcontroller, it typically requires power through a **USB port** but can also run off of battery power with different voltage inputs.

Understanding Voltage and Amperage Requirements

When selecting a power supply, two key factors to consider are **voltage** and **amperage**:

- **Voltage (V)**: This is the amount of electrical potential the power supply delivers. The **Raspberry Pi requires a 5V power supply**. Anything higher than 5V could damage the board.
- **Amperage (A)**: This is the current, or the amount of electricity flowing to the device. The amperage depends on the model:

- Raspberry Pi 4: 3A (or higher, if you're connecting power-hungry peripherals).
- Raspberry Pi 3: 2.5A.
- Raspberry Pi Zero: 1.2A.

A power supply with higher amperage than required is safe to use (e.g., using a 5V/3A supply on a Raspberry Pi 3). The Raspberry Pi will only draw the current it needs. However, using a power supply with **lower amperage** can cause instability, as the Pi won't get enough power to run properly.

What Happens if You Use the Wrong Power Supply?

Using an improper power supply can lead to several issues:

- **Insufficient Amperage**: If the power supply cannot provide enough current (amperage), the Raspberry Pi might underperform, crash, or reboot frequently. You might also see a **low voltage warning** (a rainbow square or lightning bolt) on the screen, indicating that the Pi is not receiving enough power.
- **Excessive Voltage**: Using a power supply that delivers more than 5V can permanently damage your Raspberry Pi. Higher voltage can overheat components and cause malfunctions.
- **Overheating**: Inadequate power can cause the Pi to overheat as it struggles to function properly, especially when running demanding applications or when multiple peripherals are connected.

How to Check if Your Power Supply Is Safe for Your Pi

Here are a few steps to ensure that the power supply you're using is safe and compatible with your Raspberry Pi:

- **Check the Label**: Make sure the power supply provides **5V** and the appropriate **amperage** for your Raspberry Pi model (e.g., 3A for Pi 4, 2.5A for Pi 3).
- **Official Power Supply**: The safest choice is to use the **official Raspberry Pi power supply**, which is designed

specifically for each model. These are reliable and ensure that the correct voltage and amperage are delivered.

- **Avoid Cheap or Unreliable Chargers**: Smartphone chargers or unbranded USB power supplies may not deliver stable power, especially over long periods. These can cause voltage drops, which will affect the performance of your Raspberry Pi.
- **Test with a Different Supply**: If you're experiencing crashes or a low voltage warning, try using a different power supply to see if the issue persists. This is a good indicator that the power supply is inadequate or faulty.
- **Look for Safety Certifications**: Make sure the power supply has been certified for safety standards (e.g., CE, UL). This reduces the risk of using a low-quality power adapter that could damage your Raspberry Pi.

1.6. Selecting an Operating System

Choosing the right **Operating System (OS)** for your Raspberry Pi is key to how smoothly your projects run. The OS manages the hardware and software resources on your Pi, and different operating systems are optimized for different types of tasks.

What Is an Operating System (OS)?

An **Operating System (OS)** is the software that manages all the hardware and software on your Raspberry Pi. It allows you to run programs, interact with peripherals, and manage files. Without an OS, your Raspberry Pi wouldn't be able to perform any tasks.

The OS acts as a bridge between the user and the hardware, helping you run applications like a web browser, word processor, or coding environment.

Popular Operating Systems for Raspberry Pi

There are several operating systems that can run on the Raspberry Pi, each designed for different use cases. Here are the most popular ones:

- **Raspberry Pi OS (formerly Raspbian)**: This is the official operating system for the Raspberry Pi, specifically designed to run efficiently on Pi hardware. It's based on the Linux operating system, and it comes pre-installed with useful software like Python, Scratch, and a web browser.
- **Ubuntu**: A popular Linux distribution that is more full-featured and robust but requires more system resources. Ubuntu on Raspberry Pi is great for users who are familiar with Linux or need to run more complex applications.
- **RetroPie**: Designed for gaming, RetroPie allows you to turn your Raspberry Pi into a retro gaming console. It includes emulators for a wide variety of gaming systems.
- **LibreELEC**: A lightweight OS focused on creating a media centre. It's designed to run **Kodi**, a popular home media player software, so you can easily turn your Pi into a streaming device.
- **Twister OS**: Twister OS offers a user-friendly, Windows-like interface and comes with various tools and applications, making it a good choice for those who want an easy transition into using Raspberry Pi.

Which Operating System Is Best for Beginners?

For beginners, **Raspberry Pi OS** is the best choice. It's lightweight, optimized for the Raspberry Pi hardware, and comes pre-installed with all the tools you need to get started right away.

- **Why Raspberry Pi OS?**
  - **Beginner-Friendly**: It's designed with beginners in mind, providing an easy-to-use desktop environment similar to what you'd find on a regular PC.
  - **Pre-installed Software**: It comes with essential software for programming (like Python), web browsing, and basic office tools, so you can start working on projects immediately without needing to install extra applications.
  - **Great Support**: There's a huge community and a wealth of tutorials, guides, and support forums specifically for Raspberry Pi OS, making it easier to find help when you need it.

If you're already familiar with Linux or want to explore more advanced tasks, **Ubuntu** can be a good alternative. But for most beginners, Raspberry Pi OS provides the simplest, most straightforward experience.

What Is Raspberry Pi OS and Why Use It?

Raspberry Pi OS is the official operating system created by the Raspberry Pi Foundation. It's based on Debian Linux but is optimized for Raspberry Pi hardware to provide a smooth, efficient experience. Here's why you should use it:

- **Optimised for Raspberry Pi**: Since Raspberry Pi OS is specifically designed for Pi hardware, it's optimised to run fast and efficiently, even on lower-powered models like the Pi Zero.
- **Pre-installed Applications**: It includes a variety of pre-installed software, such as:

- Programming tools: Python, Scratch, Thonny IDE, and more.
  - **Programming tools**: Python, Scratch, Thonny IDE, and more.
  - **Internet tools**: Chromium web browser, email clients, and network tools.
  - **Office software**: Word processing and spreadsheet applications.
  - **Educational tools**: Perfect for learning coding, electronics, and computing.
- **Customizable and Lightweight**: You can customise it to suit your needs while keeping the system lightweight, ensuring that even the more basic Raspberry Pi models can run smoothly.
- **User-Friendly Desktop**: It provides a desktop interface that is easy to navigate, similar to a traditional computer OS like Windows or macOS, making it approachable for beginners.

Why It's Important:

Selecting the right operating system can significantly impact your Raspberry Pi's performance and how easily you can use it. **Raspberry Pi OS** is optimized for beginners, making it a great starting point for learning and experimentation. With the right OS, you can ensure that your projects run smoothly, your Pi remains stable, and you get the most out of your experience.

1.7. How to Download and Prepare Your Operating System

To use your Raspberry Pi, you'll need to download an **Operating System (OS)** and install it onto a microSD card. Preparing the OS properly ensures that your Raspberry Pi boots up smoothly and works correctly from the start. Let's walk through the process.

Downloading the OS Image

An **OS image** is a file that contains all the necessary components to run the operating system on your Raspberry Pi. Follow these steps to download the image:

1. **Choose Your Operating System**: For beginners, it's recommended to use **Raspberry Pi OS**, which can be downloaded from the official Raspberry Pi website.
    ○ Go to the official Raspberry Pi website: Raspberry Pi Downloads
    ○ Choose **Raspberry Pi OS (32-bit)** for a simple desktop experience.
2. **Download the OS Image**: You can download the OS as an image file, which will typically be in a **.img** or compressed **.zip** format. The file size might be large (around 1-2 GB), so be patient during the download.

Using Tools like Raspberry Pi Imager

Once you've downloaded the OS image, the next step is to write it onto a microSD card. The easiest way to do this is by using a tool called **Raspberry Pi Imager**. Here's a step-by-step guide:

1. **Download Raspberry Pi Imager**:
    ○ Go to the Raspberry Pi Imager download page.
    ○ Download the version that matches your computer's operating system (Windows, macOS, or Linux).
    ○ Install it on your computer.
2. **Insert the microSD Card**: Insert a **microSD card** (at least 16GB recommended) into your computer using a card reader.

3. **Open Raspberry Pi Imager**:
   - Open the Imager tool, and you'll see a simple interface with three options: **Choose OS**, **Choose Storage**, and **Write**.
4. **Choose the Operating System**:
   - Click **Choose OS**, and select **Raspberry Pi OS** from the list of available options. If you already downloaded the OS image manually, you can select **Use custom** to choose the downloaded file.
5. **Select the microSD Card**:
   - Click **Choose Storage**, and select the microSD card you inserted.
6. **Write the Image**:
   - After selecting the OS and the microSD card, click **Write**. The Raspberry Pi Imager will format the microSD card and write the OS image to it. This may take a few minutes.
7. **Eject the microSD Card**:
   - Once the process is complete, safely eject the microSD card from your computer. You can now insert the card into your Raspberry Pi.

1.8. Writing a microSD Card with NOOBS

NOOBS (New Out Of the Box Software) is an easy-to-use operating system installer for Raspberry Pi. It's designed for beginners who want a simple way to install an operating system without worrying about technical details. NOOBS includes multiple OS options, so you can choose which one to install when you first set up your Raspberry Pi.

What Is NOOBS and Why Use It?

NOOBS is essentially a beginner-friendly installer that helps you install an operating system (or multiple OSs) on your Raspberry Pi with minimal effort. Here's why NOOBS can be useful:

- **Simplifies Installation**: NOOBS comes with several OS options, so you don't need to download and prepare each

OS manually. It offers a menu where you can pick the OS you want to install.

- **Multiple OS Options**: It includes **Raspberry Pi OS** (the official OS) and other choices like **LibreELEC** (for media centers) or **RISC OS** (for lightweight computing).
- **Easy to Switch**: If you're unsure which OS is best for you, NOOBS makes it easy to switch between different operating systems.
- **Built-In Recovery Mode**: If something goes wrong, NOOBS includes a recovery mode to help you reinstall the OS without starting from scratch.

Writing NOOBS on an SD Card

Here's how you can install NOOBS on your microSD card:

1. **Download NOOBS**:
   - Visit the official Raspberry Pi Downloads page.
   - Download **NOOBS** (offline and network install) or **NOOBS Lite** (only includes a small installer and requires an internet connection to download the OS). NOOBS Lite is recommended if you have stable Wi-Fi.
2. **Format the microSD Card**:
   - Use a tool like **SD Card Formatter** (available for free) to format your microSD card. This will prepare the card for NOOBS installation.
   - Ensure the card is formatted as **FAT32**.
3. **Extract NOOBS Files**:
   - Once the NOOBS zip file is downloaded, **extract** the contents of the zip file to a folder on your computer.
4. **Copy NOOBS to the microSD Card**:
   - Copy all the extracted files from the NOOBS folder onto the **root directory** of your microSD card. Make sure that you don't place the files inside any sub-folder.
5. **Eject the microSD Card**:
   - Safely eject the microSD card from your computer.
6. **Insert the microSD Card into Your Raspberry Pi**:

o Insert the microSD card into the **microSD slot** of your Raspberry Pi.

7. **Power on the Raspberry Pi**:
   o Connect your Raspberry Pi to a monitor, keyboard, and power supply. Power it on.

8. **Choose Your Operating System**:
   o When your Raspberry Pi boots up, you'll see the NOOBS interface. From here, you can choose which OS to install (e.g., Raspberry Pi OS, LibreELEC, etc.).
   o Select your preferred operating system and click **Install**.

9. **Wait for Installation**:
   o NOOBS will download and install the selected OS. This process may take a few minutes depending on your internet connection (if using NOOBS Lite) and the size of the OS.

10. **Restart and Begin**:
    o Once the OS installation is complete, your Raspberry Pi will restart, and you'll be taken to the OS you just installed.

Use if Needed:

NOOBS is an excellent tool if you're not sure which OS to choose or if you want a simple, guided way to install an operating system. It's also useful for beginners who might feel overwhelmed by the process of manually writing an OS image to a microSD card.

1.9. Installing an Operating System Without NOOBS

Installing an operating system manually without using NOOBS gives you more control and flexibility, but it also requires a few extra steps. This method involves downloading the operating system image and writing it to a microSD card using tools like **Etcher**. Here's a beginner-friendly guide on how to do it.

How to Install OS Manually (Using Tools like Etcher)

Here's how you can manually install an operating system on your Raspberry Pi:

1. **Download the OS Image**:
   - Go to the official Raspberry Pi website or another trusted source to download the **OS image** file for your chosen operating system (e.g., Raspberry Pi OS, Ubuntu, etc.).
   - The file will typically be in **.img** or **.zip** format.
2. **Download and Install Etcher**:
   - Visit the **Etcher website** and download the tool for your operating system (Windows, macOS, or Linux).
   - Install **Etcher** on your computer. It's an easy-to-use tool for writing OS images to microSD cards.
3. **Prepare the microSD Card**:
   - Insert a microSD card (at least 16GB is recommended) into your computer using a card reader.
   - If your card isn't already formatted, you can use a tool like **SD Card Formatter** to format it to **FAT32**.
4. **Write the OS Image to the microSD Card**:
   - Open Etcher and click on **"Flash from file."**
   - Select the **OS image** you downloaded.
   - Choose the **microSD card** as the target device.
   - Click **"Flash"** to start writing the OS to the microSD card. This process may take a few minutes depending on the size of the image.
5. **Eject the microSD Card**:
   - Once Etcher has finished, safely eject the microSD card from your computer.
6. **Insert the microSD Card into Your Raspberry Pi**:
   - Insert the microSD card into the Raspberry Pi's microSD slot, and power it on. Your Raspberry Pi will boot from the newly installed operating system.

Differences Between NOOBS and Manual Installations

- **NOOBS**:
  - Simplifies the process by offering a menu of different operating systems to choose from during installation.
  - Ideal for beginners who aren't sure which OS they want to use or if they want an easy recovery option.
- **Manual Installation**:
  - Requires downloading and writing the OS image manually.
  - Gives you more control over the installation process, but you need to decide on the operating system beforehand.
  - Generally faster once the process is understood since it skips the NOOBS installer step.

Is Manual Installation Hard for Beginners?

Manual installation isn't particularly hard, but it does require a bit more understanding of the steps involved. With tools like **Etcher**, the process is simplified to just a few clicks, making it beginner-friendly. The steps can be learned quickly, and once you've done it once, it becomes an easy and fast way to install or reinstall operating systems on your Raspberry Pi.

If you prefer more flexibility and control over your setup, learning how to manually install the OS can be valuable. The key difference is that you need to download the OS image yourself and use a tool to write it to the SD card.

How to Recover If Installation Fails

If the manual installation doesn't work (for example, if the Pi doesn't boot), here are some troubleshooting steps:

1. **Check the microSD Card**:
   - Ensure the card is properly inserted into your Raspberry Pi.

- Use a reliable, **high-quality microSD card**, as some cheaper cards may cause issues.
2. **Reformat and Reflash the OS**:
   - If your Pi isn't booting, try **reformatting the microSD card** and repeating the installation process using **Etcher**.
   - Ensure you're using the correct image for your Raspberry Pi model (e.g., Raspberry Pi 4 images won't work on Raspberry Pi Zero).
3. **Try a Different OS**:
   - If one OS image fails to work, consider downloading a different operating system (e.g., switch from Ubuntu to Raspberry Pi OS) to rule out compatibility issues.
4. **Check Power Supply**:
   - Make sure you're using the correct power supply, as an inadequate power source can cause boot issues.
5. **Use a Different SD Card**:
   - Sometimes the SD card can be faulty. If the installation fails repeatedly, try using a different microSD card to see if that resolves the issue.

1.10. How to Connect the Raspberry Pi to a Monitor, Keyboard, and Mouse

Connecting your Raspberry Pi to a monitor, keyboard, and mouse is one of the first steps in setting up your Pi for the first time. This is known as setting up a **"desktop environment"** so you can interact with the Pi just like a regular computer.

Setting Up Your First Pi System

To set up your Raspberry Pi, you'll need the following:

- **Raspberry Pi board**
- **MicroSD card with an operating system** (e.g., Raspberry Pi OS)
- **Monitor or TV**
- **HDMI cable**
- **Keyboard and mouse** (wired or wireless)

- **Power supply** (compatible with your Raspberry Pi model)

Here's how to connect everything:

1. **Insert the microSD card**: Take the microSD card with the operating system installed and insert it into the microSD slot on the Raspberry Pi.
2. **Connect the HDMI cable**: Plug one end of the HDMI cable into the Raspberry Pi's **HDMI port** (micro-HDMI for Pi 4) and the other end into the **HDMI input** on your monitor or TV.
3. **Connect the keyboard and mouse**:
   - Plug your **keyboard and mouse** into the Raspberry Pi's **USB ports**. If you are using a wireless set, plug in the wireless receiver (USB dongle) into a USB port.
   - For Raspberry Pi 4 and Pi 3, there are several USB ports available. For Pi Zero, you may need a USB OTG adapter.
4. **Power on the Raspberry Pi**: Once all the peripherals are connected, plug the power supply into the Raspberry Pi's power port. The Raspberry Pi will automatically boot up, and you should see the boot sequence on your monitor.

Using HDMI and USB Ports

Here's a simple breakdown of how the **HDMI** and **USB ports** work with the Raspberry Pi:

- **HDMI Ports**:
   - Raspberry Pi 4 has **two micro-HDMI ports**, which means it supports dual monitors. You will need a **micro-HDMI to HDMI** cable for these ports.
   - Older models (like the Pi 3) use a single **standard HDMI port**, so a regular HDMI cable is sufficient.
   - If your monitor only has a DVI or VGA input, you'll need an **HDMI to DVI** or **HDMI to VGA adapter**.
- **USB Ports**:
   - The Raspberry Pi 4 and Pi 3 have multiple USB ports (Pi 4 has USB 2.0 and faster USB 3.0 ports). These

can be used to connect peripherals like keyboards, mice, USB drives, and more.

- o If you're using a **Raspberry Pi Zero**, you'll need a **USB OTG adapter** since it only has a single micro-USB port.

What to Do If Your Devices Don't Work with Raspberry Pi

Sometimes, you might encounter issues when connecting devices to your Raspberry Pi. Here are some common problems and troubleshooting steps:

- **No Display on Monitor**:
  - o **Check the HDMI cable and connections**: Make sure the HDMI cable is firmly connected to both the Raspberry Pi and the monitor. If you're using a micro-HDMI adapter, ensure that it's properly connected.
  - o **Switch HDMI ports**: If using a Raspberry Pi 4 with dual HDMI ports, try using the other HDMI port.
  - o **Monitor input settings**: Ensure your monitor is set to the correct HDMI input channel.
  - o **Test with a different monitor**: If possible, try connecting the Raspberry Pi to a different monitor or TV to rule out monitor issues.
  - o **Power supply issues**: Ensure the Raspberry Pi is receiving enough power. If the power supply is insufficient, it may not fully boot up.
- **Keyboard/Mouse Not Working**:
  - o **Use wired peripherals**: Some wireless keyboards and mice may not work properly with the Raspberry Pi, especially during the initial setup. Try using a wired USB keyboard and mouse instead.
  - o **Check USB ports**: Test each USB port to make sure they are functioning. If one port doesn't work, try using another.
  - o **Test with another device**: Plug the keyboard/mouse into another computer to ensure they are working correctly.

- **Low Power Issues**:
    - ○ If you see a **rainbow square** or **lightning bolt icon** on the screen, this indicates a low-power supply. Make sure you're using a power supply that meets the **Raspberry Pi's power requirements** (e.g., 5V/3A for Pi 4).

1.11. Connecting to Wi-Fi or Ethernet

Getting your Raspberry Pi connected to the internet is essential for many projects, such as installing software, updating the system, or accessing your Pi remotely. Whether you prefer Wi-Fi or a wired Ethernet connection, this section will guide you through setting up internet access on your Raspberry Pi.

How to Set Up Internet on Raspberry Pi

There are two primary ways to connect your Raspberry Pi to the internet: **Wi-Fi** and **Ethernet**. Here's how to set them up:

1. Connecting via Wi-Fi:

- **For Raspberry Pi with desktop interface**:
    1. **Boot up your Raspberry Pi** and ensure you're on the desktop.
    2. In the top-right corner of the screen, click the **Wi-Fi icon**.
    3. A list of available networks will appear. Select your network from the list.
    4. Enter your **Wi-Fi password** when prompted and click **OK**.
    5. The Wi-Fi icon will update to show signal strength once connected.

- **For headless setup (without monitor)**:
    1. If you're setting up your Pi without a monitor (headless), you can configure Wi-Fi by adding a file to the **boot partition** of your microSD card.

After writing the OS to the card, insert it into your computer, and add a file named `wpa_supplicant.conf` with the following content:

```
country=US # Replace with your country code
ctrl_interface=DIR=/var/run/wpa_supplicant GROUP=netdev
update_config=1

network={
  ssid="Your_Network_Name"
  psk="Your_Network_Password"
}
```

2. Save the file and eject the microSD card.
3. Insert the card into your Raspberry Pi and boot it up. The Pi should automatically connect to the Wi-Fi network you specified.

2. Connecting via Ethernet:

- Plug an **Ethernet cable** directly into your Raspberry Pi's **Ethernet port** (available on Pi 3 and Pi 4 models).
- Connect the other end of the cable to your **router** or **network switch**.
- The Raspberry Pi will automatically connect to the network via Ethernet, and no additional setup is required.

Wi-Fi vs. Ethernet: What's Better for Your Setup?

Both Wi-Fi and Ethernet have their advantages, and the best choice depends on your setup:

- **Wi-Fi (Wireless)**:
    - **Advantages**:
        - No need for cables, making it more flexible for setups where the Pi is located far from the router.
        - Portable, especially useful for projects where the Pi might move around (e.g., mobile robots, IoT devices).
    - **Disadvantages**:

- Potentially slower and less reliable than Ethernet, depending on your Wi-Fi signal strength.
- May experience interference or dropouts, especially in crowded or weak signal areas.
- **Ethernet (Wired)**:
  - **Advantages**:
    - Provides a faster and more reliable connection than Wi-Fi.
    - Ideal for projects that require constant, high-speed internet (e.g., network servers, media centers).
  - **Disadvantages**:
    - Requires a physical connection to the router or network switch, limiting where you can place your Raspberry Pi.

Which is better?

- **For general use and convenience**, Wi-Fi is often the easiest choice, especially if your Pi will be used in a remote location or if cables are inconvenient.
- **For projects that require high performance or stable connectivity**, Ethernet is the better option because it provides faster speeds and more reliable connections.

How to Troubleshoot Wi-Fi Connection Issues

If your Raspberry Pi is having trouble connecting to Wi-Fi, here are a few troubleshooting tips:

1. **Check Signal Strength**:
   - If your Pi is too far from the router, the Wi-Fi signal may be weak. Try moving the Pi closer to the router or using an Ethernet cable to test the connection.
2. **Verify Wi-Fi Credentials**:
   - Double-check that you've entered the correct **SSID (network name)** and **password**. Even a small typo can prevent your Pi from connecting.

3. **Check Wi-Fi Configuration File (Headless Setup)**:
    ○ If you're using the headless setup, make sure the `wpa_supplicant.conf` file is correctly formatted. Even small formatting errors can prevent the Pi from connecting to Wi-Fi.
4. **Reboot the Raspberry Pi**:
    ○ Sometimes simply rebooting the Pi can resolve connection issues.
5. **Update Your System**:

Run the following commands to make sure your Raspberry Pi's Wi-Fi drivers and software are up-to-date:

```
sudo apt update
sudo apt upgrade
```

6. **Check for Interference**:
    ○ Wi-Fi signals can sometimes suffer from interference from other devices or networks. You can try changing the Wi-Fi channel on your router to reduce interference.
7. **Network Compatibility**:
    ○ Ensure that your router is compatible with the Pi's Wi-Fi standards. For example, some older routers only support 2.4GHz networks, while the Raspberry Pi 4 can connect to both 2.4GHz and 5GHz networks.
8. **Use an Ethernet Cable**:
    ○ If Wi-Fi issues persist and you need a quick solution, connect the Raspberry Pi to your router using an Ethernet cable to ensure stable internet access.

1.12. First Boot and Initial Setup

Once you've connected all the components and inserted the microSD card with the operating system, you're ready to boot up your Raspberry Pi for the first time. This section will walk you through what to expect and how to complete the initial setup.

What to Expect on First Boot

When you power on your Raspberry Pi for the first time:

1. **Startup Sequence**: You'll see the Raspberry Pi logo and a series of boot messages scrolling across the screen. This is normal—it's the system initializing all its components.
2. **Welcome Screen**: If you are using **Raspberry Pi OS**, you'll be greeted by the **Welcome to Raspberry Pi** setup screen. This will guide you through configuring your Pi for the first time.
3. **Mouse and Keyboard**: Make sure your keyboard and mouse are working. If they aren't, check the USB connections or try using a different port.

Configuring Your Raspberry Pi (Language, Time Zone, etc.)

After the boot sequence, you'll go through an initial configuration setup:

1. **Select Language and Region**:
   - You'll be prompted to select your **language**, **country**, and **keyboard layout**. For example, if you're in the United States, select **English (US)**.
   - Click **Next** to continue.
2. **Set Time Zone**:
   - Select your **time zone** from the list to ensure that your Pi displays the correct time and date.
   - Click **Next** to proceed.
3. **Change Password**:
   - By default, the username is **pi**, and the password is **raspberry**. You'll be prompted to change this to something more secure.
   - Enter a new password and click **Next**.
4. **Connect to Wi-Fi (if applicable)**:
   - If you're using Wi-Fi, you'll be asked to connect to your **Wi-Fi network**. Select your network, enter the password, and connect.
   - If you're using Ethernet, you can skip this step.

5. **Check for Updates**:
   - ○ The system will automatically check for updates to ensure your Raspberry Pi is running the latest software. It's recommended to let the system update during this step.
   - ○ Click **Next** and wait while updates are installed.
6. **Set Up Screen Resolution**:
   - ○ The system may ask you to adjust the screen resolution based on your monitor or display setup. You can select a resolution from the list or leave it as **default**.
7. **Reboot**:
   - ○ After the configuration is complete, the Raspberry Pi will prompt you to reboot to apply the settings. Click **Reboot** to finish the setup.

Updating the System for the First Time

After the first boot, it's important to make sure your system is fully updated:

1. **Open the Terminal**:
   - ○ On the Raspberry Pi desktop, click the **Terminal** icon (a black screen icon in the taskbar).
2. **Run Update and Upgrade Commands**:

To update the list of available software and upgrade to the latest versions, type the following commands into the terminal and press **Enter**:

```
sudo apt update
sudo apt upgrade
```

   - ○ The **update** command checks for the latest packages, and the **upgrade** command installs them. This process may take a few minutes.
3. **Reboot (if needed)**:

If the system suggests that you need to reboot after the updates, simply type:

```
sudo reboot
```

How to Know If Your Raspberry Pi Is Working Properly

There are a few ways to ensure that your Raspberry Pi is working correctly after the initial setup:

1. **Check the Display**:
   - If your Raspberry Pi boots up and you can see the desktop or command-line interface (CLI), that's a good sign everything is working.
2. **Responsive Keyboard and Mouse**:
   - Ensure your keyboard and mouse respond to input. Try opening applications, typing commands, and moving the mouse around.
3. **Internet Connection**:
   - Test the internet connection by opening the **web browser** and visiting a website. If it loads properly, your Pi is successfully connected to the internet.
4. **System Information**:

Open the terminal and type the following command to check system performance and usage:
```
htop
```

   - This will display real-time information about the CPU, memory usage, and processes running on the Raspberry Pi.
5. **No Warning Icons**:
   - Check for any **warning icons** (e.g., a rainbow square or lightning bolt) in the top-right corner of the screen. These indicate power supply or performance issues. If you see these, ensure your power supply meets the required specifications (5V/3A for Pi 4).
6. **Temperature Check**:

If your Raspberry Pi feels hot to the touch or you're concerned about temperature, you can check the CPU temperature by typing the following in the terminal:

```
vcgencmd measure_temp
```

- The normal operating temperature is under **60°C** for most tasks. If it's higher, consider using a heat sink or fan to cool your Pi.

1.13. How to Use the Terminal for the First Time

The **Terminal** is a command-line interface (CLI) that lets you control your Raspberry Pi by typing text commands instead of using a graphical interface like clicking icons and buttons. It's a direct way to interact with the operating system, and once you get used to it, you'll find it a quick and powerful tool for tasks like installing software, managing files, and more.

- Think of the Terminal as a **text-based control center** where you can give your Raspberry Pi instructions directly.

To open the Terminal:

- On the Raspberry Pi desktop, click the **Terminal icon** (a black screen icon) in the taskbar.

Basic Commands Every Beginner Should Know

Here are some basic commands to help you get started with the Terminal:

- **pwd** (Print Working Directory):

This command shows you the current location (directory) you are in.

```
pwd
```

- Output: /home/pi (example, this means you're in the "pi" user's home directory).

- **ls** (List):

Lists the files and directories in your current location.

```
ls
```

- Output: A list of files and folders in your current directory.
- **cd** (Change Directory):

Use this to navigate to a different directory (folder). For example, to go into a folder named "Documents":

```
cd Documents
```

To go back to the previous directory:

```
cd ..
```

- **mkdir** (Make Directory):

Creates a new folder. For example, to create a folder called "MyProject":

```
mkdir MyProject
```

- **nano** (Text Editor):

Opens a simple text editor right in the terminal. To create or edit a file called example.txt:

```
nano example.txt
```

- After editing, press **Ctrl + X**, then **Y**, then **Enter** to save and exit.
- **sudo** (Run as Superuser):
  - Allows you to run commands with superuser (administrator) privileges. This is used for installing software or making system-wide changes. (More on this below.)
- **apt** (Package Manager):

To install software, use the `apt` package manager. For example, to install `htop` (a system monitor):

```
sudo apt install htop
```

What Is Sudo and Why Should You Use It?

Sudo stands for **Superuser Do**, and it allows you to execute commands as the **superuser** (or root), which is like an administrator. Normally, your Raspberry Pi runs with restricted permissions to prevent accidental changes to important system files. Using `sudo` gives you the power to:

- **Install software**.
- **Make system-wide changes** (like updating the OS).
- **Edit system configuration files**.

For example:

To install new software, you often need superuser privileges:

```
sudo apt install software-name
```

To shut down the Raspberry Pi from the Terminal:

```
sudo shutdown now
```

You should use `sudo` carefully because commands run with superuser privileges can potentially change critical system settings.

Basic File Management Using the Terminal

You can manage files and directories (folders) directly from the Terminal. Here are some basic file management commands:

- **Creating a File**:

Use the `touch` command to create an empty file:

```
touch example.txt
```

- **Copying a File**:

To copy a file from one location to another:
```
cp example.txt /home/pi/Documents/
```

- **Moving/Renaming a File**:

To move or rename a file:
```
mv example.txt /home/pi/Documents/newname.txt
```

- **Deleting a File**:

To delete a file:
```
rm example.txt
```

- **Viewing the Contents of a File**:

To view the contents of a text file directly in the Terminal:
```
cat example.txt
```

These commands allow you to perform all the basic file management tasks without using the desktop interface. Over time, you'll find the Terminal quicker and more efficient for these tasks.

1.14. Maximising Performance

If you want to get the most out of your Raspberry Pi, there are a few ways to optimize its performance. Whether you're using your Pi for a simple project or something more demanding, there are steps you can take to improve speed and prevent issues like overheating.

1.16.1. How to Make Your Raspberry Pi Faster

To boost the performance of your Raspberry Pi, you can apply several optimization techniques:

1. **Use a Faster microSD Card**:
    o   The speed of your Raspberry Pi depends on how fast the microSD card can read and write data. Look for microSD cards with **Class 10** or **UHS-1** ratings for faster boot times and smoother operations.

2. **Use Raspberry Pi OS Lite**:
    o   If you don't need a graphical interface, use **Raspberry Pi OS Lite** (without the desktop) for command-line-based projects. This uses fewer system resources, allowing your Pi to run faster.

3. **Disable Unnecessary Services**:

If your Raspberry Pi is running slow, there might be unnecessary services running in the background. You can disable them using the `raspi-config` tool:

```
sudo raspi-config
```

    o   Navigate to **"Boot Options"** to reduce startup programs or disable services like **Bluetooth** if you're not using them.

4. **Update Your System Regularly**:

Keep your Raspberry Pi's operating system and software updated to ensure you're using the most efficient versions:

```
sudo apt update
sudo apt upgrade
```

5. **Use Ethernet Instead of Wi-Fi**:
    o   If you're running network-heavy applications (e.g., streaming, remote access), using a wired Ethernet connection instead of Wi-Fi can improve network speed and stability.

6. **Minimize Open Applications**:

- On Raspberry Pi models with limited RAM (like the 1GB Pi 4), running too many programs at once can slow down the system. Close any unnecessary applications to free up resources.

Overclocking: Is It Necessary for Beginners?

Overclocking refers to increasing the clock speed of your Raspberry Pi's processor to make it run faster than its default speed. While overclocking can boost performance, it also generates more heat and can reduce the lifespan of your Pi if done incorrectly.

For beginners, overclocking is **not necessary**. The Raspberry Pi performs well out of the box for most beginner projects like coding, media streaming, and light web browsing. However, if you're working on more resource-intensive projects like emulation or compiling large programs, overclocking may offer a noticeable performance boost.

To overclock your Raspberry Pi:

Open the **config.txt** file using the Terminal:

```
sudo nano /boot/config.txt
```

Add or modify the following lines:

```
over_voltage=2
arm_freq=1750
gpu_freq=600
```

- These settings overclock the CPU to **1.75 GHz** and the GPU to **600 MHz**. Make sure to test different settings to find what works best for your Pi.

Save and reboot your Raspberry Pi:

```
sudo reboot
```

Note: Overclocking can void your warranty and cause stability issues if done improperly. It's recommended for intermediate users who understand the risks.

How to Avoid Overheating in Your Raspberry Pi

Overheating can slow down your Raspberry Pi as it will throttle its performance to cool down. Here are some tips to prevent overheating:

1. **Use a Case with Good Ventilation**:
   - Ensure your Raspberry Pi is housed in a case that allows air to flow freely, or consider cases with built-in vents or active cooling.
2. **Install Heat Sinks**:
   - Heat sinks are small metal components that you attach to the CPU and other chips to help dissipate heat. They are easy to install and can reduce the operating temperature of your Pi by a few degrees.
3. **Keep Your Pi in a Cool Environment**:
   - Place your Raspberry Pi in a well-ventilated area, away from heat sources and direct sunlight. Avoid stacking devices on top of your Pi, as this can trap heat.
4. **Monitor Temperature**:

You can check the current temperature of your Raspberry Pi by typing this command in the Terminal:

```
vcgencmd measure_temp
```

- The temperature should ideally stay below **60°C** for most tasks. If it goes above **80°C**, your Pi will start throttling to prevent overheating.

Do You Need a Fan to Improve Performance?

While heat sinks are sufficient for basic tasks, a **fan** may be necessary for long-term use or resource-intensive projects like gaming, compiling code, or running a server. A fan provides **active cooling**, which can significantly reduce the temperature of your Raspberry Pi and prevent performance throttling.

Use if Needed:

- **For basic projects** like coding, web browsing, or using your Pi as a media player, you likely won't need a fan.
- **For resource-intensive projects** like gaming (e.g., RetroPie), running servers, or overclocking, installing a fan is highly recommended to prevent overheating and ensure stable performance over time.

There are Raspberry Pi cases available with built-in fans or you can purchase small fans that connect to the GPIO pins for power.

1.15. Changing Your Password for Security

Changing the default password on your Raspberry Pi is an important step to keep your device secure, especially if it's connected to the internet. The default username and password are well-known, making it easy for someone to gain unauthorized access to your system if it's left unchanged.

Why It's Important to Change the Default Password

When you first set up your Raspberry Pi, the default login credentials are:

- **Username**: pi
- **Password**: raspberry

Leaving these credentials unchanged poses a security risk, particularly if you're connecting your Raspberry Pi to a network. Anyone who knows these default login details could potentially access your Pi remotely, modify files, or even take control of your device. By changing the default password, you reduce the chances of unauthorized access and protect your data.

How to Change Your Password Using the Terminal

Changing your password is simple and can be done directly from the Terminal. Follow these steps:

1. **Open the Terminal**:
   - Click the **Terminal icon** on the desktop (a black screen icon).
2. **Enter the Password Change Command**:

Type the following command and press **Enter**:

```
passwd
```

3. **Enter Your Current Password**:
   - The system will prompt you to enter your **current password** (default is raspberry). Type it in and press **Enter**. The characters won't appear on the screen as you type, but it is being recorded.
4. **Enter a New Password**:
   - You'll now be prompted to type in your **new password**. Choose a strong password that you can remember, but that isn't easy to guess. Press **Enter** after typing your new password.

5. **Confirm the New Password**:
    ○ Retype the new password to confirm it, then press **Enter**.

You've successfully changed the password! Make sure to store it somewhere safe in case you forget it.

What Happens If You Forget Your Password?

If you forget your Raspberry Pi password, don't worry—you can reset it by following these steps:

1. **Power Off the Raspberry Pi**:
    ○ First, power off the Raspberry Pi and remove the microSD card.
2. **Access the microSD Card on Another Computer**:
    ○ Insert the microSD card into another computer using a card reader. Open the card and locate the **boot partition**.
3. **Modify the cmdline.txt File**:
    ○ In the **boot** directory, find the file named `cmdline.txt`. Open it with a text editor.

Add the following text to the end of the line (make sure it's all on one line with a space before it):

```
init=/bin/sh
```

    ○ Save the file and eject the microSD card safely.
4. **Boot the Raspberry Pi**:
    ○ Insert the microSD card back into your Raspberry Pi and power it on. This will boot into **single-user mode**, giving you root access without needing a password.
5. **Change the Password**:
Once the system has booted, type the following command to mount the root filesystem as read-write:

```
mount -o remount,rw /
```

Now, change the password for the `pi` user:

```
passwd pi
```

- o Enter the new password when prompted.
6. **Revert the Changes**:
    - o After resetting the password, you need to remove the changes from the `cmdline.txt` file to allow your Raspberry Pi to boot normally. Power off the Pi, remove the SD card, and open the `cmdline.txt` file again on your computer.
    - o Remove the `init=/bin/sh` part you added earlier, then save and eject the microSD card.
7. **Reboot Your Raspberry Pi**:
    - o Insert the card back into your Raspberry Pi, power it on, and boot as usual. You can now log in with the new password.

1.16. Shutting Down Your Raspberry Pi Safely

Properly shutting down your Raspberry Pi is crucial to ensure that all running processes are stopped correctly and no data is lost. An unsafe shutdown can lead to **data corruption** and other system issues that may affect the performance and stability of your Raspberry Pi.

Why Safe Shutdown Is Important

Shutting down safely ensures that your Raspberry Pi has enough time to close all open files, stop running programs, and complete any background tasks before powering off. If you simply unplug the power or turn off the device without properly shutting it down, you risk:

- **File System Corruption**: If the operating system is writing data to the microSD card when the power is suddenly cut, the file system can become corrupted. This can lead to lost files, crashes, or even a non-bootable Raspberry Pi.

- **Data Loss**: Any unsaved work or data may be lost if you don't properly shut down the system.
- **Reduced Lifespan of the SD Card**: Unsafe shutdowns can cause wear on the microSD card, which may shorten its lifespan over time.

How to Shut Down Using the Terminal

One of the easiest and safest ways to shut down your Raspberry Pi is by using the Terminal. Here's how to do it:

1. **Open the Terminal**:
   - If you're on the Raspberry Pi desktop, click the **Terminal icon** (a black screen icon) on the taskbar.
   - If you're working in command-line mode, you're already in the Terminal.
2. **Enter the Shutdown Command**:

Type the following command to safely shut down your Raspberry Pi:

```
sudo shutdown now
```

   - Press **Enter**.
3. **Wait for the System to Shut Down**:
   - After entering the command, the Raspberry Pi will start the shutdown process. You'll see messages indicating that processes are being stopped. Once the shutdown is complete, the screen will go blank, and the green activity light on the Pi will stop blinking.
4. **Remove Power**:
   - Once the Pi has fully shut down, you can safely disconnect the power supply.

Alternative Shutdown Commands:

Timed Shutdown: If you want the Pi to shut down after a delay (e.g., after 1 minute), you can use this command:

```
sudo shutdown +1
```

- This tells the Raspberry Pi to shut down in one minute. You can replace +1 with any number of minutes.

Reboot: If you want to reboot your Raspberry Pi instead of shutting it down, use this command:

```
sudo reboot
```

Additional Tips:

- **Shut Down from the Desktop**: If you're using the Raspberry Pi with a desktop interface, you can also shut down by clicking the **Raspberry Pi menu** in the top-left corner, selecting **Shutdown**, and then choosing **Shutdown** from the options.

1.17. Enclosing a Raspberry Pi

Enclosing your Raspberry Pi in a case is an important step for protecting your device from physical damage and environmental hazards. Cases come in different materials and designs, each offering various benefits depending on your project.

Why You Need a Case for Your Raspberry Pi

A case serves several key purposes, especially for beginners who might be using their Raspberry Pi in a variety of environments. Here's why it's important to have a case:

- **Protection**: A case provides a layer of protection against physical damage, such as bumps, drops, or accidental spills. Without a case, your Raspberry Pi's components are exposed, making them vulnerable to damage from handling or dust.
- **Safety**: It reduces the risk of short circuits, which can occur if the exposed board comes into contact with metal objects or conductive materials.

- **Portability**: If you're using your Raspberry Pi for mobile projects or moving it frequently, a case makes it easier and safer to transport.
- **Heat Management**: Some cases are designed to help with airflow or include built-in fans or heat sinks, preventing your Pi from overheating during intensive tasks.

Different Types of Cases: Pros and Cons

There are various types of cases available for the Raspberry Pi, each with their own strengths and weaknesses. Here's a breakdown of some common types:

1. **Plastic Cases**:
   - **Pros**:
     - Lightweight and affordable.
     - Good for basic protection against dust and minor impacts.
     - Often come in fun colors or clear designs.
   - **Cons**:
     - Limited heat dissipation; may require additional heat sinks if using for high-performance tasks.
     - Can be less durable than metal or specialized cases.
2. **Metal (Aluminum) Cases**:
   - **Pros**:
     - Excellent heat dissipation due to the metal's conductivity, reducing the need for additional cooling.
     - Durable and sturdy, providing better protection from damage.
   - **Cons**:
     - More expensive than plastic cases.
     - Heavier, which can be a drawback for portable projects.

3. **Custom or DIY Cases**:
   - **Pros**:
     - Can be built from materials like wood, 3D-printed plastic, or even Lego, allowing for creativity and customization.
     - You can design the case to fit specific project needs (e.g., including space for additional components like sensors or fans).
   - **Cons**:
     - May not offer as much protection as professionally-made cases.
     - Requires time and tools to build.
4. **Fan-Integrated Cases**:
   - **Pros**:
     - Built-in fans provide active cooling, making them ideal for projects that push the Raspberry Pi to its limits (e.g., gaming, emulation, server use).
     - Often come with additional features like GPIO pin access or easy port access.
   - **Cons**:
     - Slightly more expensive.
     - Fans may create noise, which could be a factor in quiet environments.

What Are the Benefits of Using a Case?

Using a case for your Raspberry Pi provides both practical and aesthetic benefits:

- **Protection and Durability**: A case shields your Raspberry Pi from physical damage, dust, and environmental factors, increasing the longevity of your device.
- **Improved Cooling**: Cases designed with ventilation, heat sinks, or fans help manage heat more effectively, ensuring your Pi runs efficiently and avoids throttling due to overheating.

- **Neat Appearance**: A case gives your Raspberry Pi a polished and finished look, making it ideal for showcasing your projects or leaving your Pi on display as part of a setup.
- **Easy Access to Ports and GPIO Pins**: Many cases are designed with cutouts or removable sections, allowing you to access the Pi's ports, GPIO pins, and other connectors without needing to remove the case.
- **Portability and Handling**: A case makes it easier to transport your Pi from one location to another without worrying about damaging the exposed components.

1.18. Connecting a DVI or VGA Monitor

If you have an older monitor that uses a **DVI** or **VGA** connection, you can still use it with your Raspberry Pi. The Pi's HDMI output can be adapted to work with these older display types using simple adapters.

Using Adapters to Connect Older Monitors

Raspberry Pi models like the Pi 4 come with **HDMI** (or micro-HDMI) ports, which are the standard for modern displays. However, older monitors use **DVI** or **VGA** ports, which require an adapter to work with the Pi.

Here's how you can connect your Raspberry Pi to an older monitor:

- **HDMI to DVI Adapter**:
    - DVI is a digital display standard that is similar to HDMI but doesn't carry audio signals. You can use an **HDMI to DVI adapter** or a simple **HDMI to DVI cable** to connect your Raspberry Pi to a DVI monitor.
    - **How to connect**:
        - Plug one end of the HDMI cable (or micro-HDMI for Pi 4) into the Raspberry Pi.
        - Plug the other end of the HDMI cable into the **HDMI to DVI adapter**, then connect the adapter to the DVI input on the monitor.

- **HDMI to VGA Adapter**:
  - ○ VGA is an older analog standard, so connecting a Raspberry Pi to a VGA monitor requires an **HDMI to VGA adapter**. This adapter will convert the digital HDMI signal into an analog VGA signal.
  - ○ **How to connect**:
    - ■ Plug the HDMI cable into the Raspberry Pi.
    - ■ Connect the other end to the **HDMI to VGA adapter**.
    - ■ Plug the VGA cable from your monitor into the adapter.
    - ■ Some adapters also include an additional audio output because VGA doesn't carry audio.

Things to Consider:

- **Power for Adapters**: Some HDMI to VGA adapters require external power. Look for adapters that either include a power input or work passively without additional power.
- **Audio**: HDMI carries audio, but neither DVI nor VGA transmits audio. If you need audio, you'll need to use the Raspberry Pi's 3.5mm audio jack or a separate USB audio device.

How to Adjust Display Settings for DVI/VGA

After connecting your Raspberry Pi to an older monitor, you might need to adjust the display settings for optimal resolution and performance, especially if the screen doesn't display properly or cuts off part of the image.

Here's how to adjust the display settings:

1. **Open the Terminal**:
   - ○ If you're on the desktop, open the **Terminal** by clicking the black screen icon in the taskbar.
2. **Edit the Configuration File**:

Type the following command to open the `config.txt` file where you can adjust display settings:

```
sudo nano /boot/config.txt
```

3. **Modify Resolution Settings**:
   - If the display isn't showing properly, you can force the Raspberry Pi to output at a specific resolution:

For **DVI**, find the line that says `#hdmi_group=1` and `#hdmi_mode=1` in the file. Uncomment these lines (remove the #) and set the appropriate values. For example:

```
hdmi_group=2
hdmi_mode=16
```

This sets the resolution to 1024x768, which is common for older monitors. You can find other resolution options online, based on your specific monitor.

4. **Force HDMI Output**:

If your VGA monitor isn't detected, you can force the Pi to output an HDMI signal:

```
hdmi_force_hotplug=1
```

5. **Adjust Overscan (Screen Size)**:

If the image is cut off or doesn't fit the screen, you can adjust the **overscan** settings. Look for the following lines in the `config.txt` file:

```
disable_overscan=1
```

Set this value to 0 to enable overscan adjustments. Then, you can fine-tune the overscan values:

```
overscan_left=16
overscan_right=16
overscan_top=16
overscan_bottom=16
```

6. **Save Changes**:
   ○ After making the necessary changes, press **Ctrl + X**, then **Y** to save the file, and press **Enter** to exit.
7. **Reboot the Raspberry Pi**:

To apply the changes, reboot the Raspberry Pi by typing:

```
sudo reboot
```

Once the system restarts, your Raspberry Pi should display properly on the older DVI or VGA monitor with the adjustments you've made.

Why It's Important: Understanding how to connect and configure older monitors ensures that you can make use of existing hardware and avoid purchasing new displays. Proper display settings also help avoid frustration with poor image quality or screen alignment issues.

1.19. Using a Composite Video Monitor/TV

Composite video is a standard analog video signal that combines the image data into a single channel. Unlike HDMI, which carries high-definition digital signals for both audio and video, composite video offers lower resolution and doesn't carry audio in the same signal. Composite video was widely used with older televisions before the era of HDMI and VGA.

When to Use Composite Video:

- **Older TVs and Monitors**: If you have an older CRT television or monitor that doesn't support HDMI or VGA, composite video allows you to connect your Raspberry Pi.
- **Portable Projects**: Composite video might be useful in certain DIY projects where you're repurposing old, smaller monitors or displays.
- **Budget Setups**: If you already have an older TV or monitor available, using composite video can save you the cost of purchasing a new display.

However, composite video provides lower resolution compared to HDMI, so it's best used for basic tasks or projects that don't require high-definition output.

How to Connect to Older TVs and Monitors

To connect your Raspberry Pi to a monitor or TV using composite video, follow these steps:

Check Your Raspberry Pi Model:

- **Raspberry Pi 4**: The Pi 4 uses a **4-pole 3.5mm audio and video jack** to output composite video, so you'll need a **3.5mm to RCA adapter** (also known as a TRRS cable) to connect to the composite input on your TV.
- **Older Raspberry Pi Models (Pi 3 and earlier)**: These models have a dedicated composite video output pin, but you'll still use a 3.5mm TRRS cable for connection.

Get the Right Cable:

- You'll need a **3.5mm TRRS to RCA cable**. This is a 3.5mm jack on one end (which connects to your Pi) and RCA connectors (typically yellow for video, red and white for audio) on the other end, which connect to your TV or monitor.
- Make sure the cable is specifically for video and audio; regular audio-only 3.5mm to RCA cables won't work.

Connect the Cable to Your Pi and TV:

- Insert the **3.5mm end** of the TRRS cable into the **audio/video port** on your Raspberry Pi.

- Connect the **yellow RCA plug** (video) to the corresponding **video input** on your TV or monitor.
- Optionally, connect the **red and white RCA plugs** (audio) to the audio inputs on your TV or speakers to get sound.

Configure the Raspberry Pi for Composite Output:

- By default, your Raspberry Pi may output video via HDMI. To force it to use composite video, follow these steps:

Modify the config.txt file:

Open the **Terminal** on your Raspberry Pi or insert the SD card into your computer and access the `config.txt` file.

```
sudo nano /boot/config.txt
```

- Find the line `#hdmi_force_hotplug=1`. You'll need to **uncomment** and modify a few lines to enable composite video.

To force composite video:

```
sdtv_mode=0  # for NTSC (North America)
sdtv_mode=2  # for PAL (Europe)
hdmi_ignore_hotplug=1
```

- **Save and exit** the file by pressing **Ctrl + X**, then **Y**, and pressing **Enter**.

Reboot the Raspberry Pi:

Reboot your Raspberry Pi to apply the new settings:

```
sudo reboot
```

Tune the TV:

   ○ On your TV, switch to the correct **input source** (usually labeled "AV" or "Video") to view the Raspberry Pi's output.

After completing these steps, your Raspberry Pi should display through the composite video connection on your older TV or monitor.

1.20. Adjusting the Picture Size on Your Monitor

When connecting your Raspberry Pi to a monitor or TV, you might find that the display doesn't fit properly on the screen. You may see black borders around the image or parts of the screen being cut off. This is usually due to a setting called **overscan**, which can be adjusted to fix the display size and alignment issues.

What to Do If the Display Doesn't Fit

If the image on your Raspberry Pi isn't fitting your screen correctly (e.g., it's too large or too small), you can adjust the settings to make it fit. This often happens when using different types of monitors (e.g., older TVs, VGA, or HDMI displays).

Common issues include:

- **Black borders around the display**: The image doesn't extend to the edges of the screen.
- **Cut-off edges**: Part of the screen (like the taskbar or text) is missing.

The solution to both issues usually involves adjusting **overscan settings**.

Adjusting Overscan Settings

Overscan refers to the practice of displaying the image slightly larger than the physical screen, which was common in older TVs. By default, Raspberry Pi uses overscan, which can lead to black borders or cut-off edges on certain monitors.

Here's how to adjust the overscan settings:

1. **Open the Terminal**:
   - On the desktop, click the **Terminal icon** in the taskbar, or press **Ctrl + Alt + T** to open it.
2. **Edit the config.txt File**:

The display settings are stored in the `config.txt` file, which controls how your Raspberry Pi displays the image on the monitor. Open this file with the following command:

```
sudo nano /boot/config.txt
```

3. **Disable Overscan**:

Look for the line in the file that says `disable_overscan=1`. If this line is commented out (with a # in front of it), remove the # to enable it. This should disable overscan and remove the black borders.

```
disable_overscan=1
```

4. **Fine-Tune the Overscan Settings**:

If disabling overscan doesn't completely fix the display issue, or if part of the screen is still cut off, you can manually adjust the overscan values. Look for lines like this:

```
overscan_left=16
overscan_right=16
overscan_top=16
overscan_bottom=16
```

- You can change the numbers to adjust the image size on each side of the screen. **Decrease** the value to make the image larger and **increase** the value to shrink the image.

5. **Save and Exit**:
    ○ After making your changes, press **Ctrl + X** to exit, then press **Y** to confirm saving the file, and press **Enter**.
6. **Reboot the Raspberry Pi**:

For the changes to take effect, reboot your Raspberry Pi:

```
sudo reboot
```

After rebooting, your Raspberry Pi should display properly on the monitor. If the image still isn't right, you can go back to the config.txt file and adjust the overscan values further until the screen fits properly.

What to Do If the Screen Is Too Small or Too Large

If the display is still too small (with black borders) or too large (cutting off parts of the screen) after adjusting overscan, here are additional steps to fine-tune the display:

1. **Set a Specific Resolution**:
    ○ You can manually set the resolution to fit your monitor by editing the config.txt file again.

Look for the following lines:

```
#hdmi_group=1
#hdmi_mode=1
```

   ○ Uncomment these lines and change the values to match your monitor's resolution.
      ■ **hdmi_group=1** is for CEA (common with TVs), and **hdmi_group=2** is for DMT (common with computer monitors).

For example, to set the resolution to **1920x1080**, you'd use:

```
hdmi_group=1
hdmi_mode=16
```

2. **Test Different HDMI Modes**:
   - ○ You can try different HDMI modes by referencing this table:
     - ■ **hdmi_mode=16** is **1080p, 60Hz**.
     - ■ **hdmi_mode=4** is **720p, 60Hz**.
   - ○ Adjust these settings to fit your display's capabilities.
3. **Use tvservice to Check Available Resolutions**:

You can check what resolutions are supported by your monitor by using the `tvservice` command in the terminal:

```
tvservice -m CEA
tvservice -m DMT
```

   - ○ These commands will display a list of supported modes, and you can adjust the `hdmi_mode` and `hdmi_group` based on these results.

4. **Check Your Monitor's Settings**:
   - ○ Some monitors and TVs have their own settings for picture size, such as "Zoom," "Wide," or "Full." Ensure that your monitor is set to the correct display mode for a normal, unmodified picture.

Why It's Important:

Getting the display size right is crucial for usability, especially when working on projects or coding. Properly adjusting the picture ensures you have full access to the screen without missing important details. By knowing how to adjust overscan and resolution settings, you can make sure your Raspberry Pi displays correctly on any monitor or TV.

1.21. Installing the Raspberry Pi Camera Module

The **Raspberry Pi Camera Module** is a powerful accessory that allows you to capture photos, record videos, and even create projects like security cameras, time-lapse photography, or computer vision systems. Installing and using the camera module is simple, and this guide will walk you through the process.

What Can You Do with a Camera Module?

The **Raspberry Pi Camera Module** opens up many possibilities for creative projects, including:

- **Photography and Videography**: You can use the camera module to take high-quality photos and videos, which can be saved directly onto the Raspberry Pi.
- **Time-Lapse Photography**: Capture long-term projects like plant growth or cloud movement by taking pictures at regular intervals and compiling them into a video.
- **Security Camera**: Set up a motion-detecting security camera that can capture footage when movement is detected.
- **Computer Vision**: Use the camera with software like **OpenCV** to create face detection, object recognition, or other image processing projects.
- **Live Streaming**: Stream video from the camera module in real-time, useful for video conferencing or remote monitoring.

How to Set Up and Use the Camera

Here's a installing and using the **Raspberry Pi Camera Module**.

1. Gathering the Required Materials:

- **Raspberry Pi Camera Module**.
- **Raspberry Pi** (any model with a camera port, such as the Pi 3 or Pi 4).
- **Ribbon cable** (usually comes with the camera module).
- **microSD card** with Raspberry Pi OS installed.
- **Power supply**.

2. Installing the Camera Module:

1. **Power Off the Raspberry Pi**: Always make sure your Raspberry Pi is powered off before connecting the camera module to avoid any damage.
2. **Locate the Camera Port**: On your Raspberry Pi board, find the camera port (usually labeled **CAMERA** or **CSI**). It's a small, flat connector located near the HDMI port on models like the Raspberry Pi 3 or 4.
3. **Insert the Ribbon Cable**:
    o   Gently lift the tabs on both sides of the camera port to open it.
    o   Insert the ribbon cable from the camera module into the port, ensuring that the metal contacts on the cable are facing the HDMI port.
    o   Once the cable is properly seated, push the tabs back down to secure it in place.
4. **Attach the Other End of the Ribbon Cable**:
    o   Attach the other end of the ribbon cable to the camera module's connector. Make sure the metal contacts are aligned correctly and securely fastened.

3. Enable the Camera on Raspberry Pi OS:

*   Power on your Raspberry Pi and boot into **Raspberry Pi OS**.

Open the **Terminal** and type the following command to open the Raspberry Pi configuration tool:

```
sudo raspi-config
```

*   Navigate to **Interfacing Options** and select **Camera**.
*   Choose **Enable** to activate the camera.

Reboot your Raspberry Pi for the changes to take effect:

```
sudo reboot
```

4. Testing the Camera:

- Once the Pi has rebooted, you can test the camera by using the built-in `raspistill` and `raspivid` commands.

To take a photo:

```
raspistill -o image.jpg
```

- This command takes a photo and saves it as `image.jpg` in your home directory.

To record a video:

```
raspivid -o video.h264 -t 10000
```

- This command records a **10-second** video (`-t 10000` means 10,000 milliseconds) and saves it as `video.h264`.

5. Adjusting Camera Settings:

- You can control various settings such as resolution, brightness, contrast, and more using additional options in the `raspistill` and `raspivid` commands. For example:

Set resolution to 1920x1080:

```
raspistill -o image.jpg -w 1920 -h 1080
```

Set video recording length to 20 seconds:

```
raspivid -o video.h264 -t 20000
```

6. Using the Camera for Projects:

- With the camera module set up, you can now use it for various projects. For instance, you can install software like **Motion** to create a security camera or use Python with libraries like **OpenCV** for computer vision projects.

Why It's Important:

The Raspberry Pi Camera Module adds a powerful functionality to your Raspberry Pi, allowing you to explore creative projects involving photography, video recording, or even more complex tasks like computer vision. Setting it up is straightforward, and once you're familiar with the basics, you can integrate the camera into a variety of Raspberry Pi projects.

1.22. Using Bluetooth

Bluetooth is a useful feature on the Raspberry Pi, allowing you to connect wireless devices such as keyboards, mice, headphones, and speakers. This guide will help you understand how to pair devices, connect audio devices, and troubleshoot common Bluetooth issues.

How to Pair Devices Using Bluetooth

Pairing Bluetooth devices with your Raspberry Pi is a straightforward process, and the steps are similar to those on other systems like Windows or macOS.

Steps to Pair a Bluetooth Device:

1. **Ensure Bluetooth Is Enabled**:
    - On Raspberry Pi OS with a desktop interface, click the **Bluetooth icon** on the taskbar (usually in the top-right corner).
    - If Bluetooth is off, turn it on by selecting **Turn Bluetooth On**.
2. **Set the Device in Pairing Mode**:
    - Put your Bluetooth device (e.g., keyboard, mouse, or speaker) into **pairing mode**. This process varies by device, so check the instructions for the specific device you're using.
3. **Find and Pair the Device**:
    - Click the **Bluetooth icon** again and choose **Add Device**.

- A list of available devices will appear. Find the name of your device in the list and click on it.
- If prompted, confirm the pairing request by clicking **Yes** or **Pair**.
- For devices like keyboards, you may be asked to enter a pairing code.

4. **Confirm Connection**:
   - Once the device is paired, it should automatically connect to your Raspberry Pi. You can check the status by clicking the **Bluetooth icon** and seeing if the device is listed as connected.

Command-Line Alternative (if you prefer using the terminal):

Open the terminal and install the Bluetooth management tool:

```
sudo apt install pi-bluetooth
```

Run the Bluetooth management tool:

```
bluetoothctl
```

- Use the following commands in the `bluetoothctl` prompt:

Turn on Bluetooth:

```
power on
```

Scan for devices:

```
scan on
```

Pair and connect a device (replace XX:XX:XX:XX:XX:XX with the actual Bluetooth address of your device):

```
pair XX:XX:XX:XX:XX:XX
connect XX:XX:XX:XX:XX:XX
```

Trust the device so it connects automatically in the future:

```
trust XX:XX:XX:XX:XX:XX
```

Common Issues and Fixes with Bluetooth Devices

While pairing Bluetooth devices is usually easy, you might encounter a few common issues. Here's how to troubleshoot them:

- **Device Not Appearing**:
  - **Solution**: Make sure the device is in pairing mode. Some devices only stay in pairing mode for a limited time, so you may need to reset the pairing process by turning the device off and back on.

Try this: Restart the Bluetooth service on the Pi:

```
sudo systemctl restart bluetooth
```

- **Failed to Pair**:
  - **Solution**: Ensure that the device is not already paired with another device (such as your phone). Unpair it from other devices if necessary and try pairing with the Raspberry Pi again.
- **Connection Drops Frequently**:
  - **Solution**: Ensure that the device is within range and fully charged. Bluetooth has a limited range, so try moving the device closer to the Raspberry Pi.

Try this: Remove the device and pair it again:

```
bluetoothctl
remove XX:XX:XX:XX:XX:XX
```

- **Audio Issues with Bluetooth Speakers/Headphones**:
  - **Solution**: Sometimes audio profiles may not be correctly set. This can be fixed by ensuring the right Bluetooth profile is used for audio devices.

How to Connect Wireless Headphones or Speakers to Your Pi

Using Bluetooth for audio devices such as headphones or speakers can be a great way to enhance your Raspberry Pi experience. Here's how to connect audio devices:

1. **Enable Bluetooth and Put Device in Pairing Mode**:
   - Make sure your Bluetooth speaker or headphones are in pairing mode.
2. **Pair the Device**:
   - Follow the pairing steps outlined in **1.24.1** to pair the audio device with your Raspberry Pi.
3. **Set the Audio Output**:
   - After pairing, you need to set the Raspberry Pi to use your Bluetooth device as the audio output.
   - Click the **Bluetooth icon** in the taskbar, and you should see your paired audio device listed.
   - Go to the **Volume control** or **Audio Output** settings and select your Bluetooth device as the output.
4. **Test the Audio**:
   - Play a video or music file to check if the sound is coming through your Bluetooth headphones or speaker.

Command-Line Alternative:

After pairing the Bluetooth audio device, you can install and configure **PulseAudio** for better management of Bluetooth audio:

```
sudo apt install pulseaudio pulseaudio-module-bluetooth
```

Then, load the Bluetooth module in PulseAudio:

```
pactl load-module module-bluetooth-discover
```

How to Troubleshoot Bluetooth Connection Issues

If your Bluetooth connection isn't working properly, here are some common troubleshooting steps:

1. **Restart Bluetooth**:

Restarting the Bluetooth service often fixes connection problems:

```
sudo systemctl restart bluetooth
```

2. **Check for Interference**:
   o Other wireless devices (like Wi-Fi routers) can interfere with Bluetooth connections. Try moving your Pi and Bluetooth device closer together or away from other electronics.
3. **Re-Pair the Device**:
   o If the device was paired but isn't connecting, remove the device and pair it again using the **Bluetooth menu** or **bluetoothctl**.
4. **Update Raspberry Pi OS**:

Keeping your system updated ensures that any Bluetooth bugs are fixed in the latest version of the operating system:

```
sudo apt update
sudo apt upgrade
```

5. **Check Bluetooth Power**:

Ensure that the Bluetooth interface is powered on using bluetoothctl:

```
power on
```

By following these steps, you should be able to successfully connect and manage Bluetooth devices with your Raspberry Pi, enhancing its functionality and wireless convenience.

1.23. How to Power Off Your Raspberry Pi Properly

Properly shutting down your Raspberry Pi is crucial to prevent data loss, file system corruption, and potential damage to the operating system. Turning off the Raspberry Pi without following the proper shutdown procedure can cause issues, especially if files or programs are still running in the background.

Why Powering Off Safely Matters

Just like with any computer, it's important to follow a proper shutdown process on the Raspberry Pi. Here's why:

- **Prevents Data Corruption**: If you simply unplug your Raspberry Pi while it's running, there's a high risk that files on the microSD card could become corrupted, especially if the Pi was in the middle of writing data to the card.
- **Avoids System Errors**: Improper shutdowns can cause the operating system to malfunction, leading to boot issues or even requiring you to reinstall the operating system.
- **Protects the microSD Card**: The microSD card is constantly being read from and written to by the operating system. Safely shutting down ensures that no data is being accessed during power-off, reducing the risk of corrupting the card.

Powering Off

Powering off your Raspberry Pi is easy, and you have multiple ways to do it depending on whether you're using the desktop environment or the terminal.

1. Powering Off from the Desktop (Raspberry Pi OS):

If you're using the Raspberry Pi desktop interface, follow these steps:

1. **Click the Raspberry Pi menu** (the Raspberry icon in the top-left corner).
2. **Select Shutdown** from the dropdown menu.
3. In the pop-up window, choose **Shutdown** to safely power off your Raspberry Pi.
4. Wait for the screen to go blank and for the green activity light on your Pi to stop blinking. Once this happens, you can safely unplug the power supply.

2. Powering Off Using the Terminal:

If you're working in the terminal or command-line interface, you can safely power off your Raspberry Pi using the following command:

1. **Open the Terminal**:
   - If you're in the desktop environment, click the **Terminal icon** in the taskbar.
   - If you're already in command-line mode, you're ready to proceed.
2. **Enter the Shutdown Command**:

Type the following command and press **Enter**:

```
sudo shutdown now
```

   - This command initiates a safe shutdown process. The system will close all running programs, finish writing any data to the SD card, and then turn off.
3. **Wait for the Shutdown to Complete**:
   - After you issue the shutdown command, wait for the screen to go blank and for the **green activity light** to stop blinking. This indicates that the Raspberry Pi has fully powered off.

4. **Unplug the Power Supply**:
   - Once the Raspberry Pi has powered off, you can safely disconnect the power supply.

Alternative Command for Delayed Shutdown:

If you want to delay the shutdown for a specific amount of time (e.g., 1 minute), use this command:

```
sudo shutdown +1
```

- This will shut down the Raspberry Pi in 1 minute. You can replace +1 with any number of minutes.

Rebooting Instead of Shutting Down:

If you want to restart your Raspberry Pi instead of powering it off, use the **reboot** command:

```
sudo reboot
```

By following these steps, you ensure that your Raspberry Pi powers off safely, protecting the integrity of your system and data. Proper shutdowns are especially important if you're using your Raspberry Pi for projects involving sensitive data or continuous operations, like servers or media centers.

Chapter 2: Connecting Raspberry Pi to the Internet

2.0. Networking

Networking is a key aspect of using your Raspberry Pi effectively, allowing you to connect it to the internet, communicate with other devices, and enable remote access for a variety of projects. Understanding basic networking concepts is essential for both simple setups, like connecting your Pi to Wi-Fi, and more advanced uses, such as building a local server or managing devices across a network.

Why Networking Is Important for Your Raspberry Pi

Networking allows your Raspberry Pi to:

- **Access the internet**: This is essential for downloading updates, installing software, or using your Pi as a web browsing device.
- **Communicate with other devices**: You can connect your Raspberry Pi to other computers, printers, or networked devices, which is important for projects like file sharing or network printing.
- **Remote access and control**: Networking enables you to control your Raspberry Pi from anywhere using tools like SSH, VNC, or RDP. This means you don't need a monitor or keyboard directly attached to your Pi to work with it.
- **Internet of Things (IoT) projects**: Many IoT projects require your Raspberry Pi to communicate with other devices or sensors across a network or over the internet.

Basic Networking Concepts for Beginners

Before diving into setting up your Raspberry Pi's network, let's cover some essential concepts to help you understand how networking works.

What Is an IP Address?

An **IP address** is a unique identifier assigned to each device on a network. It's similar to a street address, allowing devices to communicate with each other by sending and receiving data.

There are two main types of IP addresses:

- **IPv4**: A common format consisting of four numbers separated by periods (e.g., `192.168.1.100`).
- **IPv6**: A newer format designed to accommodate more devices, consisting of hexadecimal numbers (e.g., `fe80::1ff:fe23:4567:890a`).

Every device on your local network, including your Raspberry Pi, is assigned an IP address by the router.

What Is the Difference Between Static and Dynamic IPs?

- **Static IP Address**: A static IP address is manually assigned and doesn't change over time. This is useful when you need a reliable and fixed address to access your Raspberry Pi, for example, for remote access or hosting a server.
- **Dynamic IP Address**: A dynamic IP address is automatically assigned by the router's **DHCP server** and can change over time. Most devices on a home network use dynamic IPs by default, but this can make accessing your Pi remotely more difficult since the IP might change.

Understanding Routers, Modems, and Switches

- **Router**: A router directs data between devices on a local network and also connects them to the internet. It assigns IP addresses to devices and ensures that data reaches the correct destination.
- **Modem**: A modem connects your home network to your internet service provider (ISP). It translates data between your network and the wider internet.
- **Switch**: A switch is a device that allows multiple devices to be connected to the same network. Unlike a router, it doesn't

assign IP addresses or connect to the internet but allows for efficient communication within a local network.

What Is a Local Area Network (LAN) vs. Wide Area Network (WAN)?

- **Local Area Network (LAN)**: A LAN is a network of devices (e.g., computers, printers, Raspberry Pis) within a limited area, such as your home or office. Devices on the same LAN can communicate with each other without needing to go through the internet.
- **Wide Area Network (WAN)**: A WAN covers a much larger area and often connects multiple LANs. The internet is a good example of a WAN. Devices on a LAN connect to a WAN through a router.

Why It's Important: Knowing the difference between LAN and WAN helps you understand how your Raspberry Pi fits into your home network and how it connects to the wider internet. This is particularly important for projects that involve remote access or data sharing across networks.

2.1. Setting Up a Wireless Connection

Setting up a wireless connection on your Raspberry Pi allows you to connect to the internet without needing a physical Ethernet cable. This gives you the flexibility to use your Pi anywhere within your Wi-Fi range, which is especially useful for portable projects or if your Pi is located far from the router.

What You Need to Set Up Wi-Fi

To connect your Raspberry Pi to a wireless network, you'll need:

- **Raspberry Pi** with built-in Wi-Fi (Raspberry Pi 3, 4, or Zero W). If you're using an older model without built-in Wi-Fi, you'll need a **USB Wi-Fi adapter**.
- **Wi-Fi network name (SSID)** and **password**.
- **Raspberry Pi OS** installed on your Pi.

Note: If you're setting up Wi-Fi on a headless Raspberry Pi (without a monitor), the steps are slightly different and involve pre-configuring the Wi-Fi settings on the SD card.

Why It's Important: Provides Mobility and Flexibility

Using Wi-Fi with your Raspberry Pi offers several benefits:

- **Mobility**: You can place your Raspberry Pi anywhere within the Wi-Fi range, making it ideal for projects where your Pi needs to move or be set up away from the router.
- **Cable-Free Setup**: Avoids the hassle of dealing with Ethernet cables, making the setup tidier and more flexible.
- **On-the-Go Access**: With Wi-Fi, you can also connect your Raspberry Pi to mobile hotspots when you need internet access while traveling.

Connecting to Wi-Fi

If you're using the Raspberry Pi desktop interface, connecting to Wi-Fi is easy:

1. **Boot Up Your Raspberry Pi**:
   - Power on your Raspberry Pi and wait for it to boot to the desktop.
2. **Open the Wi-Fi Menu**:
   - On the top-right corner of the taskbar, click the **network icon** (a series of bars indicating signal strength).
3. **Select Your Wi-Fi Network**:
   - A list of available networks will appear. Click on your network name (SSID).
4. **Enter the Wi-Fi Password**:
   - Enter your Wi-Fi password when prompted and click **OK**.
5. **Confirm Connection**:
   - Once connected, the network icon will change to show the strength of the connection. You can now access the internet from your Raspberry Pi.

For Headless Setup (without monitor):

1. Insert the **microSD card** into your computer after flashing Raspberry Pi OS.

In the **boot** partition of the microSD card, create a file named `wpa_supplicant.conf` with the following content:

```
country=US # Your country code
ctrl_interface=DIR=/var/run/wpa_supplicant GROUP=netdev
update_config=1

network={
  ssid="Your_Network_Name"
  psk="Your_WiFi_Password"
}
```

2. Save the file, eject the microSD card, and insert it into your Raspberry Pi. On boot, the Pi will connect to your Wi-Fi automatically.

How to Troubleshoot Wi-Fi Issues

Sometimes you may encounter issues when connecting to Wi-Fi. Here are some common problems and solutions:

- **Can't Find Wi-Fi Network**:
  - Ensure your Wi-Fi network is broadcasting, and the Pi is within range. If you're using a headless setup, double-check the `wpa_supplicant.conf` file for any typos in the network name or password.
- **Connection Drops Frequently**:
  - Wi-Fi signal strength might be weak. Try moving the Raspberry Pi closer to the router or use an external antenna if your Wi-Fi adapter supports it.
- **Incorrect Password Error**:
  - Verify that you're entering the correct Wi-Fi password. If the problem persists, try reconnecting to the network by removing and re-adding it from the network settings.

- **No Internet Access**:
  - If your Pi connects to the Wi-Fi network but can't access the internet, check if other devices connected to the same network can access the internet. You can also try restarting the router.
- **Reboot the Pi and Router**:
  - A simple reboot can often fix connectivity issues.

Connecting Raspberry Pi to Mobile Hotspots

If you're on the go or don't have access to a regular Wi-Fi network, you can connect your Raspberry Pi to a mobile hotspot for internet access.

Why It's Useful:

- **Portable Projects**: Great for mobile projects or if you're using your Raspberry Pi outdoors or in areas where regular Wi-Fi isn't available.
- **Flexibility**: Enables internet access in remote locations or during travel.

Step-by-Step Guide:

1. **Enable Hotspot on Your Mobile Device**:
   - On your smartphone, enable the **mobile hotspot** feature from the settings. Note the network name (SSID) and password.
2. **Connect Raspberry Pi to the Hotspot**:
   - On the Raspberry Pi, open the **Wi-Fi menu** as described above and select the name of your mobile hotspot.
   - Enter the hotspot password when prompted and click **OK**.
3. **Confirm Connection**:
   - Once connected, the Pi will use your mobile hotspot to access the internet. Keep in mind that data usage will count toward your mobile data plan.

How to Monitor Data Usage:

When using your Raspberry Pi with a mobile hotspot, you'll want to monitor your data usage to avoid exceeding your mobile data plan limits.

- **On Android**:
    - Most Android devices have a built-in data usage monitor that shows how much data the hotspot is using.
    - Go to **Settings** > **Connections** > **Data usage** > **Mobile hotspot usage** to track how much data your Raspberry Pi is using.
- **On iPhone**:
    - Go to **Settings** > **Cellular** > **Personal Hotspot** to see data usage statistics for your mobile hotspot.

2.2. Connecting to a Wired Network

While using Wi-Fi with your Raspberry Pi offers mobility, a wired Ethernet connection provides faster and more reliable internet access. Wired connections are particularly useful for projects that require stable, high-speed data transfer or when you're setting up your Raspberry Pi as a server.

What You Need for a Wired Connection

To connect your Raspberry Pi to a wired network, you'll need:

- **Ethernet cable**: A standard Ethernet cable (also known as an RJ-45 cable) is required to connect your Raspberry Pi to your router or network switch.
- **Router or network switch**: You'll need a router or switch with available Ethernet ports to connect the Pi to your local network.
- **Raspberry Pi with an Ethernet port**: Raspberry Pi models 3, 4, and higher come with built-in Ethernet ports. If you're using a Raspberry Pi Zero, you'll need a **USB to Ethernet adapter**.

Why It's Important: Wired Connections Are More Stable and Faster

Using a wired Ethernet connection for your Raspberry Pi has several key benefits:

- **Higher Speeds**: Ethernet typically provides faster data transfer speeds than Wi-Fi, which is crucial for data-heavy tasks like running a file server or streaming HD video.
- **More Reliable Connection**: Ethernet is less prone to interference and signal drops compared to Wi-Fi, making it more suitable for projects where a constant connection is critical.
- **Low Latency**: Wired connections have lower latency, which is beneficial for gaming, video conferencing, or other real-time applications.

For projects where speed, reliability, and stability are important, a wired connection is generally preferred over Wi-Fi.

Connecting via Ethernet

Connecting your Raspberry Pi to a wired network is straightforward:

1. **Power Off Your Raspberry Pi**:
   - Although you can connect the Ethernet cable while the Raspberry Pi is powered on, it's generally a good practice to power off the device before connecting new cables.
2. **Connect the Ethernet Cable**:
   - Plug one end of the **Ethernet cable** into the **Ethernet port** on your Raspberry Pi.
   - Plug the other end into an available Ethernet port on your **router** or **network switch**.

3. **Power On Your Raspberry Pi**:
   - Once the Ethernet cable is connected, power on your Raspberry Pi. It will automatically detect the wired

connection and attempt to obtain an IP address from your router's DHCP server.

4. **Check the Connection**:
    o   If you're using the desktop interface, click on the **network icon** (a series of bars or an Ethernet symbol) in the top-right corner of the screen. It should indicate that the Pi is connected via **Wired Network**.

To confirm the connection in the terminal, open the **Terminal** and use the following command to view network details:

```
ifconfig
```

    o   Look for the **eth0** section, which shows the IP address assigned to your Pi and confirms that it's connected to the network.

How to Troubleshoot Ethernet Issues

If you encounter problems while connecting your Raspberry Pi via Ethernet, here are some common troubleshooting steps:

No Network Connection:

*   Check if the **Ethernet cable** is securely plugged in at both ends (Pi and router).
*   Ensure that the router or network switch has available Ethernet ports.
*   Try using a different Ethernet cable to rule out a faulty cable.

No IP Address Assigned:

*   If your Raspberry Pi isn't receiving an IP address, your router's DHCP server may not be functioning correctly. Restart the router and check if it assigns an IP address.
*   You can manually set a **static IP address** (see **2.4 Setting a Static IP Address**) if DHCP isn't working.

Slow or Unstable Connection:

- Ensure that your Ethernet cable is **Cat5e** or higher for better speeds, especially if you're using a Raspberry Pi 4 with **gigabit Ethernet**.
- Try connecting the Pi directly to the router (bypassing any switches) to see if the issue is with intermediate network devices.

Check Link Lights:

- Look at the **link lights** (small LED lights) near the Ethernet port on the Raspberry Pi. A **blinking green light** typically indicates network activity, while a **solid orange light** shows that the connection is established. If the lights are off, there may be an issue with the physical connection.

Verify Network Settings:

- If you're comfortable using the terminal, use the following commands to check your network configuration:

To check the current IP address:

```
ip addr show eth0
```

To ping the router and check network connectivity:

```
ping 192.168.1.1
```

- (Replace 192.168.1.1 with the IP address of your router.)

By following these steps, you can quickly establish a stable, high-speed Ethernet connection for your Raspberry Pi, making it ideal for tasks that require reliable networking performance.

2.3. Finding Your IP Address

Knowing your Raspberry Pi's IP address is crucial for many networking tasks, especially when you want to access your Pi remotely, transfer files, or connect it to other devices. The IP address acts as your Pi's unique identifier on your local network or the internet, allowing other devices to communicate with it.

Why You Need to Know Your Pi's IP Address

Your Raspberry Pi's IP address is important for several reasons:

- **Remote Access**: To access your Raspberry Pi remotely via SSH, VNC, or RDP, you need to know its IP address.
- **File Sharing**: If you're using your Raspberry Pi as a server for file sharing or media streaming, devices on your network will connect using its IP address.
- **Networking Projects**: Many IoT and networking projects require communication between multiple devices, which is only possible when you know the IP addresses of each device, including your Pi.
- **Troubleshooting Network Issues**: Knowing the IP address helps diagnose and fix network problems, such as identifying connectivity or routing issues.

How to Find Your Pi's IP Address via Command Line

If you're comfortable using the **command line** or are working with a headless Raspberry Pi (without a monitor), you can easily find the IP address by running a few simple commands.

1. **Open the Terminal**:
    - If you're using the Raspberry Pi desktop, click the **Terminal icon** in the taskbar.
    - If you're connecting remotely via SSH, you're already in the terminal.

2. **Use the ifconfig Command**:

Type the following command and press **Enter**:

```
ifconfig
```

- ○ This command displays network information for all network interfaces on the Raspberry Pi.
3. **Locate the IP Address**:
   - ○ Look for the section labeled **eth0** (for wired connections) or **wlan0** (for wireless connections).

The IP address is shown next to `inet`, for example:
```
inet 192.168.1.100
```

- ○ In this case, the IP address of the Raspberry Pi is **192.168.1.100**.
4. **Alternative Command: ip addr**:

If `ifconfig` is not available, you can use the following command:

```
ip addr show
```

- ○ Look for the IP address under **eth0** (for Ethernet) or **wlan0** (for Wi-Fi). It will appear next to `inet`.

How to Find Your IP Address Using the Desktop Interface

If you're using the Raspberry Pi desktop interface, finding the IP address is even simpler. Follow these steps:

1. **Click on the Network Icon**:
   - ○ In the top-right corner of the Raspberry Pi desktop, click the **network icon** (it looks like a Wi-Fi symbol for wireless connections or an Ethernet symbol for wired connections).

2. **View IP Information**:
   ○ A drop-down menu will appear. Click on **Network Information** or **Status**.
   ○ A window will pop up displaying details about the network connection, including the **IP address**.
3. **Alternative Method via Terminal**:

If you prefer using the terminal, you can use the `hostname` command to quickly find the IP address:

```
hostname -I
```

   ○ This command will return the IP address of your Raspberry Pi without displaying additional network details.

2.4. Setting a Static IP Address

By default, your Raspberry Pi's IP address is assigned dynamically by your router's DHCP server. This means that the IP address can change each time the Pi connects to the network, which can make remote access more difficult. To avoid this, you can assign a **static IP address**, ensuring that your Pi always uses the same IP on your local network.

Why It's Important: Prevents Your Pi's IP from Changing

A **static IP address** is a fixed address assigned to your Raspberry Pi, which will not change even after restarting the Pi or router. This is important because:

- **Consistent Remote Access**: For remote control using SSH, VNC, or RDP, having a static IP ensures you always know how to reach your Pi on the network.
- **Network Services**: If your Pi is being used as a server (e.g., file server, web server, or media server), a static IP ensures that other devices on your network can consistently access the Pi.

- **Prevents Network Confusion**: Avoids situations where devices connected to the network can't find your Pi due to a change in its IP address.

How Static IPs Help with Remote Access

Using a static IP address simplifies **remote access**:

- **SSH (Secure Shell)**: When accessing your Raspberry Pi via SSH, you need to know its IP address. A static IP means you don't have to check the address every time you want to connect.
- **VNC (Virtual Network Computing)**: For graphical remote access, VNC requires the Pi's IP address. A static IP ensures your VNC client always connects to the correct address.
- **Web Servers**: If your Raspberry Pi is running as a web server or hosting any service on your local network, a static IP allows other devices to reliably connect to the server.

Setting a Static IP

There are a few ways to set a static IP address for your Raspberry Pi. The method below will walk you through setting a static IP directly on the Pi using **Raspberry Pi OS**.

1. **Find Your Network Details**:
    - You'll need the following information to set a static IP:
        - **Current IP address of your Pi** (use the command `ifconfig` or `hostname -I` to find this).
        - **Subnet Mask** (usually `255.255.255.0`).
        - **Router (Gateway) IP address** (this is the IP address of your router, typically `192.168.1.1` or similar).
        - **DNS server address** (this is also typically the router IP, but you can use Google's DNS: `8.8.8.8`).

2. Open the dhcpcd.conf File:

To set the static IP, you need to edit the **dhcpcd.conf** file. Open the terminal and type the following command:

```
sudo nano /etc/dhcpcd.conf
```

3. Configure the Static IP:

Scroll to the bottom of the file and add the following lines, replacing the example IP addresses with the ones that suit your network:

```
interface eth0
static ip_address=192.168.1.100/24   # Replace with your desired static
IP
static routers=192.168.1.1            # Replace with your router's IP
address
static domain_name_servers=192.168.1.1 8.8.8.8  # Use your router's IP
or a public DNS
```

For **Wi-Fi (wlan0)**, use the same configuration but under the `interface wlan0` section.

4. Save and Exit:

After entering your network details, save the changes by pressing **Ctrl + X**, then press **Y** to confirm, and hit **Enter** to exit the editor.

5. Reboot Your Raspberry Pi:

Reboot your Raspberry Pi for the changes to take effect:

```
sudo reboot
```

6. Verify the Static IP:

After rebooting, check if the static IP was successfully applied by using the following command:

```
ifconfig
```

Look under the **eth0** or **wlan0** section to see if the **IP address** matches the static IP you set.

Additional Notes:

- **Choosing the Right IP Address**: Make sure the static IP you choose is within the same range as your router's network but not within the range of IPs assigned by DHCP to avoid conflicts. For example, if your router assigns IP addresses from `192.168.1.2` to `192.168.1.100`, you could choose something like `192.168.1.150` for your Raspberry Pi.
- **Router-Based Static IP Assignment**: Some routers allow you to assign a static IP directly through the router's interface (often called **DHCP reservation**). This ensures the Pi gets the same IP every time it connects, without having to change settings on the Pi itself.

2.5. Setting the Network Name of a Raspberry Pi

The **hostname** of your Raspberry Pi is the name it uses on your network, making it easier to identify and connect to, especially if you have multiple devices. By default, the Raspberry Pi hostname is set to "raspberrypi", but you can change it to something more descriptive to suit your needs.

Why It's Important: Helps You Identify Your Pi on the Network

Changing the **hostname** (network name) of your Raspberry Pi has several benefits:

- **Easier Identification**: If you have multiple Raspberry Pi devices or other network devices, giving each a unique hostname makes it easier to identify and manage them.
- **Simplifies Remote Access**: Instead of needing to remember the IP address of your Pi for remote access, you can use the hostname (e.g., `pi.local`) in SSH or VNC connections.

- **Custom Naming**: You can name your Pi based on its function (e.g., "mediaserver" or "webpi") to reflect its role in your network.

How to Change the Hostname (Network Name) of Your Pi

Changing the hostname on your Raspberry Pi is a simple process and can be done through either the desktop interface or the command line.

Method 1: Using the Raspberry Pi Configuration Tool (Desktop Interface)

1. **Open the Raspberry Pi Configuration Tool**:
   - If you're using the desktop interface, click the **Raspberry Pi icon** (menu) in the top-left corner.
   - Navigate to **Preferences** > **Raspberry Pi Configuration**.
2. **Change the Hostname**:
   - In the configuration window, click on the **System** tab.
   - You'll see a field labeled **Hostname**. Enter your new desired hostname (e.g., "mypi" or "webserver").
3. **Click OK and Reboot**:
   - After entering the new hostname, click **OK**.
   - You'll be prompted to **reboot** the Raspberry Pi for the changes to take effect. Click **Yes** to reboot.

Method 2: Using the Command Line

If you prefer working with the terminal or are using a headless setup, you can change the hostname through the command line.

1. **Open the Terminal**:
   - If you're using the Raspberry Pi desktop, click the **Terminal icon** in the taskbar.
   - If you're connecting remotely via SSH, open your SSH client and log in to your Raspberry Pi.

2. **Edit the Hostname File**:

The hostname is stored in a file called `hostname`. Open this file for editing with the following command:

```
sudo nano /etc/hostname
```

3. **Change the Hostname**:
   - You'll see the current hostname (likely "raspberrypi"). Delete it and enter your new hostname (e.g., "mypi").
   - Press **Ctrl + X**, then **Y**, and **Enter** to save and exit the editor.
4. **Update the Hosts File**:

You also need to update the **/etc/hosts** file to reflect the new hostname. Open the file for editing:

```
sudo nano /etc/hosts
```

Find the line that looks like this:
```
127.0.1.1    raspberrypi
```

   - Replace "raspberrypi" with your new hostname (e.g., "mypi").
5. **Save and Exit**:
   - Press **Ctrl + X**, then **Y**, and **Enter** to save and exit.
6. **Reboot the Raspberry Pi**:

For the hostname change to take effect, reboot your Raspberry Pi:
```
sudo reboot
```

Using the New Hostname for Remote Access:

After rebooting, you can now use the new hostname to access your Raspberry Pi on the network. For example, if your new hostname is "mypi", you can connect via SSH using:
```
ssh pi@mypi.local
```

Notes:

- Hostnames must be unique on your network to avoid conflicts.
- Hostnames can contain letters, numbers, and hyphens but no spaces or special characters.

By changing your Raspberry Pi's hostname, you make it easier to manage and identify your Pi on the network, particularly when working with multiple devices or remote access tools.

2.6. Controlling the Pi Remotely with SSH

SSH (**Secure Shell**) is a powerful tool that allows you to control your Raspberry Pi from another computer over a network. It provides access to the Pi's command line, so you can run commands, install software, and manage the Pi without needing to attach a monitor, keyboard, or mouse.

What is SSH and Why Use It?

SSH (Secure Shell) is a protocol used to securely connect to and control remote computers, like your Raspberry Pi, over a network. SSH encrypts the communication between your device and the Pi, ensuring that sensitive data like passwords are protected.

Why Use SSH:

- **Remote Control**: SSH allows you to manage your Raspberry Pi from any device connected to the same network (or even over the internet) without needing a monitor or keyboard attached to the Pi.
- **Headless Setup**: If you're using your Raspberry Pi without a display (headless setup), SSH is the most convenient way to interact with it.
- **Command Line Access**: SSH provides full access to the Raspberry Pi's command line, allowing you to install software, update the system, manage files, and run programs remotely.

Why It's Important: Enables Remote Control via the Command Line

Using SSH to control your Raspberry Pi is important because it:

- **Saves Space**: You don't need extra peripherals like a monitor or keyboard attached to the Pi.
- **Increases Flexibility**: You can access your Pi from anywhere, even outside your home, by enabling port forwarding on your router (or using cloud-based services).
- **Streamlines Workflow**: Developers, hobbyists, and system administrators often use SSH to manage multiple devices remotely, making it an essential tool for advanced projects and server setups.

Enabling and Using SSH

Step 1: Enable SSH on Your Raspberry Pi

SSH is disabled by default for security reasons, but you can easily enable it.

- **On Raspberry Pi with Desktop Interface**:
    1. Click the **Raspberry Pi menu** (top-left corner) and select **Preferences** > **Raspberry Pi Configuration**.
    2. In the **Interfaces** tab, find **SSH** and click **Enable**.
    3. Click **OK** and reboot the Pi if prompted.
- **On Raspberry Pi Without a Monitor (Headless Setup)**:
    1. Insert your Raspberry Pi's SD card into your computer.
    2. In the **boot** partition of the SD card, create a blank file called ssh (with no file extension).
    3. Eject the SD card and insert it back into the Raspberry Pi. SSH will be enabled when the Pi boots.

Step 2: Find Your Raspberry Pi's IP Address

You need the IP address of your Raspberry Pi to connect via SSH. You can find it using the methods in **2.3 Finding Your IP Address** (e.g., by running `ifconfig` or `hostname -I` in the terminal, or checking your router's connected devices).

Step 3: Connect to Your Raspberry Pi Using SSH

Once SSH is enabled and you have the Pi's IP address, follow these steps to connect:

- **On Linux or macOS**:
    1. Open the **Terminal**.

Type the following command (replace `192.168.1.100` with your Pi's IP address):

```
ssh pi@192.168.1.100
```

    2. If prompted, type **yes** to accept the Pi's fingerprint.
    3. Enter the **default password** for the Pi (if you haven't changed it, it's `raspberry`).
- **On Windows**:
    1. Download and install an SSH client like **PuTTY**.
    2. Open PuTTY, enter your Pi's IP address under **Host Name**, and click **Open**.
    3. When the terminal window opens, log in with the username `pi` and password `raspberry`.

Once connected, you'll have full access to the Raspberry Pi's command line, and you can manage the Pi as if you were using it directly.

How to Troubleshoot SSH Connectivity Issues

If you're having trouble connecting to your Raspberry Pi via SSH, here are some common issues and how to fix them:

- **SSH Not Enabled**:
  - Make sure SSH is enabled. If you can't access the Raspberry Pi, try using the headless setup method by creating the `ssh` file in the boot partition of the SD card.
- **Incorrect IP Address**:
  - Double-check the Raspberry Pi's IP address. Use `ifconfig` or `hostname -I` on the Pi, or check the connected devices list on your router to find the correct address.
- **Network Issues**:
  - Ensure both your Raspberry Pi and the computer you're using to connect are on the same network.
  - Restart your router and check the network cables if you're using Ethernet.
- **Firewall Blocking SSH**:
  - If you're trying to access the Raspberry Pi from another network (e.g., over the internet), check that your router is forwarding port 22 (the default SSH port) to the Pi's IP address.
- **Connection Refused**:

If you see a "connection refused" error, SSH may not be running. You can try restarting the SSH service by running:

```
sudo systemctl restart ssh
```

By enabling and using SSH, you can control your Raspberry Pi remotely, manage it without needing a direct monitor connection, and easily integrate it into larger projects or network setups.

2.7. Controlling the Pi Remotely with VNC

While SSH is great for command-line control, **VNC (Virtual Network Computing)** allows you to control your Raspberry Pi remotely using its full graphical interface. This means you can interact with your Pi's desktop as if you were using a monitor, making VNC ideal for projects where you need the GUI or want to run graphical applications.

What is VNC and When to Use It?

VNC (Virtual Network Computing) is a system that allows you to remotely control another computer's desktop interface over a network. With VNC, you can view and interact with your Raspberry Pi's graphical desktop from another device, such as a PC, Mac, or even a smartphone.

When to Use VNC:

- **Graphical Applications**: If you're running programs that require a graphical interface (such as a web browser or media player) on your Raspberry Pi, VNC allows you to control those applications remotely.
- **Beginners**: For those who prefer working with a desktop interface rather than the command line, VNC makes remote management easier and more visual.
- **Managing a Headless Pi**: If your Pi doesn't have a monitor attached (headless setup), VNC provides full desktop access without needing to be physically connected to a display.

Why It's Important: Provides Remote Access to the Graphical Interface

VNC provides several important benefits:

- **Full Desktop Access**: Unlike SSH, which only provides command-line access, VNC lets you interact with the Pi's desktop, run graphical programs, and access all visual tools.

- **Cross-Platform Access**: You can use VNC to control your Raspberry Pi from any device, including Windows, macOS, Linux, or even mobile devices.
- **Multitasking**: VNC allows you to run multiple desktop applications simultaneously, enabling you to use your Raspberry Pi as a remote workstation, media center, or even as a teaching tool.

How to Set Up and Use VNC

Setting up VNC on your Raspberry Pi is straightforward, and Raspberry Pi OS comes with VNC software pre-installed.

Step 1: Enable VNC on the Raspberry Pi

- **On the Raspberry Pi Desktop**:
  1. Click the **Raspberry Pi menu** (top-left corner) and select **Preferences** > **Raspberry Pi Configuration**.
  2. Go to the **Interfaces** tab.
  3. Find **VNC** and click **Enable**.
  4. Click **OK** and restart the Raspberry Pi if prompted.
- **On a Headless Raspberry Pi**:
  1. Open an SSH session (see **2.6. Controlling the Pi Remotely with SSH**).

Run the following command to enable VNC:

```
sudo raspi-config
```

  2. Navigate to **Interfacing Options**, select **VNC**, and choose **Enable**.
  3. Exit and reboot the Pi if necessary.

Step 2: Install a VNC Viewer on Your Computer

- **On Windows, macOS, or Linux**:
  - Download **VNC Viewer** from the RealVNC website.
  - Install VNC Viewer on your computer or device.

- **On Mobile Devices**:
  - You can download VNC Viewer from the **App Store** (iOS) or **Google Play** (Android).

Step 3: Find Your Raspberry Pi's IP Address

You'll need the IP address of your Raspberry Pi to connect. You can find this using the methods in **2.3 Finding Your IP Address**.

Step 4: Connect to the Raspberry Pi via VNC

1. Open **VNC Viewer** on your computer or mobile device.
2. In the address bar, enter the Raspberry Pi's IP address, followed by **:1** (e.g., `192.168.1.100:1`).
3. Press **Enter** or click **Connect**.
4. A window will appear asking for your Raspberry Pi's login credentials. Enter your **Pi's username** (typically `pi`) and **password** (default is `raspberry` unless you've changed it).
5. Once connected, you'll see the Raspberry Pi's desktop interface, and you can now control it remotely.

Customizing VNC Settings:

- You can adjust the resolution for your VNC session by going to **VNC Server** > **Options** > **Troubleshooting** and selecting a virtual desktop resolution. This is useful if the default resolution doesn't fit well on your screen.

How to Troubleshoot VNC Issues

If you're having trouble connecting to your Raspberry Pi via VNC, here are some common issues and how to resolve them:

- **VNC Not Enabled**:
  - Ensure VNC is enabled in the **Raspberry Pi Configuration** tool or by running the command `sudo raspi-config` and enabling VNC under **Interfacing Options**.

- **Incorrect IP Address**:
  - Double-check the Raspberry Pi's IP address. Use the command `hostname -I` on the Pi to get the correct IP address.
  - Make sure you're on the same network as your Raspberry Pi.
- **Connection Refused**:

If you get a "connection refused" error, it could mean that VNC isn't running. You can restart VNC with the following command:

```
sudo systemctl restart vncserver-x11-serviced
```

- **Black Screen on VNC**:
  - If you get a black screen when connecting, it might be due to resolution issues. Go to **VNC Server > Options > Troubleshooting** in the VNC Viewer and adjust the **virtual desktop resolution**.
- **Firewall Issues**:
  - Ensure that your router or firewall isn't blocking port **5900**, which is the default port used by VNC.
- **Lag or Poor Performance**:
  - If your VNC session is slow, reduce the screen resolution or lower the image quality in the VNC Viewer settings to improve performance.

By setting up VNC, you can access your Raspberry Pi's desktop interface from any device, making it easier to work on graphical projects and manage your Pi remotely with full visual control.

2.8 Controlling the Pi Remotely Using RDP

Remote Desktop Protocol (RDP) is another way to control your Raspberry Pi from another computer, specifically from Windows devices. RDP allows you to connect to your Pi's graphical desktop environment remotely, making it ideal for users who want to work with the Pi's interface without needing a physical monitor attached.

What is RDP and How Is It Different from VNC?

RDP (Remote Desktop Protocol) is a protocol developed by Microsoft that allows users to remotely connect to another computer's graphical interface. This is similar to VNC (Virtual Network Computing), but there are some differences:

- **RDP is integrated into Windows**: This makes it especially useful for Windows users who can use the built-in Remote Desktop client to connect to their Raspberry Pi.
- **VNC is platform-independent**: It can be used across different operating systems like Windows, macOS, and Linux. RDP is more focused on Windows-to-Pi connections.
- **Performance**: RDP often provides better performance for graphical desktops, especially over slower network connections, because it is optimized for Windows systems.

Why It's Important: Ideal for Remote Access from Windows Devices

RDP is particularly useful for:

- **Windows users**: Since Remote Desktop is built into Windows, you don't need to install any additional software on your Windows machine to access your Raspberry Pi.
- **Graphical Interface**: RDP allows you to fully interact with your Raspberry Pi's graphical interface, which is useful for tasks that require more than just command-line control (such as using a web browser or graphical applications).
- **Performance**: RDP is often smoother and faster than VNC when used over a local network, making it ideal for everyday remote tasks.

Using RDP

Here's how to set up and use RDP to control your Raspberry Pi from a Windows device:

Step 1: Install XRDP on Raspberry Pi

1. Boot up your Raspberry Pi and open the terminal.

Install the XRDP package, which allows your Raspberry Pi to communicate using the RDP protocol:

```
sudo apt update
sudo apt install xrdp
```

Once the installation is complete, XRDP will start automatically. You can confirm this by checking the status:

```
sudo systemctl status xrdp
```

Step 2: Find Your Raspberry Pi's IP Address

You'll need your Pi's IP address to connect via RDP. To find the IP address, run the following command in the terminal:

```
hostname -I
```

1. Make a note of this IP address.

Step 3: Connect from Windows Using Remote Desktop

1. On your Windows machine, press `Windows + R` to open the Run dialog.
2. Type `mstsc` and press Enter. This will open the Remote Desktop Connection app.
3. In the "Computer" field, enter your Raspberry Pi's IP address (e.g., `192.168.1.100`), then click **Connect**.

4. A login window will appear. Enter your Raspberry Pi's username (`pi` by default) and password (the default password is `raspberry` unless you've changed it).
5. After logging in, you will be connected to the Raspberry Pi's desktop, and you can control it just as if you were using a monitor directly connected to the Pi.

Step 4: Customize Your RDP Session (Optional)

- You can adjust the resolution and display settings in the Remote Desktop Connection window before connecting, making it easier to match your screen preferences.

How to Troubleshoot RDP Issues

If you encounter problems while using RDP, here are some common solutions:

- **Can't Connect to the Raspberry Pi**:

Ensure XRDP is running on your Pi. You can restart the service with the following command:

```
sudo systemctl restart xrdp
```

  - Double-check that the Raspberry Pi is on the same network as your Windows machine.
  - Verify that your Pi's IP address hasn't changed by running `hostname -I` again.
- **Black Screen After Connecting**:

This can happen if there's a conflict with the desktop environment. Try restarting the Raspberry Pi or use the following command to ensure the graphical interface is running properly:

```
sudo systemctl restart lightdm
```

- **Incorrect Username or Password**:
  - Make sure you're entering the correct username and password for your Raspberry Pi. If you've changed the password from the default `raspberry`, ensure you use the updated one.
- **Laggy or Slow Performance**:
  - If your connection feels slow, try reducing the display resolution in the Remote Desktop settings or limiting the color depth to improve speed.

By following these steps, you can successfully set up and troubleshoot RDP to control your Raspberry Pi remotely from a Windows device, giving you a smooth graphical interface experience.

2.9 Using a Raspberry Pi for Network Attached Storage (NAS)

Network Attached Storage (NAS) allows you to store and access files over a local network, making it easy to share documents, media, and backups between devices. By using a Raspberry Pi as a NAS, you can create a simple, cost-effective file server that is accessible from anywhere on your network.

What is NAS and Why Use a Pi for It?

NAS (Network Attached Storage) is a centralized storage device connected to a network that allows multiple devices to access its files. It works like a file server, letting you store data in one place and access it from different computers, smartphones, or tablets.

Why use a Raspberry Pi for NAS?

- **Low-cost solution**: The Raspberry Pi is an inexpensive computer, making it a great option for setting up a basic NAS without breaking the bank.
- **Low power consumption**: Compared to a full-size server, the Raspberry Pi uses very little power, making it ideal for a 24/7 file server.
- **Flexible storage options**: You can connect external hard drives or USB storage devices to the Pi to expand storage.

Why It's Important: Transforms Your Pi into a Cost-Effective File Server

Using a Raspberry Pi as a NAS can:

- **Centralize your storage**: All your files, media, and backups are stored in one place, accessible from multiple devices.
- **Streamline backups**: A NAS setup is perfect for automatically backing up files from your computer or other devices on the network.
- **Media server**: Your Pi can act as a media server, streaming music, videos, or photos to devices across the network.

Setting Up Your Pi as a NAS

Here's how to turn your Raspberry Pi into a NAS using **Samba**, which allows devices running different operating systems to share files over a network.

Step 1: Set Up Your Raspberry Pi

Boot up your Raspberry Pi and ensure that your Raspberry Pi OS is up to date:

```
sudo apt update
sudo apt upgrade
```

Step 2: Install Samba Samba is software that allows file sharing between different systems (Windows, macOS, and Linux).

Install Samba by running the following command:

```
sudo apt install samba samba-common-bin
```

Step 3: Configure Samba for File Sharing

Create a folder to share. For example, you can create a folder called "nas" in your home directory:

```
mkdir ~/nas
```

Open the Samba configuration file to add this folder as a shared directory:

```
sudo nano /etc/samba/smb.conf
```

Scroll to the bottom of the file and add the following configuration:

```
[NAS]
path = /home/pi/nas
browseable = yes
writeable = yes
only guest = no
create mask = 0777
directory mask = 0777
public = yes
```

1. Save the file by pressing Ctrl + X, then Y, and Enter.

Step 4: Set a Samba Password

To secure the shared folder, set a password for the pi user on Samba:

```
sudo smbpasswd -a pi
```

1. Follow the prompt to enter and confirm your password.

Step 5: Restart Samba

Restart the Samba service to apply your changes:

```
sudo systemctl restart smbd
```

Step 6: Access the NAS Folder from Other Devices

1. On a Windows computer:
   - Open File Explorer and type `\\<Your_Pi's_IP_Address>\NAS` in the address bar (e.g., `\\192.168.1.100\NAS`).
   - Enter the username (`pi`) and the password you set earlier.
2. On a macOS or Linux machine:
   - Open Finder (macOS) or File Manager (Linux), and select **Go > Connect to Server**.
   - Enter `smb://<Your_Pi's_IP_Address>/NAS`.

How to Access NAS Files Remotely

To access your NAS files remotely from outside your home network, you'll need to take some additional steps:

Option 1: Port Forwarding (Advanced)

1. Log in to your router's settings and set up port forwarding for Samba (port 445) to your Raspberry Pi's IP address.
2. Once configured, you can access the NAS remotely by entering your public IP address followed by the shared folder in your file manager (e.g., `\\<Public_IP>\NAS`).

Note: Be cautious when exposing your NAS to the internet, as it could open security vulnerabilities. Consider setting up a VPN for safer remote access.

Option 2: Use a VPN for Secure Remote Access

1. Set up a VPN (Virtual Private Network) on your Raspberry Pi using tools like **OpenVPN** or **WireGuard**.
2. Connect to your VPN from any device while you're away, and you'll be able to access your NAS as if you were on the same local network.

2.10 File Sharing on a Network

File sharing on a network allows you to easily exchange and access files between different devices connected to the same network, such as computers, smartphones, or Raspberry Pi. This is particularly useful for collaborative projects, backups, and centralized storage solutions.

Why File Sharing Is Useful on Networks

File sharing makes it easy to:

- **Access files from multiple devices**: You can store files on a central device (like a Raspberry Pi) and access them from other devices, such as computers, tablets, or phones.
- **Collaborate easily**: Multiple users can access and modify the same files, streamlining collaborative work or shared projects.
- **Backup files centrally**: By sharing files over a network, you can back up important data to a centralized location, such as a Raspberry Pi acting as a file server.
- **Stream media**: Easily stream music, videos, or other media files from one device to another without physically transferring files.

How to Set Up File Sharing Between Your Raspberry Pi and Other Devices

To set up file sharing between your Raspberry Pi and other devices on your local network, you can use **Samba**. This is a popular software tool that allows file sharing between Linux, Windows, and macOS devices.

Step 1: Install Samba on Raspberry Pi

1. Open the terminal on your Raspberry Pi.

Install Samba and the necessary components:

```
sudo apt update
sudo apt install samba samba-common-bin
```

Step 2: Create a Shared Folder

Choose or create a folder on your Raspberry Pi that you want to share. For example, create a folder called "shared":

```
mkdir ~/shared
```

Step 3: Configure Samba for File Sharing

Open the Samba configuration file to set up file sharing:

```
sudo nano /etc/samba/smb.conf
```

Scroll to the bottom of the file and add the following lines to define your shared folder:

```
[Shared]
path = /home/pi/shared
browseable = yes
writeable = yes
only guest = no
create mask = 0777
directory mask = 0777
public = yes
```

1. Save and close the file by pressing `Ctrl + X`, then `Y`, and Enter.

Step 4: Set Samba Password

Set a password for your Raspberry Pi user (`pi`) to use for file sharing:

```
sudo smbpasswd -a pi
```

1. Enter and confirm the password.

Step 5: Restart Samba

Restart the Samba service to apply the new settings:

```
sudo systemctl restart smbd
```

Step 6: Access the Shared Folder from Other Devices

- **On Windows**:
    1. Open File Explorer and type `\\<Your_Pi's_IP_Address>\Shared` into the address bar (e.g., `\\192.168.1.100\Shared`).
    2. Enter the Raspberry Pi username (`pi`) and password when prompted.
- **On macOS**:
    1. Open Finder and click **Go > Connect to Server**.
    2. Enter `smb://<Your_Pi's_IP_Address>/Shared`, and log in with the Raspberry Pi credentials.
- **On Linux**:
    1. Open the File Manager and select **Go > Enter Location**.
    2. Type `smb://<Your_Pi's_IP_Address>/Shared` to access the shared folder.

How to Troubleshoot File Sharing Issues

Here are some common issues you might encounter while setting up file sharing and how to resolve them:

- **Can't Access Shared Folder**:

Make sure that Samba is installed and running on your Raspberry Pi. You can check its status with:

```
sudo systemctl status smbd
```

- o Verify the IP address of your Raspberry Pi by running hostname -I in the terminal, and ensure you're using the correct IP to connect.
- **Incorrect Username or Password**:
  - o Ensure that you're using the correct Raspberry Pi credentials (username and password). If you haven't set a Samba password yet, run sudo smbpasswd -a pi to create one.
- **Permission Denied**:

Make sure the shared folder has the correct permissions to allow file sharing. You can set the necessary permissions with:

```
chmod 777 ~/shared
```

- **Connection Refused**:

If you're seeing a "connection refused" error, it's possible that the Samba service isn't running. Restart it with:

```
sudo systemctl restart smbd
```

- **No Access from Different Operating Systems**:
  - ○ Ensure that Samba is configured to allow connections from Windows, macOS, or Linux by ensuring `public = yes` is set in the Samba configuration file. Restart Samba after making changes.

2.11 Network Printing

Network printing allows you to share a printer across multiple devices on the same network. Using a Raspberry Pi as a print server is an affordable and convenient solution to make any USB printer accessible to all devices connected to your home or office network.

Why Network Printing Is Convenient

Network printing is highly convenient because:

- **Shared access**: Multiple devices (laptops, desktops, smartphones, etc.) can print to the same printer without needing a direct connection.
- **Wireless printing**: You can print from any device on your network, eliminating the need to physically connect the printer to each device.
- **Cost-effective**: Using a Raspberry Pi to set up a network printer is far cheaper than purchasing a dedicated network printer.
- **Centralized management**: With one printer shared across the network, it simplifies management and maintenance, as there's no need for multiple printers for different devices.

How to Set Up Network Printing with Raspberry Pi

You can turn your Raspberry Pi into a print server by using **CUPS (Common UNIX Printing System)**, which allows printers to be shared over a network.

Step 1: Install CUPS on Raspberry Pi

1. Open the terminal on your Raspberry Pi.

Update your Raspberry Pi's package list:

```
sudo apt update
```

2. Install CUPS:

```
sudo apt install cups
```

3. Add the `pi` user to the `lpadmin` group so you can manage printers:

```
sudo usermod -aG lpadmin pi
```

Step 2: Configure CUPS

Open the CUPS configuration file:

```
sudo nano /etc/cups/cupsd.conf
```

Look for the following sections and change them to allow network access:

```
# Allow remote access
Listen *:631
<Location />
  Order allow,deny
  Allow all
</Location>

<Location /admin>
  Order allow,deny
  Allow all
</Location>

<Location /admin/conf>
  AuthType Default
  Require valid-user
  Order allow,deny
  Allow all
</Location>
```

1. Save the changes by pressing `Ctrl + X`, then `Y`, and Enter.

Restart CUPS to apply the changes:

```
sudo systemctl restart cups
```

Step 3: Access the CUPS Web Interface

1. Open a web browser on your Raspberry Pi or any device connected to the same network.

Enter the following URL in the address bar to access the CUPS web interface:

```
http://<Your_Pi's_IP_Address>:631
```

2. (e.g., `http://192.168.1.100:631`)
3. Log in with your Raspberry Pi's username and password (usually `pi` and `raspberry` unless you've changed them).

Step 4: Add Your Printer

1. In the CUPS web interface, click on the **Administration** tab.
2. Under the **Printers** section, select **Add Printer**.
3. You will see a list of detected printers, including USB-connected printers. Select your printer and follow the on-screen instructions to add it.
4. Set the printer as **shared** so other devices on your network can access it.

Step 5: Install Printer on Other Devices

1. **Windows**:
   - Open **Settings > Devices > Printers & Scanners** and click **Add a Printer**. Windows should automatically detect the network printer. Select it and install the necessary drivers.

2. **macOS**:
   - Go to **System Preferences > Printers & Scanners** and click **+** to add a new printer. The network printer should appear, and you can add it by selecting the appropriate driver.
3. **Linux**:
   - Open the **Printers** settings and select **Add a Printer**. The CUPS server should automatically detect the printer, allowing you to add it.

How to Troubleshoot Network Printing Issues

If you encounter problems with network printing, here are some common issues and solutions:

- **Printer Not Detected**:
  - Ensure that the printer is properly connected to the Raspberry Pi via USB and turned on.
  - Check the printer's connection in the CUPS interface (http://<Your_Pi's_IP_Address>:631) to confirm it is listed.
- **Can't Access the CUPS Interface**:

Verify that CUPS is running on your Raspberry Pi by restarting the service:

```
sudo systemctl restart cups
```

  - Ensure you're using the correct IP address of the Raspberry Pi. You can find it by running hostname -I.
- **Devices Can't Find the Printer**:
  - Make sure the printer is shared in the CUPS settings.
  - Ensure that CUPS is configured to allow network access (Allow all in the /etc/cups/cupsd.conf file).

- Restart both the Raspberry Pi and the printer to refresh the connection.
- **Print Jobs Stuck in Queue**:
  - Check if there are any errors in the CUPS interface under the **Jobs** section.
  - Ensure the printer is online and that no physical issues (like low ink or paper jams) are causing the problem.

2.12 Introduction to Security in Networking

When connecting your Raspberry Pi to a network, security is crucial to protect your device and data from unauthorized access. Even if your Pi is on a home network, it's important to enable some basic security features to safeguard it from external threats.

Why It's Important to Secure Your Pi on a Network

Security is critical for a few reasons:

- **Prevent unauthorized access**: By default, Raspberry Pi OS uses default login credentials (pi and raspberry), which are widely known and could be exploited by attackers.
- **Protect sensitive data**: If you're using your Pi for file sharing, a web server, or any project with personal or sensitive data, securing it helps prevent data breaches.
- **Avoid being compromised**: An unsecured Raspberry Pi could be used as a launch point for attacks on other devices on your network or for malicious activities over the internet.

Key risks include:

- Unsecured **remote access** through SSH.
- Weak default passwords.
- Lack of protection against external attacks, especially if the Pi is exposed to the internet.

How to Enable Basic Security Features

To secure your Raspberry Pi, follow these basic security steps:

Changing Default Passwords

By default, the Raspberry Pi OS uses `pi` as the username and `raspberry` as the password. Changing this password is a fundamental step to protect your Pi from unauthorized access.

Step-by-Step Guide:

1. Open a terminal on your Raspberry Pi.

Change the default password by running:

```
passwd
```

2. You will be prompted to enter your current password (default is `raspberry`) and then enter a new, secure password twice. Ensure that your new password is strong, using a combination of letters, numbers, and special characters.

Disabling SSH When Not in Use

SSH (Secure Shell) allows you to remotely access your Raspberry Pi's terminal from another computer. While SSH is very useful, leaving it enabled when not in use could allow attackers to try logging into your Pi. To enhance security, disable SSH when you don't need it.

Step-by-Step Guide:

To check if SSH is enabled, use this command:

```
sudo systemctl status ssh
```

If you aren't using SSH, disable it:

```
sudo systemctl disable ssh
sudo systemctl stop ssh
```

If you need to use SSH later, you can re-enable it by running:

```
sudo systemctl enable ssh
sudo systemctl start ssh
```

By disabling SSH when it's not needed, you close a potential entry point for attackers.

Enabling a Simple Firewall

A firewall helps to block unauthorized connections to your Raspberry Pi by filtering incoming and outgoing traffic. One easy-to-use firewall tool on Linux is **UFW (Uncomplicated Firewall)**.

Step-by-Step Guide:

Install UFW on your Raspberry Pi:

```
sudo apt install ufw
```

Allow SSH through the firewall if you plan to use it. This ensures you don't lock yourself out when the firewall is active:

```
sudo ufw allow ssh
```

Enable UFW to block any other unwanted connections:

```
sudo ufw enable
```

Check the status of the firewall to ensure it's active:

```
sudo ufw status
```

If you want to allow other services, like web servers or file sharing, you can specify them:

```
sudo ufw allow http
sudo ufw allow samba
```

By enabling a firewall, you ensure that only specific types of traffic can access your Raspberry Pi, providing an additional layer of protection.

2.13 Understanding Common Networking Commands

Networking commands are essential tools for checking the status of your network connection and troubleshooting issues on your Raspberry Pi. These commands help you diagnose problems and understand the current state of your network.

Basic Commands for Checking Network Status

Here are some commonly used networking commands and what they do:

1. `ifconfig` (Interface Configuration)

- **What it does**: Displays the current network configuration of your Raspberry Pi, including IP addresses, subnet masks, and active network interfaces (such as `eth0` for Ethernet or `wlan0` for Wi-Fi).

How to use it:

```
ifconfig
```

- This command will show all active network interfaces, their IP addresses, and connection status. It's particularly useful for checking whether your Pi has a valid IP address.

---

2. `ping` (Packet Internet Groper)

- **What it does**: Sends a small packet of data to another device on the network or the internet to check if it is reachable. It helps you test if your Raspberry Pi is connected to a network and if a specific server or website is online.

How to use it:

```
ping google.com
```

- This will send packets to Google's server and display the time it takes to get a response. You can also use it to test connectivity with other devices on your network by replacing "google.com" with an IP address.

3. `netstat` (Network Statistics)

- **What it does**: Provides detailed information about network connections, routing tables, and active ports. It can be used to see all active connections to and from your Raspberry Pi.

How to use it:

```
netstat
```

- This command shows you a list of active connections, the ports in use, and which services are listening for incoming connections.

---

4. `hostname -I` (Hostname IP Address)

- **What it does**: Displays your Raspberry Pi's IP address quickly without additional network details.

How to use it:

```
hostname -I
```

- This is a simple way to find out your Pi's IP address if you need it for file sharing, remote access, or troubleshooting.

---

5. `traceroute` (Trace Route)

- **What it does**: Traces the path packets take to reach a destination. It helps you understand if there are any bottlenecks or issues between your Raspberry Pi and another device on the network or the internet.

How to use it:

```
traceroute google.com
```

- This command shows each step (or "hop") your packets take on the way to Google's server, revealing any delays or issues along the way.

---

6. nslookup (Name Server Lookup)
- **What it does**: Resolves domain names to IP addresses, helping you check if your Pi can communicate with DNS servers.

How to use it:

```
nslookup google.com
```

- This will return the IP address associated with "google.com," showing that your DNS resolution is working properly.

Chapter 3: Using the Raspberry Pi Operating System

3.0. Introduction

An **Operating System (OS)** is the software that allows your Raspberry Pi to function, just like Windows or macOS on other computers. The OS is responsible for managing hardware (like your keyboard, mouse, and screen), running programs, and handling files. For beginners, understanding the basics of the OS is key to using your Raspberry Pi effectively.

Why Understanding the Operating System is Crucial

Understanding the OS is essential for controlling your Raspberry Pi. It lets you:

- **Install software**: The OS helps you add new applications or tools.
- **Manage files**: You'll learn how to organize and navigate your files.
- **Run programs**: You can control what tasks your Pi performs, such as creating a web server or running games.
- **Troubleshoot issues**: Understanding the OS helps you fix common problems and keep your Pi running smoothly.

Even basic knowledge of the OS gives you the power to unlock your Raspberry Pi's full potential, whether for personal projects, learning, or experimenting.

Overview of Raspberry Pi Operating Systems

There are several operating systems available for the Raspberry Pi, each tailored to different uses:

- **Raspberry Pi OS** (formerly called Raspbian):
  - **Most popular** and **official OS** for the Raspberry Pi.
  - **Beginner-friendly** and perfect for general use, learning to code, and basic tasks like web browsing.
  - Comes in different versions (with a desktop environment or Lite for command-line-only use).
- **Ubuntu**:
  - A popular Linux-based OS that is **more powerful** but also a bit more complex.
  - Useful for advanced users who want to run servers or more intensive applications.
- **Other OS options**:
  - **RetroPie** for turning your Pi into a retro gaming console.

- ○ **LibreELEC** for media center projects (e.g., using your Pi as a home theater).
- ○ **Windows IoT Core** for running IoT (Internet of Things) applications.

Basic Terminology

Here are some key terms that are useful when working with your Raspberry Pi's OS:

- **Terminal**:
    - ○ A text-based interface where you can type commands to control your Raspberry Pi. Think of it as the "control center" for your Pi.
    - ○ You can open the terminal to install software, manage files, or even shut down the system.

- **File Manager**:
    - ○ A graphical tool that lets you visually browse and manage files and folders (just like the file explorer on Windows or Finder on macOS).
    - ○ Helpful for beginners who are not yet comfortable using the terminal.
- **Permissions**:
    - ○ Determines who can read, write, or execute files. Files and folders have different levels of access control, ensuring that sensitive system files are protected.
- **Superuser**:
    - ○ The user with administrative privileges. Running commands as the superuser (with sudo in the terminal) allows you to perform system-level tasks, like installing software or changing important settings.

Basic Commands

Here are some essential commands to help you get started with your Raspberry Pi's terminal. Learning these commands will give you more control over your system, making tasks like navigating directories, copying files, and editing text much easier.

`ls` – List Files and Directories

- **What it does**: Displays the files and folders in your current directory.
- **Why It's Useful**: Helps you see what's in the current folder and check if the files you're looking for are present.

How to use it:

```
ls
```

This will show a list of files and folders. For more details, you can use:

```
ls -l
```

`cd` – Change Directories

- **What it does**: Moves you into a different directory (folder) in the file system.
- **Why It's Important**: Allows you to navigate through the various folders on your Raspberry Pi.

How to use it:

```
cd /path/to/directory
```

For example, to move to the "Documents" folder:

```
cd Documents
```

pwd – Print the Working Directory

- **What it does**: Tells you the full path of the folder you are currently in.
- **Why It's Important**: Helps you know where you are in the file system, which is essential when moving between directories.

cp – Copy Files and Directories

- **What it does**: Copies files or folders from one location to another.
- **Why It's Useful**: Ideal for backing up files or transferring them to a different directory.

How to use it:

```
cp file.txt /path/to/destination
```

To copy an entire directory:

```
cp -r folder_name /path/to/destination
```

mv – Move or Rename Files and Directories

- **What it does**: Moves files or folders to another location or renames them.
- **Why It's Useful**: Useful for organizing files or changing their names.

How to use it:

```
mv old_name.txt new_name.txt
```

To move a file to another folder:

```
mv file.txt /path/to/destination
```

rm – Remove Files and Directories

- **What it does**: Deletes files or directories.
- **Why It's Important**: Clears up space by removing unnecessary files.

How to use it:

```
rm file.txt
```

To remove an entire folder and its contents, use:

```
rm -r folder_name
```

- **Warning**: Be careful when using rm, as deleted files cannot be easily recovered.

mkdir – Create Directories

- **What it does**: Creates a new folder.
- **Why It's Important**: Organizes files by placing them into specific folders for easy access.

How to use it:

```
mkdir new_folder
```

touch – Create an Empty File

- **What it does**: Creates an empty file.
- **Why It's Useful**: Useful for creating configuration files or placeholders.

How to use it:

```
touch newfile.txt
```

---

nano – Open and Edit Files with the Nano Text Editor

- **What it does**: Opens the **Nano** text editor to create or edit text files.
- **Why It's Useful**: Nano is a simple and beginner-friendly text editor that lets you directly modify text files from the terminal.

How to use it:

```
nano file.txt
```

- Once in Nano, you can edit the file and press $Ctrl + O$ to save, then $Ctrl + X$ to exit.

---

sudo – Execute Commands with Superuser Privileges

- **What it does**: Runs commands as a superuser (admin).
- **Why It's Important**: Required for system-level tasks like installing software or modifying important files.

How to use it:

```
sudo command
```

For example, to update your Raspberry Pi's software, you would run:

```
sudo apt-get update
```

Common Mistakes to Avoid

- **Navigating to non-existent directories with** `cd`: Double-check the path before navigating.
- **Accidentally deleting important files with** `rm`: Be cautious when using the `rm` command. Always double-check the files you're removing.

3.1 Browsing Files Graphically

For those who are new to the Raspberry Pi or computers in general, browsing files graphically is often the easiest way to manage files and folders. The **File Manager** provides a visual interface, similar to File Explorer on Windows or Finder on macOS, where you can click to open, move, or delete files without needing to type commands in the terminal.

Using the File Manager

Here's how you can browse files graphically on your Raspberry Pi:

1. **Open the File Manager**:
   - On the Raspberry Pi's desktop, look for an icon that looks like a folder. This is the **File Manager**.
   - Double-click the folder icon to open the File Manager.

2. **Navigating Directories**:
   - Once the File Manager is open, you'll see different directories (folders).
   - You can **double-click** on a folder to open it and see its contents.
   - If you want to go back to the previous folder, click the **back arrow** at the top or the **up arrow** to move up one directory level.

3. **Opening Files**:
   - ○ To open a file, simply **double-click** on it. If it's a text file, it will open in the default text editor. Images, videos, and other file types will open in their respective programs.
4. **Copying and Moving Files**:
   - ○ To **copy** a file, right-click on the file and select **Copy**. Then, navigate to the folder where you want to place the copy, right-click again, and select **Paste**.
   - ○ To **move** a file, right-click and select **Cut** instead of Copy. Then navigate to the destination folder and right-click to **Paste** the file there.
5. **Creating Folders**:
   - ○ To create a new folder, **right-click** inside the directory where you want the folder and select **Create New Folder**. Name the folder and press Enter.
6. **Renaming Files**:
   - ○ To rename a file or folder, right-click on it and choose **Rename**. Enter the new name and press Enter.
7. **Deleting Files**:
   - ○ Right-click on a file or folder you want to delete and select **Move to Trash**. Be careful, as once files are deleted, they might be permanently removed if you empty the trash.

3.2 Copying Files onto a USB Flash Drive

Using a USB flash drive to copy files between systems is a simple way to transfer data, back up important files, or share content between devices. Here's an easy, copying files from your Raspberry Pi to a USB flash drive.

Copying Files

1. **Insert the USB Flash Drive**:
   - ○ Plug your USB flash drive into one of the USB ports on your Raspberry Pi.

- After a few moments, your Raspberry Pi should automatically recognize the drive, and an icon will appear on the desktop.

2. **Open the USB Drive**:
   - Double-click the USB flash drive icon on the desktop. This will open the drive in the **File Manager**.

3. **Open the Source Folder**:
   - In another File Manager window (you can open a second one by clicking the folder icon on the desktop again), navigate to the folder containing the file(s) you want to copy.

4. **Copy the File**:
   - Right-click on the file you want to copy and select **Copy**.

5. **Paste the File to the USB Drive**:
   - Switch to the File Manager window displaying your USB flash drive.
   - Right-click anywhere in the open space in the USB drive window and select **Paste**. The file will now be copied to your USB flash drive.

6. **Safely Eject the USB Drive**:
   - Before physically removing the USB flash drive, right-click on the USB drive icon on the desktop and select **Eject**.
   - Wait until the system confirms that it's safe to remove the USB flash drive (the drive icon may disappear from the desktop).

Why It's Useful

Copying files onto a USB flash drive is useful because:

- It allows you to **transfer files between different systems**, like moving documents, images, or media files from your Raspberry Pi to another computer.
- You can easily create **backups** of important files on a USB drive, which can later be stored safely.
- It's a great method for **sharing files** with others when cloud services aren't available or suitable.

Common Mistakes

- **Not ejecting the USB drive properly**: Removing the USB flash drive without ejecting it first can result in data loss or file corruption. Always eject the drive to ensure the transfer is complete and the data is safe.
- **Copying large files without checking available space**: Make sure your USB flash drive has enough space for the files you're copying. You can check available space by right-clicking the USB drive in the File Manager and selecting **Properties**.

3.3 Starting a Terminal Session

The **Terminal** is a powerful tool that lets you interact with your Raspberry Pi through text commands rather than using a graphical interface. It may seem intimidating at first, but with a little practice, it becomes a great way to control your Raspberry Pi and perform tasks more efficiently.

Why Use It?

The **Terminal** is a command-line interface that allows you to communicate with your Raspberry Pi by typing commands. It provides direct access to the operating system, allowing you to:

- **Install software**: The terminal is often the quickest way to install or update applications.
- **Manage files**: Move, copy, or delete files with just a few commands.
- **Perform administrative tasks**: Many system-level tasks require terminal commands for full control.

Using the terminal is especially helpful when:

- You need more control than the graphical interface provides.
- You want to work faster, as some tasks are quicker to perform through the terminal.
- You're troubleshooting an issue, as the terminal can provide detailed information.

How to Start a Terminal Session

Step-by-Step Guide:

1. **Opening the Terminal**:
    - On the Raspberry Pi's desktop, look for the terminal icon, which looks like a black screen or command prompt.
    - **Click the terminal icon** to open a terminal window. This will bring up a blank window with a prompt (usually ending in $), where you can start typing commands.
2. If you prefer, you can also open the terminal by pressing Ctrl + Alt + T on your keyboard.
3. **Running a Command**:

Once the terminal is open, you can start typing commands. For example, to see your current location in the file system, type:

```
pwd
```

Then, press Enter. The terminal will display the current directory (folder) you're working in.

3.4 Navigating the Filesystem Using a Terminal

Navigating the Raspberry Pi's filesystem through the terminal is an essential skill that helps you manage your files efficiently. Instead of relying on a graphical interface, you'll be using simple commands to move between directories, view files, and organize your folders.

Navigating the Filesystem

Here are some basic commands for navigating and managing the filesystem on your Raspberry Pi through the terminal.

---

1. pwd – Print Working Directory

- **What it does**: Shows the full path of your current location in the filesystem.

How to use it:

```
pwd
```

- This command tells you exactly where you are, which is especially useful if you get lost while navigating through folders.

---

2. ls – List Files and Directories

- **What it does**: Lists all files and directories in the current folder.

How to use it:

```
ls
```

This will display all files and folders in your current directory. To view more details (such as file size and modification date), use:

```
ls -l
```

3. cd – Change Directory

- **What it does**: Allows you to move to different directories in the filesystem.

How to use it:

```
cd /path/to/directory
```

For example, to move to the **Documents** folder:

```
cd Documents
```

To move up one directory (to the parent folder):

```
cd ..
```

To move directly to your home directory:

```
cd ~
```

4. mkdir – Make Directory

- **What it does**: Creates a new folder in your current directory.

How to use it:

```
mkdir new_folder
```

For example, to create a folder called "Projects":

```
mkdir Projects
```

.3.5 Copying a File or Folder

Copying files and folders using the terminal is a simple but important skill for managing your Raspberry Pi's filesystem. The **cp** command allows you to create backups, organize files, or transfer them from one folder to another.

How to Copy Files or Folders via Terminal

Basic Command: cp

The cp command is used to copy files or directories from one location to another.

1. Copying a File:

Command format:

```
cp source_file destination_directory
```

Example: If you want to copy a file named file.txt from your home directory to the Documents folder, the command would look like this:

```
cp file.txt Documents/
```

This will make a copy of `file.txt` and place it in the Documents folder. The original file will remain in its original location.

2. Copying a Folder:

Command format: To copy an entire directory (folder), use the `-r` option (which stands for "recursive") to ensure all contents of the folder are copied.

```
cp -r source_folder destination_directory
```

Example: To copy a folder named `MyFolder` into the Documents directory:

```
cp -r MyFolder Documents/
```

This will copy the `MyFolder` directory, along with all its contents, into the Documents folder.

Common Mistakes

Forgetting to include the destination path: If you don't specify the full destination path, the `cp` command won't know where to copy the file. Always ensure you include both the file to be copied and the folder where you want it to go.

For example, running:

```
cp file.txt
```

- will result in an error because the command is missing the destination directory.
- **Not using `-r` for copying folders**: If you forget the `-r` option when copying directories, the command will fail. Always use `-r` when copying a folder.

3.6 Renaming a File or Folder

Renaming files and folders using the terminal is a quick and easy way to keep your files organized. The `mv` command, which is primarily used for moving files, can also be used to rename them.

How to Rename Files Using the Terminal

Basic Command: `mv`

The `mv` command allows you to rename files and folders by "moving" them to a new name.

---

1. Renaming a File:

Command format:

```
mv old_name new_name
```

Example: To rename a file called document.txt to notes.txt, use:

```
mv document.txt notes.txt
```

This command changes the name of the file without moving it to a different directory.

---

2. Renaming a Folder:

Command format:

```
mv old_folder_name new_folder_name
```

Example: To rename a folder called `OldFolder` to `NewFolder`, use:

```
mv OldFolder NewFolder
```

Common Mistakes

Accidentally overwriting files: If a file with the new name already exists, the `mv` command will overwrite it without warning. Always check that the new file name does not already exist before renaming.

For example, if `notes.txt` already exists, the following command will replace it:

`mv document.txt notes.txt`

- **Confusing paths**: When renaming, make sure you're in the correct directory and using the correct file paths. If you try to rename a file that doesn't exist in the current directory, you'll see an error message.

3.7 Creating a Directory

Creating directories (folders) is an essential task for organizing your files on a Raspberry Pi. The `mkdir` command allows you to easily create new folders using the terminal, helping you keep your files organized and accessible.

Creating Directories

Basic Command: `mkdir`

The `mkdir` command is used to create new directories (folders) in the current or specified location.

1. Creating a New Directory:
Command format:

```
mkdir directory_name
```

Example: To create a folder named NewFolder in your current directory:

```
mkdir NewFolder
```

This will create a new directory called **NewFolder** in the location you are currently in.

2. Creating a Directory in a Specific Path:

Command format: If you want to create a directory in a specific location (not your current directory), you can specify the path:

```
mkdir /path/to/directory_name
```

Example: To create a folder named Projects inside the **Documents** folder:

```
mkdir Documents/Projects
```

Common Mistakes
Typing errors in directory names: It's easy to make a mistake while typing directory names. Double-check the name before hitting Enter, especially if it contains multiple words or special characters. For example, if you type:

```
mkdir myfoler
```

- instead of `myfolder`, the directory will be created with the wrong name.

Creating directories in the wrong location: Make sure you are in the correct directory before creating a new folder. You can check your current location using the `pwd` command:

`pwd`

3.8 Deleting a File or Directory

Deleting unnecessary files and directories is important for keeping your Raspberry Pi's storage clean and organized. The `rm` command allows you to safely delete files and directories via the terminal.

How to Safely Delete Files and Directories

Basic Command: `rm`

The `rm` command is used to remove (delete) files and directories.

---

1. Deleting a File:

Command format:

```
rm file_name
```

Example: To delete a file named `example.txt`:

```
rm example.txt
```

This will permanently delete the file, so double-check the file name before pressing Enter.

2. Deleting a Directory:

Command format: To delete an entire directory and its contents, use the `-r` option (recursive), which tells the terminal to delete the folder and everything inside it.

```
rm -r folder_name
```

Example: To delete a folder called `OldFolder`:

```
rm -r OldFolder
```

This will permanently delete the folder and all its contents, including files and subfolders.

Common Mistakes

Accidentally deleting important files: Be careful when using the `rm` command, as it **permanently** deletes files without sending them to a trash bin. Always double-check the file or folder you're about to delete.

To avoid mistakes, you can use the `rm -i` command, which prompts you to confirm each deletion:

```
rm -i file_name
```

- **Using `rm` on the wrong file or folder**: Typing errors in file or folder names can lead to unintended deletions. Double-check the name of the file or directory before running the command.

3.9 Editing a File

Editing files on your Raspberry Pi is a crucial skill, especially when you need to make configuration changes, write scripts, or adjust settings. The **Nano** text editor is a simple and beginner-friendly tool for editing text files directly from the terminal. For those who want to dive deeper, **Vim** is also available, but Nano is easier for beginners.

How to Edit Files Using Nano

Basic Command: nano

The nano command opens a file for editing within the terminal. Nano is a lightweight text editor that's easy to use, making it ideal for beginners.

1. Opening a File with Nano:

Command format:

```
nano file_name
```

Example: To open a file called config.txt for editing:

```
nano config.txt
```

This will open the config.txt file in the Nano editor, where you can make changes.

2. Making Changes in Nano:

- Once the file is open in Nano, you can start typing or editing the text.
- Use the arrow keys to move around within the file.

3. Saving Changes in Nano:

- After editing the file, press Ctrl + O to save your changes.

- You'll be prompted to confirm the file name. Just press **Enter** to save the file.

---

4. Exiting Nano:

- To exit Nano, press `Ctrl + X`. This will close the editor and return you to the terminal.

Common Mistakes

- **Forgetting to save changes**: It's easy to forget to save your work before exiting Nano. Always press `Ctrl + O` to save your changes before pressing `Ctrl + X` to exit.
- **Typing errors**: When editing configuration files or scripts, a small typo can cause errors. Be careful when editing important system files and double-check your changes.

3.10 Understanding File Permissions

File permissions control who can read, write, or execute a file or directory on your Raspberry Pi. Understanding how permissions work is crucial for ensuring the security and proper management of your files.

How to Check File Permissions

Basic Command: `ls -l`

The `ls -l` command lists files and directories along with detailed information, including their permissions.

1. Checking File Permissions:

Command format:

```
ls -l
```

Example: To check the permissions of the files in your current directory, type:

```
ls -l
```

This will output something like this:

```
-rw-r--r--   1 pi    pi    1234   Jan 1 12:34
example.txt
```

The output can be broken down as follows:

- `-rw-r--r--`: File permissions (explained below)
- `pi pi`: The owner and group
- `1234`: File size in bytes
- `Jan 1 12:34`: Last modified date
- `example.txt`: File name

Understanding File Permissions

Permissions are typically shown as a string of 10 characters (e.g., `-rw-r--r--`).

- The first character indicates whether it's a **file** (`-`) or **directory** (`d`).
- The next three characters (`rw-`) show the permissions for the **file owner**.
- The following three characters (`r--`) show the permissions for the **group**.
- The final three characters (`r--`) show the permissions for **everyone else** (others).

Here's what the individual letters mean:

- **r** = Read: The user can view the file or list the directory's contents.
- **w** = Write: The user can modify or delete the file.
- **x** = Execute: The user can run the file (if it's a program or script) or enter the directory.
- **-** = No permission.

For example, `-rw-r--r--` means:

- The owner can read and write the file.
- The group can only read the file.
- Others (everyone else) can only read the file.

3.11 Performing Tasks with Superuser Privileges

Certain tasks on your Raspberry Pi, such as installing software or making system-wide changes, require **superuser privileges**. The sudo command allows you to temporarily act as the superuser (also called root) to perform these administrative tasks.

How to Use sudo for Admin Tasks

Basic Command: sudo

The sudo command allows you to run commands with superuser (admin) privileges. It's used when you need to install, update, or modify system files that a normal user can't change.

---

1. Running a Command with sudo:

Command format:

```
sudo command
```

Example: To install software or update your system, you would use sudo. For example, to update your system's package list:

```
sudo apt-get update
```

- Here, apt-get update is the command to update the system's package list, and adding sudo at the beginning gives you the necessary permissions to perform the task.

3.12 Installing Software with apt-get

One of the key benefits of using a Raspberry Pi is the ability to install new software easily, expanding its functionality. The apt-get tool is the default package manager for Raspberry Pi OS (based on Debian) and is used to install, update, and remove software packages.

Installing Software

Basic Command: sudo apt-get install

To install software, you need to use apt-get along with the install option, followed by the name of the software package. Since installing software requires admin privileges, you will need to use sudo.

1. Updating the System's Package List: Before installing new software, it's a good idea to update the package list to ensure you're getting the latest version of the software.
Command:

```
sudo apt-get update
```

This command updates the list of available software and versions from the repositories, ensuring you get the most current version.

2. Installing Software:

Command format:

```
sudo apt-get install package_name
```

Example: To install a simple system monitoring tool called htop:

```
sudo apt-get install htop
```

This command will download and install the htop package from the repositories.

Chapter 4: Getting Started with Python Programming

4.0 Introduction

Python is a powerful, high-level, and easy-to-learn programming language, widely recognized for its simplicity and readability. Its beginner-friendly syntax makes it an excellent choice for both novice and experienced programmers. Python is versatile and supports a range of programming paradigms, including procedural, object-oriented, and functional programming.

Why Does This Matter for Raspberry Pi?

Python is the go-to language for many Raspberry Pi projects due to its simplicity and efficiency. The Raspberry Pi community often uses Python for tasks like automating hardware (sensors, LEDs, etc.), building small web applications, or creating IoT (Internet of Things) projects. By learning Python, you'll unlock the ability to write your own programs, automate tasks, and control hardware components on your Raspberry Pi.

Why Learn Python for Raspberry Pi?

- **Control Hardware**: Use Python to interface with Raspberry Pi's GPIO pins and interact with various sensors, LEDs, and motors.
- **Automate Tasks**: Write scripts to automate repetitive tasks, manage files, or perform system maintenance.
- **Build Projects**: Whether you want to create games, web applications, or smart devices, Python is a great starting point for building your own Raspberry Pi projects.
- **Extensive Community Support**: Python is one of the most popular languages, with extensive documentation and a large community of developers. There are countless tutorials, code samples, and libraries tailored to Raspberry Pi.

Key Concepts You Will Learn:

- Python syntax and how to write simple programs
- How to control the Raspberry Pi's hardware using Python
- Reading inputs (like sensors) and producing outputs (like controlling lights or motors)

4.1 Assigning Names to Values (Variables)

Variables are used to store data in a program. They act as containers that hold values, such as names, numbers, or any other type of data.

Why Does This Matter?

Variables are essential for working with data in programs. They allow you to store, update, and manipulate information efficiently.

Syntax:

Here is the basic syntax to create a variable and assign a value

```
variable_name = value
```

This assigns the `value` to the `variable_name`.

Example:

Here's how to assign a name and age to variables:

```
name = "Alice"
age = 25
```

In this case:

- The variable `name` holds the value `"Alice"`.
- The variable `age` holds the number `25`.

Common Mistakes:

- **Starting variable names with numbers**: Variables cannot start with numbers. For example, `1name` is invalid, but `name1` is allowed.
- **Using spaces in variable names**: Variable names cannot contain spaces. Instead, use underscores (_), like `first_name`.

4.2 Variable Reassignment

Variable reassignment allows you to change the value stored in a variable after it has been initially assigned.

Why Does This Matter?

Reassigning variables is important because it lets you update the value stored in a variable as your program runs.

Syntax:
Here's how to reassign a variable:

```
variable_name = new_value
```

Example:

```
age = 25
print(age)  # Output: 25

age = 30  # Reassigning the value
print(age)  # Output: 30
```

Explanation of the Code:

- Initially, age is assigned the value 25.
- Later, age is reassigned to 30.

Common Mistakes:

- **Confusing reassignment with creating a new variable**: Reassigning changes the existing variable's value, it does not create a new variable.

4.3 Variable Types

Variables can hold different types of data, such as numbers, strings (text), and more. These are called "data types."

Why Does This Matter?

Understanding variable types helps you work with different kinds of data, like numbers for calculations or strings for text.

Syntax:

Python supports multiple data types for variables, such as:

- **Integer** (whole numbers): age = 25
- **Float** (decimal numbers): price = 19.99
- **String** (text): name = "Alice"
- **Boolean** (True/False): is_student = True

Example:

```
age = 25  # Integer
price = 19.99  # Float
name = "Alice"  # String
is_student = True  # Boolean
```

Explanation of the Code:

- `age` is an integer (whole number).
- `price` is a float (decimal number).
- `name` is a string (text).
- `is_student` is a boolean (True/False value).

4.4 Constants

Constants are variables whose values are not meant to change during the execution of a program.

Why Does This Matter?

Using constants makes your code more readable and helps avoid accidental changes to important values.

Syntax:

By convention, constants are written in all uppercase letters:

```
PI = 3.14159
MAX_USERS = 100
```

Example:

```
PI = 3.14159
print("The value of PI is:", PI)
```

Common Mistakes:

- **Treating constants like regular variables**: Constants are supposed to remain unchanged, so avoid reassigning them.

4.5 Multiple Variable Assignment

Python allows you to assign values to multiple variables in one line.

Why Does This Matter?
Multiple variable assignment can make your code cleaner and more concise.

Syntax:
You can assign values to several variables at once:

```
a, b, c = 5, 10, 15
```

Example:

```
x, y, z = 1, 2, 3
print(x, y, z)
```

Common Mistakes:

- **Assigning the wrong number of values**: Make sure the number of variables matches the number of values you're assigning.

4.6 Swapping Values Between Variables

Swapping values means exchanging the values of two variables.

Why Does This Matter?
Swapping values is useful in many algorithms and problem-solving situations.

Syntax:

You can swap two variables easily in Python:

```
a, b = b, a
```

Example:

```
x = 5
y = 10
x, y = y, x   # Swapping values
print(x, y)   # Output: 10 5
```

4.7 Displaying Output

Displaying output refers to using the `print()` function in Python to show information or results on the screen.

Why Does This Matter?

Output is crucial because it helps you understand what your program is doing, whether it's producing the correct results or providing the right feedback.

Syntax:

The `print()` function can display many types of information, such as strings, numbers, variables, and even expressions. Here are the common ways to use `print()`:

Printing Strings (Text):

```
print("Your message here")
```

Printing Numbers:

```
print(123)
```

Printing Variables:

```
        my_variable = "Hello"
print(my_variable)
```

Printing Multiple Items: You can print several things at once by separating them with commas:

```
print("Name:", "Alice", "Age:", 25)
```

Printing Expressions: You can also print the result of an expression:

```
print(5 + 3)   # Outputs: 8
```

Printing with String Concatenation: You can combine strings using the + operator:

```
print("Hello, " + "World!")   # Outputs: Hello, World!
```

Formatted String (f-strings): Python allows you to embed variables directly inside strings using f-strings:

```
name = "Alice"
age = 25
print(f"Name: {name}, Age: {age}")
```

1. **Printing with sep and end Parameters**:
   o sep controls how multiple items are separated (by default, it's a space).
   o end controls what is printed at the end of the output (by default, it's a newline).

Example using `sep`:

```
print("Alice", "Bob", "Charlie", sep=" | ")  # Outputs: Alice | Bob |
Charlie
Example using end:
print("Hello", end="!")
print(" World")  # Outputs: Hello! World (instead of on a new line)
```

Example:

```
print("Welcome to Python!")
```

Explanation of the Code:

- The `print()` function will display the message `"Welcome to Python!"` on the screen.

Common Mistakes:

- **Forgetting parentheses in Python 3**: In Python 2, `print` could be used without parentheses, but in Python 3, you must always use parentheses. So, `print "Hello"` (Python 2) is now written as `print("Hello")` in Python 3.

4.8 Reading User Input

The `input()` function allows your program to receive information from the user by prompting them to enter something. This makes programs interactive, letting the user provide data that the program can use.

Why Does This Matter?

User input is essential for creating interactive programs that adapt to different users' inputs, making your programs more dynamic and useful.

Syntax:

The `input()` function is used to ask the user for input. Here's the basic syntax:

```
input("Your prompt message here")
```

Syntax Explanation:

- `input`: This function pauses the program and waits for the user to type something.
- `"Your prompt message here"`: This is the message that appears to the user, prompting them to enter something. It should be placed inside parentheses and quotes.

Example:

```
name = input("What's your name? ")
print("Hello, " + name + "!")
```

Explanation of the Code:

- `input("What's your name? ")`: This prompts the user to type their name. The input is stored in the variable `name`.
- `print("Hello, " + name + "!")`: This prints a personalized greeting using the name the user entered.

Handling Different Data Types:
Reading Strings (Text Input):

```
name = input("Enter your name: ")
print("Hello, " + name + "!")
```

1. **Reading Numbers**: If you expect the user to enter a number, you need to convert the input from a string to an integer or float, as the `input()` function always returns a string.

For integers (whole numbers):

```python
age = int(input("Enter your age: "))
print("You are", age, "years old.")
```

For floats (decimal numbers):

```python
height = float(input("Enter your height in meters: "))
print("Your height is", height, "meters.")
```

Reading Booleans: You can convert the user's input into a boolean by comparing it to expected values:

```python
is_student = input("Are you a student? (yes/no): ").lower() == "yes"
print("Student status:", is_student)
```

Common Mistakes:

Forgetting to convert input to numbers: The `input()` function always returns data as a string. If you're asking for numbers (like age or height), you must convert it using `int()` or `float()` for calculations.
For example:

```python
age = input("Enter your age: ")   # Returns a string
print(age * 2)   # This will repeat the string, not multiply the number
```

To fix this, convert it to an integer:

```python
age = int(input("Enter your age: "))   # Converts input to an integer
print(age * 2)   # Correctly multiplies the age by 2
```

4.9 Arithmetic

Arithmetic in Python involves using basic math operations like addition, subtraction, multiplication, and division to perform calculations.

Why Does This Matter?

Arithmetic is essential because it allows programs to handle numbers and perform operations that are often needed for various calculations.

Syntax

You can perform arithmetic operations like this:

```
result = 5 + 3
```

Explanation: This adds 5 and 3 together, storing the result in the variable `result`.

Examples

Addition:

```
total = 5 + 7
print(total)   # Outputs: 12
```

Subtraction:

```
difference = 10 - 3
print(difference)   # Outputs: 7
```

Multiplication:

```
product = 10 * 2
print(product)   # Outputs: 20
```

Division:

```
result = 8 / 2
print(result)   # Outputs: 4.0
```

Modulus (to find the remainder of a division):

```
remainder = 9 % 2
print(remainder)   # Outputs: 1
```

Exponentiation (raising a number to a power):

```
power = 2 ** 3
print(power)   # Outputs: 8
```

Floor Division (division that rounds down):

```
floor_div = 7 // 2
print(floor_div)  # Outputs: 3
```

Common Mistakes

- **Confusing + for string concatenation**: Remember that + is used for addition with numbers, but it can also join strings. Make sure you know when you're adding numbers vs. combining text.

4.10 Creating Strings

A string in Python is a sequence of characters used to store text, such as names, messages, or any form of textual data.

Why does this matter?
Strings are essential because most programs need to work with text. Whether it's displaying messages, accepting user input, or storing information like names or emails, strings are widely used.

Syntax
To create a string, you enclose the text in quotes:

```
my_string = "Hello"
```

Explanation: Here, the word "Hello" is stored in the variable my_string.

Example:

```
name = "Alice"
print(name)
```

Explanation: This stores the name "Alice" in the variable name, and print(name) displays the value of the name variable, which is "Alice".

Common Mistakes

- **Forgetting to use quotes around strings**: Always remember to enclose text in either double (" ") or single (' ') quotes. Without quotes, Python will think you are referring to a variable or command.

4.11 Concatenating (Joining) Strings

Concatenation refers to joining two or more strings together into one continuous string.

Why does this matter?
This is helpful for creating dynamic messages, combining user input, or generating longer strings from smaller pieces.

Syntax
You can join strings using the + operator:

```
full_name = first_name + " " + last_name
```

Explanation: This combines `first_name` and `last_name` with a space in between.

Example:

```
first_name = "John"
last_name = "Doe"
full_name = first_name + " " + last_name
print(full_name)  # Outputs: John Doe
```

Explanation: The first and last names are stored separately in variables, and then concatenated using the + operator, with a space in between, to form the full name.

Common Mistakes

Forgetting spaces between concatenated strings: When joining strings like names, you must manually add spaces if needed. For example:

```
full_name = first_name + last_name   # Will output: JohnDoe (without
space)
```

4.12 Converting Numbers into Strings

Converting numbers into strings means turning numerical values (like integers or floats) into text so they can be used with other strings in a program.

Why does this matter?
You can't directly combine numbers and text in Python. To display a number alongside text in a message, you first need to convert the number into a string.

Syntax
You can convert a number to a string using the str() function:

```
str(25)
```

Explanation: The str() function converts the number 25 into a string "25".

Example:

```
age = 25
print("I am " + str(age) + " years old.")
```

Explanation: The integer age is converted to a string using str(age) before it is concatenated with the other text.

Common Mistakes
Forgetting to convert numbers to strings before concatenating:
If you try to combine numbers with strings without converting the number to a string first, you'll get an error. For example:

```
age = 25
print("I am " + age + " years old.")  # This will cause an error
```

4.13 Converting Strings into Numbers

Converting strings into numbers means transforming text that represents numbers (like "25") into actual numbers (like 25) so you can perform calculations with them.

Why does this matter?
User input is usually in the form of strings, even when numbers are entered. If you want to perform any calculations, you need to convert these strings into integers or floats.

Syntax
To convert a string into an integer (whole number), you use the `int()` function:

```
int("25")
```

To convert a string into a float (decimal number), you use the `float()` function:

```
float("25.5")
```

Example:

```
user_age = input("Enter your age: ")
age_in_five_years = int(user_age) + 5
print("In five years, you will be " + str(age_in_five_years))
```

Explanation:

- `input("Enter your age: ")`: This prompts the user to enter their age.

- `int(user_age)`: Converts the input (which is a string) into an integer so you can perform the addition.
- `str(age_in_five_years)`: Converts the result back into a string to display the message.

Common Mistakes

Forgetting to convert user input to numbers: When using input for calculations, forgetting to convert the string into a number will cause errors. For example:

```
user_age = input("Enter your age: ")
age_in_five_years = user_age + 5   # This will
cause an error
```

4.14 Finding the Length of a String

The length of a string refers to how many characters are in the string, including letters, numbers, spaces, punctuation, and special characters.

Why does this matter?
Determining the length of a string is important for:

- **Validating input**: For example, checking if a password is long enough.
- **Manipulating text**: Knowing the length can help when slicing or modifying a string.
- **Counting characters**: This is useful when analyzing text, like counting how many letters are in a message.

Syntax
To find the length of a string, you use the `len()` function:

```
len(my_string)
```

- `len()`: This is the built-in Python function that returns the number of characters in the string.
- `my_string`: This is the string whose length you want to find.

Detailed Syntax Explanation

Let's break down how the `len()` function works:

```python
my_string = "Hello, World!"
length = len(my_string)
print(length)  # Outputs: 13
```

- **Step 1**: We create a string `my_string` that contains the text "Hello, World!".
- **Step 2**: The `len()` function calculates the number of characters in `my_string`, which includes letters, spaces, and punctuation (total of 13 characters).
- **Step 3**: The result, `13`, is stored in the variable `length`.
- **Step 4**: We print the length using the `print()` function.

Counting Spaces and Special Characters

The `len()` function counts all characters in a string, including spaces and punctuation. For example:

```python
phrase = "I love Python!"
length = len(phrase)
print(length)  # Outputs: 14
```

Explanation: The phrase "I love Python!" has 14 characters, including the spaces and the exclamation mark.

Example:

```python
word = "Python"
print(len(word))  # Outputs: 6
```

Explanation: The word "Python" consists of 6 characters, so `len(word)` returns `6`.

Using `len()` with Variables

You can use the `len()` function with a variable that stores a string:

```python
name = "Alice"
name_length = len(name)
print("The length of the name is:", name_length)  # Outputs: The length
of the name is: 5
```

Explanation: The `len()` function counts the number of characters in the variable `name` ("Alice"), which is 5.

Common Mistakes

- **Using `len()` on non-string data types**:
    - The `len()` function works on strings, lists, tuples, and dictionaries. However, using `len()` on a number will result in an error.

```
number = 12345
print(len(number))  # This will cause an error because `len()` does not
work on integers
```

To avoid this error, convert the number to a string first:

```
number = 12345
print(len(str(number)))  # Outputs: 5
```

- Here, `str(number)` converts the number `12345` into the string `"12345"`, which allows `len()` to count the characters.

Confusing spaces or punctuation with letters: Remember that `len()` counts all characters, not just letters. For example:

```
sentence = "Hello, World!"
print(len(sentence))  # Outputs: 13 (includes space and punctuation)
```

Advanced Use Cases

Counting characters in user input: You can use `len()` to check if a user's input meets certain length criteria. For example, validating the length of a username:

```
username = input("Enter your username: ")
if len(username) < 5:
    print("Username must be at least 5 characters long.")
else:
    print("Username is valid.")
```

Using `len()` with lists: The `len()` function can also be used to find the number of elements in a list:

```
fruits = ["apple", "banana", "cherry"]
print(len(fruits))  # Outputs: 3
```

4.15 Extracting Part of a String

Extracting part of a string, also known as string slicing, allows you to retrieve a portion of a string.

Why does this matter?
It's useful when you need to work with or manipulate specific parts of text, such as extracting initials from a name or getting specific sections of a sentence.

Syntax
You can extract part of a string using slicing:

```
my_string[start:end]
```

- `start`: The index where the slice begins (inclusive).
- `end`: The index where the slice ends (exclusive).

Syntax Explanation

```
first_name = "John"
print(first_name[0:2])  # Output: "Jo"
```

Explanation:

- `first_name[0:2]` retrieves the characters starting from index 0 up to but not including index 2. In this case, it extracts the first two letters of "John", which are "Jo".

4.15 Replacing One String of Characters with Another

String replacement allows you to change part of a string by replacing one set of characters with another.

Why does this matter?
Replacing parts of a string is useful for modifying or cleaning text, such as updating a name or correcting spelling mistakes.

Syntax
To replace part of a string, use the `replace()` function:

```
my_string.replace("old", "new")
```

- `"old"`: The substring you want to replace.
- `"new"`: The substring that will replace the old one.

Syntax Explanation

```
greeting = "Hello, John!"
print(greeting.replace("John", "Alice"))  # Output: "Hello, Alice!"
```

Explanation:

- The `replace("John", "Alice")` function replaces the word "John" with "Alice" in the string `"Hello, John!"`, resulting in `"Hello, Alice!"`.

Common Mistakes

- **Forgetting that `replace()` doesn't modify the original string**: The `replace()` function creates a new string with the replacements, but it doesn't change the original string unless you assign it to a new variable.

4.16 Converting a String to Uppercase or Lowercase

This refers to changing the case of the characters in a string, either converting all letters to **uppercase** or **lowercase**.

Why does this matter?
Standardizing text case is useful when comparing strings (like checking if two names are the same, regardless of their case) or when you need to format text in a specific way.

Syntax
To convert a string to uppercase:

```
my_string.upper()
```

- This returns a new string with all letters in uppercase.

To convert a string to lowercase:

```
my_string.lower()
```

- This returns a new string with all letters in lowercase.

Syntax Explanation

```
name = "john"
print(name.upper())   # Output: JOHN
```

Explanation:
- The upper() function converts all characters in the string name to uppercase and prints "JOHN".

For lowercase:

```
name = "JOHN"
print(name.lower())   # Output: john
```

Explanation:
- The lower() function converts all characters to lowercase and prints "john".

Common Mistakes

- **Assuming the original string is modified**: The `upper()` and `lower()` functions return a new string with the changed case, but they do not modify the original string. You need to assign the result to a new variable if you want to keep the modified version.

4.17 Running Python Programs from the Terminal

Running Python programs from the terminal means executing `.py` files (Python scripts) directly using the command line. Instead of running code from an integrated development environment (IDE) like VS Code or PyCharm, you can use the terminal to run scripts.

Why does this matter?
Learning to run Python scripts from the terminal is important for:

- **Automation**: You can create and run scripts to automate repetitive tasks.
- **Deployment**: Running Python programs from the terminal is common in real-world applications when deploying code to servers.
- **Efficiency**: Once scripts are written, running them from the terminal can be faster and more efficient.

Syntax Explanation
To run a Python script from the terminal, the basic command is:

```
python3 script.py
```

- `python3`: This tells the terminal to use Python 3 to run the script.
- `script.py`: This is the name of the Python file you want to run. You should replace `script.py` with the actual name of your file.

Example:

Create a Python file called `hello.py` with the following code:

```
print("Hello from Python!")
```

1. Open the terminal (or command prompt) and navigate to the folder where the `hello.py` file is saved.

Run the Python script using the command:

```
python3 hello.py
```

The output will be displayed in the terminal:

```
Hello from Python!
```

Steps to Run a Python Script from the Terminal

1. **Write a Python Script**: Open a text editor or IDE and write some Python code. Save the file with a `.py` extension (e.g., `my_script.py`).
2. **Open the Terminal**:
    - On **Windows**, search for "Command Prompt" or "PowerShell".
    - On **Mac/Linux/RaspberryPI**, open the "Terminal" app.

Navigate to the Script Location: Use the `cd` (change directory) command to navigate to the folder where your Python script is saved. For example:

```
cd /path/to/your/folder
```

Run the Script: Once you are in the correct folder, run the script using:

```
python3 script.py
```

3. (Replace `script.py` with the name of your Python file.)

Common Mistakes

- **Forgetting to specify** `python3`: Many systems have both Python 2 and Python 3 installed. If you just use `python` instead of `python3`, the system might run Python 2 instead of Python 3, causing compatibility issues. Always use `python3` to ensure you are running the correct version.
- **Not being in the right directory**: If you're not in the same folder as the script, the terminal won't be able to find and run it. Make sure to `cd` into the directory where your `.py` file is located.

4.19 Using the Python Console

The Python console (also called the Python interactive shell) is a command-line environment that allows you to run Python code interactively. You can type and execute Python commands one at a time, making it a great tool for testing, experimenting, and learning Python concepts.

Why does this matter?
Using the Python console is a fast and easy way to try out new Python commands, test small bits of code, and immediately see the results. It's perfect for learning and understanding Python syntax or debugging small snippets of code without writing a full script.

Syntax Explanation

To open the Python console, you simply type `python3` in your terminal:

```
python3
```

This command will start an interactive Python session, where you can enter and execute Python commands line by line.

Example:

1. **Open the Python Console**:
    - On **Windows**, open the Command Prompt or PowerShell.
    - On **Mac/Linux**, open the Terminal.

Type:

```
python3
```

You'll enter the Python interactive mode and see something like this:

```
Python 3.x.x (default, ...)
Type "help", "copyright", "credits" or "license"
for more information.
>>>
```

- The `>>>` symbol is the Python prompt, indicating that it is waiting for your input.

Test a Simple Command: Type the following in the Python console:

```
print("Hello from the Python console!")
```

You should see the output:

```
Hello from the Python console!
```

Perform a Simple Calculation: You can use the Python console to run calculations instantly:

```
5 + 3
```

Benefits of Using the Python Console

- **Interactive Testing**: You can test Python commands one at a time, which is helpful for quickly trying out ideas or debugging code.
- **Learning and Experimentation**: The Python console is a great place to experiment with new functions, data types, and syntax as you learn Python.
- **Immediate Feedback**: Every time you enter a command, Python executes it immediately and shows the result.

Exiting the Python Console

When you're done using the Python console, you can exit by typing:

```
exit()
```

Or, you can use the keyboard shortcut **Ctrl + D** (on Mac/Linux) or **Ctrl + Z** followed by **Enter** (on Windows).

Common Mistakes

- **Forgetting to run** `python3`: Make sure you're using Python 3 by typing `python3` in the terminal. Using just `python` may open Python 2 if it's still installed on your system.
- **Forgetting to exit the console**: When you're finished testing code in the Python console, remember to type `exit()` to return to your normal terminal prompt.

4.20 Running Commands Conditionally (if statements)

An **if statement** is a way to make decisions in a Python program. It runs certain code only if a specified condition is **True**. This allows your program to respond differently based on user input or other factors.

Why does this matter?

Conditional logic is essential because it lets your program make decisions. For example, you can run code to check if a user is old enough to perform an action (like voting or driving) or respond to different situations in a program.

Syntax Explanation

Here's the basic structure of an `if` statement in Python:

```
if condition:
            # code to execute if condition is true
```

- `if condition:`: This checks whether the condition is True. The condition is usually a comparison (e.g., $x > 10$) or a boolean value (True or False).
- **Indented code block**: The code inside the if statement is indented (moved over by 4 spaces). This code will only run if the condition is True.

Example:

Here's an example that checks if someone is old enough to vote:

```
age = 18
if age >= 18:
    print("You can vote!")
```

Explanation:

- The condition age >= 18 checks if the value of age is greater than or equal to 18.
- If the condition is True, the indented code block (print("You can vote!")) runs, and the message "You can vote!" is printed.

Common Mistakes

- **Forgetting the colon (:)**: Every if statement must end with a colon after the condition. Without it, you'll get a syntax error.
- **Improper indentation**: The code inside the if block must be indented by 4 spaces. If it's not indented, Python won't know which code to execute as part of the condition.

Adding an Else Statement

You can use an else statement to run code when the condition is False

```
age = 16
if age >= 18:
    print("You can vote!")
else:
    print("You are too young to vote.")
```

In this example, the `else` block runs if the condition `age >= 18` is not met.

Other Conditional Statements

Elif (else if): If you want to check multiple conditions, you can use `elif` (short for "else if"):

```python
age = 15
if age >= 18:
    print("You can vote.")
elif age >= 16:
    print("You can drive but not vote.")
else:
    print("You are too young to drive or vote.")
```

4.21 Comparing Values

In Python, **comparison operators** are used to compare two values. These operators return `True` or `False` based on whether the comparison is correct. Comparisons are essential for making decisions in your programs, especially when used with `if` statements to determine the flow of the program.

Why does this matter?
Comparing values is important when your program needs to check conditions, such as comparing numbers, verifying if something is equal, or seeing if a value falls within a certain range. This is essential for logic-based decisions like user validation, calculating scores, and more.

Syntax Explanation
The most common comparison operators in Python are:
- `==`: Equal to
- `!=`: Not equal to
- `>`: Greater than
- `<`: Less than
- `>=`: Greater than or equal to
- `<=`: Less than or equal to

Here's an example of comparing two values:

```
if x == y:
    print("Equal")
```

- x == y checks if x and y are equal. If they are, the statement inside the if block is executed.
- **Remember**: == checks for equality, while = is used to assign values.

Example:

Here's an example that checks if 5 is greater than 3:

```
if 5 > 3:
    print("5 is greater than 3")
```

Explanation:

- The condition 5 > 3 checks if the number 5 is greater than 3.
- Since this is True, the program prints "5 is greater than 3".

Common Comparison Operators and Examples
- **== (Equal to):**

```
if 10 == 10:
    print("Both numbers are equal")
```

- **!= (Not equal to):**

```
if 10 != 5:
    print("10 is not equal to 5")
```

- **> (Greater than):**

```
if 8 > 3:
    print("8 is greater than 3")
```

- **< (Less than)**:

```
if 2 < 5:
    print("2 is less than 5")
```

- **>= (Greater than or equal to)**:

```
if 7 >= 7:
    print("7 is greater than or equal to 7")
```

- **<= (Less than or equal to)**:

```
if 3 <= 10:
    print("3 is less than or equal to 10")
```

Common Mistakes

Using = instead of ==: Remember, = is for assigning values, while == is for comparing values.

```
if x == 5:   # Correct
if x = 5:    # Incorrect
```

- **Forgetting to compare values of the same type**:
  Comparing a string with a number won't work, so ensure the types are compatible.

4.22 Logical Operators

Logical operators like **and**, **or**, and **not** are used to combine multiple conditions in a single if statement. This allows for more complex decision-making in programs.

- **and**: Both conditions must be **True** for the overall condition to be **True**.
- **or**: At least one of the conditions must be **True** for the overall condition to be **True**.
- **not**: Reverses the result of a condition (i.e., **True** becomes **False** and vice versa).

Why does this matter?

Logical operators allow you to check multiple conditions at once, which is crucial for making more complex decisions. For example, you can check if a number is within a specific range, if a user meets certain criteria, or if a value is either one thing or another.

Syntax Explanation

Here's how you use logical operators:

and: Both conditions must be true.

```
if x > 5 and x < 10:
    print("Within range")
```

- This checks if x is greater than 5 **and** less than 10.

or: At least one condition must be true.

```
if x < 5 or x > 10:
    print("Out of range")
```

- This checks if x is less than 5 **or** greater than 10.

not: Reverses the condition.

```
if not x > 5:
    print("x is not greater than 5")
```

- This checks if x is **not** greater than 5.

Example:

Here's an example that checks if a number is between 5 and 10 using the and operator:

```
x = 7
if x > 5 and x < 10:
    print("x is within the range of 5 and 10")
```

Explanation:

- The and operator ensures that both conditions (x > 5 **and** x < 10) must be true for the program to print "x is within the range of 5 and 10".

Using the or Operator

Here's an example that checks if a number is either less than 5 or greater than 15:

```
x = 3
if x < 5 or x > 15:
    print("x is outside the range of 5 to 15")
```

Explanation:

- The or operator allows the condition to be true if either x < 5 **or** x > 15 is true.

Using the not Operator

The not operator is used to reverse a condition:

```
x = 4
if not x > 5:
    print("x is not greater than 5")
```

Explanation:

- The `not` operator reverses the condition, so it prints "x is not greater than 5" because `x` is actually less than 5.

Common Mistakes

- **Misunderstanding the difference between `and` and `or`:**
  - `and`: Both conditions must be true.
  - `or`: At least one condition must be true.

Forgetting parentheses when using multiple conditions: Parentheses are not required for basic conditions but can help clarify complex logic:

```
if (x > 5 and y < 10) or z == 3:
    # code to run
```

4.23 Repeating Instructions an Exact Number of Times (for loops)

A **for loop** in Python allows you to repeat a block of code a set number of times. This is useful for automating repetitive tasks, like printing a message multiple times or processing a list of items.

Why does this matter?
For loops help you avoid writing the same code over and over. They are an essential part of programming when you need to repeat an action a certain number of times or when you want to process items in a sequence like a list or a range of numbers.

Syntax Explanation

Here's the basic structure of a `for` loop in Python:

```
for i in range(5):
    print("Hello!")
```

- `for i in range(5)::` This creates a loop that runs **5 times**. The `range(5)` generates numbers from 0 to 4 (a total of 5 numbers), and `i` takes on each value of the range in each iteration.
- **Indented code block**: The code inside the loop (indented) will be executed once for each value of `i`. In this case, it prints "Hello!" five times.

Example:

Here's an example that prints "Hello!" five times:

```
for i in range(5):
    print("Hello!")
```

Explanation:

- The loop runs 5 times because `range(5)` generates the numbers 0, 1, 2, 3, and 4.
- For each iteration of the loop, it prints "Hello!".

Understanding `range()`

- `range(n)`: Generates numbers from 0 to `n-1`.

`range(start, stop)`: Generates numbers from `start` to `stop-1`.

```
for i in range(2, 6):
    print(i)  # Outputs: 2, 3, 4, 5
```

Common Mistakes

Forgetting to indent: The code inside the loop must be indented by 4 spaces, or Python will give an error.

```
for i in range(5):
print("Hello!")  # This will cause an error because the print statement
is not indented
```

- **Misunderstanding** `range()`: Remember that `range(n)` generates numbers from 0 to `n-1`. If you want to include `n`, use `range(n+1)`.

Advanced Example: Looping Over a List

You can also use `for` loops to iterate over a list of items:

```python
fruits = ["apple", "banana", "cherry"]
for fruit in fruits:
    print(fruit)
```

This loop prints each fruit in the list.

4.24 Repeating Instructions Until Some Condition Changes (while loops)

A **while loop** in Python repeats a block of code as long as a specified condition is **True**. Unlike a `for` loop, which repeats a set number of times, a `while` loop keeps running until a condition changes. This makes it useful for tasks where the number of repetitions isn't known beforehand.

Why does this matter?
While loops are essential when you need your program to continue running until a certain condition is met. This is useful for tasks like continuously asking a user for input or monitoring some data until it meets a specific requirement.

Syntax Explanation
Here's the basic structure of a `while` loop:

```python
while condition:
    # code to repeat
```

- `while condition::` The loop will run as long as the condition is `True`. Once the condition becomes `False`, the loop stops.
- **Indented code block**: The code inside the loop (indented) will be executed repeatedly while the condition is `True`.

Example:

Here's an example where the loop continues until the user types "exit":

```
user_input = ""
while user_input != "exit":
    user_input = input("Type something (or 'exit' to quit): ")
```

Explanation:

- The loop continues asking for input until the user types `"exit"`.
- The condition `user_input != "exit"` checks if the user's input is not equal to `"exit"`. As long as the input is not `"exit"`, the loop keeps running.

How While Loops Work

- A `while` loop keeps running as long as the condition is true. Once the condition becomes false, the loop stops.
- You can make the loop stop by changing the condition inside the loop. For example, by using user input or variables that change with each iteration.

Example with Numbers

Here's a loop that prints numbers from 1 to 5:

```
i = 1
while i <= 5:
    print(i)
    i += 1  # Increment i by 1 in each loop
```

Explanation:

- The loop starts with `i = 1` and continues as long as `i <= 5`.
- In each loop iteration, `i` is incremented by 1 using `i += 1`.

Common Mistakes

Forgetting to update the condition: If the condition inside the loop never changes, the loop will run forever (infinite loop). Always ensure that the loop condition will eventually become `False` to stop the loop.

```
i = 1
while i <= 5:
    print(i)
    # Missing i += 1 causes an infinite loop
```

- **Using = instead of ==**: Remember, = is for assignment and == is for comparison.

```
while user_input = "exit":  # Incorrect
while user_input == "exit":  # Correct
```

- **Using Break to Stop a Loop**

You can use the `break` statement to exit a loop immediately:

```
while True:
    user_input = input("Type something (or 'exit' to stop): ")
    if user_input == "exit":
        break
    print("You typed:", user_input)
```

Explanation:

- This loop will run forever (`while True`) until the `break` statement is triggered when the user types `"exit"`.

4.25 Breaking Out of a Loop

The `break` statement is used to stop a loop before it has finished all its repetitions.

Why does this matter?

Sometimes you want to stop a loop early, and `break` gives you control to do that. For example, you may want to stop asking for input once a user types "exit."

Syntax Explanation

```
while True:
    if condition:
        break
```

- `break`: Stops the loop.
- `while True:`: Keeps the loop running until `break` is triggered.

Example:

```
while True:
    user_input = input("Type something (or 'stop' to exit): ")
    if user_input == "stop":
        break
    print("You typed:", user_input)
```

- This loop will keep asking for input until you type `"stop"`, which triggers the `break` and ends the loop.

4.26 Defining a Function in Python

A **function** is a way to group code together so you can use it again and again without re-writing it.

Why does this matter?
Functions make your code **easier to use** and **reusable**. Instead of
repeating the same code, you put it in a function and run it whenever
you need.

Syntax Explanation

```
def function_name():
    # code inside the function
```

- `def`: Starts the function definition.
- `function_name`: This is the name of the function. You
  choose this name.
- `()`: These hold any information you want to give the function
  (optional).
- `::` Shows the start of the function's code.
- **Indented code**: The code you want to run inside the
  function.

Example:
Create a simple function that prints a greeting

```
def greet():
    print("Hello, welcome to Python!")
```

Now, to **run** the function, you need to **call** it like this:
```
greet()   # Output: Hello, welcome to Python!
```

Python Lists and Dictionaries

4.27 Creating a List

A **list** is a data structure in Python that stores multiple items in a
single variable. It can contain numbers, words, or a mix of different
data types.

Why does this matter?

Lists are useful because they allow you to store and work with a collection of items in an organized way. Instead of creating separate variables for each item, you can group them together in one list.

Syntax

```
my_list = [item1, item2, item3]
```

- `my_list`: The name of your list.
- `[item1, item2, item3]`: Items inside the list, separated by commas. These can be numbers, strings (words), or even other lists!

Syntax Explanation

Here's an example of a list in Python:

```
fruits = ["apple", "banana", "cherry"]
```

- `fruits` is the list name.
- `["apple", "banana", "cherry"]` contains three string items: `"apple"`, `"banana"`, and `"cherry"`.

Example:

```
fruits = ["apple", "banana", "cherry"]
print(fruits)
```

This creates a list of three fruit names and prints it out.

Simple Explanation of the Code

- This code creates a list called `fruits` with three items: `"apple"`, `"banana"`, and `"cherry"`.
- The `print(fruits)` command will show the list in the output.

Common Mistakes
Forgetting to use square brackets: Make sure you always use square brackets [ ] when creating a list. For example:

```
my_list = [1, 2, 3]   # Correct
my_list = 1, 2, 3     # Incorrect
```

4.28 Accessing Elements of a List

A **list** in Python is a collection of items (like numbers, words, etc.). You can access any item from the list by using its **index** (position number).

Why does this matter?
When working with lists, it's important to know how to **retrieve** and **manipulate** individual items. For example, if you have a list of sensor readings or names, you need to be able to access specific values to use them in your project.

Syntax

```
my_list[index]
```

- `my_list`: The name of your list.
- `index`: The position number of the item you want to access. **Indexing starts at 0**.

Syntax Explanation

Let's break this down with an example:

```python
fruits = ["apple", "banana", "cherry"]
print(fruits[0])  # Output: "apple"
```

- `fruits[0]`: This accesses the **first** item in the list, which is "apple". The **index** 0 refers to the first position in the list.
- `fruits[1]`: This would access the **second** item, "banana", because lists are indexed starting from **0**.

Detailed Example:

Let's look at how to access items in a list:

```python
fruits = ["apple", "banana", "cherry", "orange"]
print(fruits[0])  # Output: "apple" (first item)
print(fruits[1])  # Output: "banana" (second item)
print(fruits[3])  # Output: "orange" (fourth item)
```

- `fruits[0]` gives you the first item, "apple".
- `fruits[1]` gives you the second item, "banana".
- `fruits[3]` gives you the fourth item, "orange".

How Indexing Works

Index Starts at 0: The first item in a list is at index 0, the second item is at index 1, and so on.

```python
my_list = ["a", "b", "c", "d"]
print(my_list[0])  # Output: "a" (first item)
print(my_list[2])  # Output: "c" (third item)
```

Negative Indexing: You can also access list items from the **end** using negative numbers. For example, -1 gives you the **last** item, -2 gives the second-last, and so on.

```
print(my_list[-1])  # Output: "d" (last item)
print(my_list[-2])  # Output: "c" (second-last item)
```

Common Mistakes
Forgetting that indexing starts at 0:
A list's first item is at index 0, not 1. So, to access the second item, you would use index 1:

```
my_list = ["apple", "banana", "cherry"]
print(my_list[1])  # Outputs: "banana" (second
item)
```

- **Indexing beyond the list length**:
  If you try to access an item at an index that doesn't exist (e.g., index 5 in a list with only 3 items), you will get an **IndexError**.

4.29 Finding the Length of a List

The **len()** function in Python returns the number of elements in a list. It tells you how many items are inside the list.

Why does this matter?
Knowing the length of a list is important when you want to **loop through** all the items, make decisions based on how many items are in the list, or ensure you have enough data.

Syntax

```
len(my_list)
```

- **my_list**: The name of the list you want to find the length of.
- **len()**: This function returns the number of items in the list.

Syntax Explanation

Here's how you use the `len()` function:

```
fruits = ["apple", "banana", "cherry"]
print(len(fruits))   # Output: 3
```

- **len(fruits)**: This counts the number of items in the fruits list and returns 3 because there are three items in the list.

Example:

```
fruits = ["apple", "banana", "cherry"]
print(len(fruits))   # Output: 3
```

This example prints the number of items in the fruits list, which is 3.

Simple Explanation of the Code

- **len(fruits)** returns the total number of elements in the list fruits. In this case, the list contains "apple", "banana", and "cherry", so the result is 3.

Common Mistakes

- **Using `len()` on non-list objects**: The `len()` function works with lists and other data types like strings, but if you accidentally try to use it on a number or an object that doesn't have a length, it will give you an error.

4.30 Adding Elements to a List

You can add new items to a list using the **append()** method. This is useful when you want to add data to a list **dynamically** without needing to rewrite the entire list.

Why does this matter?
In many situations, like when you're processing data on a Raspberry Pi, you may need to **add items** to a list as they come in (e.g., adding new sensor readings or user input). The append() method lets you do this easily.

Syntax

```
my_list.append(new_item)
```

- `my_list`: The list you want to add an item to.
- `append()`: This method adds the new item to the **end** of the list.
- `new_item`: The item you want to add to the list.

Syntax Explanation

Here's how you add an item to a list:

```python
fruits = ["apple", "banana", "cherry"]
fruits.append("orange")
print(fruits)  # Output: ["apple", "banana", "cherry", "orange"]
```

- `fruits.append("orange")`: This adds `"orange"` to the end of the `fruits` list.

Example:

```python
fruits = ["apple", "banana", "cherry"]
fruits.append("orange")
print(fruits)  # Output: ["apple", "banana", "cherry", "orange"]
```

This example adds `"orange"` to the `fruits` list, making the list longer by one item.

Simple Explanation of the Code

- `fruits.append("orange")` adds `"orange"` to the end of the `fruits` list. After appending, the list will contain four items: `"apple"`, `"banana"`, `"cherry"`, and `"orange"`.

Common Mistakes

Confusing `append()` with `extend()`: The `append()` method adds **one item** to the list, while `extend()` adds multiple items from another list or iterable. For example:

```python
fruits.append(["grape", "melon"])  # Adds the
entire list as one item
```

```
fruits.extend(["grape", "melon"])  # Adds each
item separately
```

4.31 Removing Elements from a List

You can remove items from a list using Python's built-in `remove()` or `pop()` methods. These methods help manage lists by allowing you to delete specific items or items at certain positions.

Why does this matter?
When working with data (such as sensor readings or user inputs), you may need to **clean up** your list by removing items that are no longer needed. This is particularly useful when processing lists that change over time.

Syntax

`remove(item)`: Removes the **first occurrence** of `item` from the list.

```
my_list.remove(item)
```

`pop(index)`: Removes the **item at a specific index**. If no index is provided, it removes the **last item** by default.
```
my_list.pop(index)
```

Syntax Explanation

`remove(item)`: You specify the exact item you want to remove from the list. If that item appears more than once, only the first occurrence is removed.

```
fruits = ["apple", "banana", "cherry", "banana"]
fruits.remove("banana")
print(fruits)  # Output: ["apple", "cherry", "banana"] (only the first
"banana" is removed)
```

`pop(index)`: You specify the **position** of the item you want to remove. Lists use **0-based indexing**, meaning the first item is at index 0, the second at index 1, and so on.

```
fruits = ["apple", "banana", "cherry"]
fruits.pop(1)
print(fruits)  # Output: ["apple", "cherry"]
```

Common Mistakes

Trying to remove an item that isn't in the list: If you try to remove an item that doesn't exist in the list, Python will throw an error.

```
fruits = ["apple", "banana", "cherry"]
fruits.remove("grape")  # This will cause an error
since "grape" isn't in the list.
```

4.32 Creating a List by Parsing a String

You can convert a string into a list by **splitting** it into smaller parts using a delimiter (like commas or spaces). This method is helpful when you need to break down a large string into individual elements.

Why does this matter?

Parsing a string into a list is useful when working with **text data**, such as when you're reading data from a file or receiving input from users that needs to be processed further. For example, you might receive data in the form of a string: `"apple,banana,cherry"`, and want to break it into a list: `["apple", "banana", "cherry"]`.

Syntax

```
my_list = my_string.split(delimiter)
```

- `my_list`: The new list you create.
- `my_string`: The original string.
- `delimiter`: The character(s) used to split the string (e.g., " , " for a comma, " " for a space).

Syntax Explanation

Here's an example of splitting a string into a list using commas:

```
sentence = "apple,banana,cherry"
fruits = sentence.split(",")
print(fruits)  # Output: ["apple", "banana", "cherry"]
```

- `split(",")`: The string is split at each comma " , ", creating a list with three items: `"apple"`, `"banana"`, and `"cherry"`.

Common Mistakes

Forgetting to use the correct delimiter: The `split()` function looks for a specific character to break up the string. If you forget to specify the correct delimiter, the string won't be split as expected.

```
sentence = "apple,banana,cherry"
fruits = sentence.split(" ")  # Output:
["apple,banana,cherry"] (because there are no
spaces to split by)
```

4.33 Iterating Over a List

Iterating over a list means going through each item in the list one by one. This is done using a `for` **loop**, which is an essential tool for working with collections of data.

Why does this matter?
When working with lists, you often need to perform actions on each item, such as printing, modifying, or analyzing the data. For example, if you have a list of sensor readings or items in a shopping cart, you might need to process each one individually.

Syntax

```
for item in my_list:
    # code to run for each item
```

- `item`: Represents each individual element in the list as the loop goes through it.
- `my_list`: The list you are iterating over.

Syntax Explanation

Here's an example of looping through a list of fruits and printing each one:

```
fruits = ["apple", "banana", "cherry"]
for fruit in fruits:
    print(fruit)
```

- `for fruit in fruits:`: This line sets up a loop that goes through each item (`fruit`) in the list `fruits`.
- `print(fruit)`: Prints each fruit during the loop.

Example:

```
fruits = ["apple", "banana", "cherry"]
for fruit in fruits:
    print(fruit)
```

This code will print:

```
apple
banana
cherry
```

Common Mistakes
- **Misunderstanding how loops work**: Some beginners try to use `range()` or `while` loops incorrectly when working with lists. A `for` loop is simpler and works directly with the list items without needing to worry about the list's length or index numbers.

4.34 Enumerating a List

The `enumerate()` function allows you to loop through a list and get both the **index** (position) and the **item** at the same time. This is helpful when you need to know the **position** of each item in the list along with the **item's value**.

Why does this matter?

In some cases, you not only want to access the items in a list, but you also need to know **where** the item is in the list. For example, if you're processing a list of tasks and need to know the task number and its name.

Syntax

```
for index, item in enumerate(my_list):
    print(index, item)
```

- `enumerate(my_list)`: Returns both the index and the item.
- `index`: The position of the item in the list.
- `item`: The actual value of the list item.

Syntax Explanation

Here's how to use `enumerate()` to loop through a list:

```
fruits = ["apple", "banana", "cherry"]
for index, fruit in enumerate(fruits):
    print(index, fruit)
```

This will output:

```
0 apple
1 banana
2 cherry
```

- `enumerate(fruits)`: This gives both the index (0, 1, 2) and the corresponding fruit (`"apple"`, `"banana"`, `"cherry"`).

Common Mistakes

- **Forgetting that indexing starts at 0**: The first item has an index of 0, not 1. So the first printed item will have an index of 0.

4.35 Sorting a List

The `sort()` method sorts the items in a list in either **ascending** or **descending** order. This is useful when you need to **organize** data, such as arranging numbers from smallest to largest or sorting words alphabetically.

Why does this matter?
Sorting is important when you need to display data in a particular order, like showing a list of names alphabetically or arranging a list of scores from highest to lowest.

Syntax
Sort in ascending order:

```
my_list.sort()
```

Sort in descending order:

```
my_list.sort(reverse=True)
```

Syntax Explanation

Here's how to sort a list of fruits alphabetically:

```
fruits = ["banana", "cherry", "apple"]
fruits.sort()
print(fruits)  # Output: ['apple', 'banana', 'cherry']
```

- `sort()`: Sorts the list in ascending order (A to Z for strings, smallest to largest for numbers).

For descending order:

```
fruits.sort(reverse=True)
print(fruits)  # Output: ['cherry', 'banana', 'apple']
```

- `sort(reverse=True)`: Sorts the list in descending order (Z to A for strings, largest to smallest for numbers).

Common Mistakes

- **Confusing `sort()` with `sorted()`:**
  - `sort()` modifies the original list.
  - `sorted()` returns a new sorted list without changing the original.

4.36 Cutting Up a List (Slicing)

Slicing is a way to **extract** specific parts of a list. You can select a **range of items** from a list by specifying their starting and ending positions.

Why does this matter?
Sometimes, you don't need the whole list—just part of it. For example, you might want the first 3 items in a list or the middle portion. Slicing helps you work with **sections** of a list.

Syntax

```
my_list[start:end]
```

- `start`: The starting index (inclusive, meaning it starts at this position).
- `end`: The stopping index (exclusive, meaning it stops just before this position).

Syntax Explanation

Here's how to extract part of a list:

```python
fruits = ["apple", "banana", "cherry", "date"]
print(fruits[1:3])  # Output: ['banana', 'cherry']
```

- `[1:3]`: This retrieves items starting from index 1 (`"banana"`) up to but not including index 3 (`"date"`), so it gives `"banana"` and `"cherry"`.

Example
Starting and stopping indices:

```python
fruits = ["apple", "banana", "cherry", "date", "fig"]
print(fruits[2:4])  # Output: ['cherry', 'date']
```

- `fruits[2:4]`: Starts at index 2 (`"cherry"`) and stops just before index 4 (`"fig"`).
2. **Leaving out the start or end**:

If you leave out the **start index**, Python will start at the beginning of the list:

```python
print(fruits[:3])  # Output: ['apple', 'banana', 'cherry']
```

If you leave out the **end index**, Python will go to the end of the list:

```
print(fruits[2:])   # Output: ['cherry', 'date',
'fig']
```

Common Mistakes

- **Misunderstanding indices**: Remember that slicing goes **up to but doesn't include** the end index. For example, `fruits[1:3]` gives you the items at index 1 and 2, but not index 3.

4.37 Applying a Function to a List

The `map()` function allows you to apply a function to **every item** in a list, creating a new list with the modified items.

Why does this matter?
When working with data, you often need to **manipulate** or **transform** each item in a list. Using `map()` lets you efficiently apply a function to each item without needing to write a loop.

Syntax

```
new_list = list(map(function, my_list))
```

- `function`: The function you want to apply to each item in the list.
- `my_list`: The list you want to apply the function to.
- `list()`: This is necessary to convert the result of `map()` into a list.

Syntax Explanation

Here's an example where we apply a function to **square** every number in a list:

```python
numbers = [1, 2, 3]
squared_numbers = list(map(lambda x: x ** 2, numbers))
print(squared_numbers)  # Output: [1, 4, 9]
```

- `map(lambda x: x ** 2, numbers)`: This applies the function `x ** 2` to each number in the `numbers` list.
- `list()`: Converts the result from `map()` into a list.

Example:

Let's say you have a list of numbers and want to square each number:

```python
numbers = [1, 2, 3]
squared_numbers = list(map(lambda x: x ** 2, numbers))
print(squared_numbers)  # Output: [1, 4, 9]
```

- The `lambda x: x ** 2` is a simple function that squares each number.
- `map()` applies this function to each number in the list, and `list()` converts the result into a new list.

Common Mistakes

Forgetting to convert `map()` to a list: The `map()` function doesn't return a list directly. You need to wrap it in `list()` to create a list.

```python
result = map(lambda x: x * 2, [1, 2, 3])
print(result)  # Output: <map object at 0x...>
(This is not a list!)
```

Correct way:
```
result = list(map(lambda x: x * 2, [1, 2, 3]))
print(result)   # Output: [2, 4, 6]
```

4.38 Creating a Dictionary

A **dictionary** in Python is a collection of **key-value pairs**. Each key is unique, and it is associated with a specific value. Think of a dictionary as a real-world dictionary where each word (the key) is connected to a definition (the value).

Why does this matter?
Dictionaries are extremely useful for storing and retrieving data efficiently. Instead of remembering the exact position of an item (like in a list), you can look up a value using its **key**.

Syntax

```
my_dict = {"key1": "value1", "key2": "value2"}
```

- `my_dict`: The name of the dictionary.
- `"key1"`: The unique identifier for the value (like a label).
- `"value1"`: The data or information associated with the key.

Syntax Explanation
Here's an example of creating a dictionary with information about a person:

```
person = {"name": "Alice", "age": 30}
```

- `"name"` is the key, and `"Alice"` is the value.
- `"age"` is another key, and `30` is the value.

Example:

```
person = {"name": "Alice", "age": 30}
print(person)
```

- This dictionary contains two key-value pairs: `"name"`: `"Alice"` and `"age"`: `30`.

Explanation of the Code

- The dictionary `person` stores two pieces of information about Alice: her name and age. You can use these keys (`"name"` and `"age"`) to look up the values (`"Alice"` and `30`).

Common Mistakes

Forgetting to use curly brackets {}: In Python, dictionaries use **curly brackets** {} instead of square brackets [ ] (used for lists).

```
my_dict = {"key": "value"}   # Correct
my_dict = ["key", "value"]   # Incorrect
```

4.39 Accessing a Dictionary

You can **access** the value of a dictionary using its **key**. This allows you to look up and retrieve information quickly.

Why does this matter?
Being able to retrieve values from dictionaries is essential when you need to access specific data based on a key. For example, you can get the value of `"age"` in a dictionary without knowing its position.

Syntax

```
my_dict["key"]
```

     `my_dict`: The dictionary name.

     `"key"`: The key whose value you want to access.

Syntax Explanation

Here's an example of accessing the `"name"` value from the `person` dictionary

```
person = {"name": "Alice", "age": 30}
print(person["name"])  # Output: "Alice"
```

- `person["name"]`: Retrieves the value `"Alice"` from the dictionary.

Example:

```
person = {"name": "Alice", "age": 30}
print(person["age"])  # Output: 30
```

- This retrieves the value associated with the key `"age"`, which is `30`.

Common Mistakes

Using a key that doesn't exist: If you try to access a key that isn't in the dictionary, Python will raise a **KeyError**.

```
person = {"name": "Alice", "age": 30}
print(person["address"])  # Error! "address" key
doesn't exist
```

4.40 Removing Entries from a Dictionary

You can remove items (key-value pairs) from a dictionary using either the `del` keyword or the `pop()` method. This is helpful when you no longer need certain data in the dictionary.

Why does this matter?
When managing dynamic data, it's often necessary to **remove outdated or unnecessary entries** from a dictionary. For example, if a user deletes their account, you would want to remove their information from the dictionary.

Syntax

`del`: Removes the key-value pair.

```
del my_dict["key"]
```

1. `pop()`: Removes the key-value pair and returns the value.
   ```
   my_dict.pop("key")
   ```

Syntax Explanation

Here's an example of how to remove the `"age"` entry from the `person` dictionary:

```python
person = {"name": "Alice", "age": 30}
del person["age"]
print(person)  # Output: {"name": "Alice"}
```

- `del person["age"]`: Removes the `"age"` key and its value `30` from the dictionary.

Example:

Using the `pop()` method:

```python
person = {"name": "Alice", "age": 30}
age = person.pop("age")
print(age)  # Output: 30
print(person)  # Output: {"name": "Alice"}
```

- `person.pop("age")`: Removes `"age"` from the dictionary and returns its value (`30`).

Common Mistakes

Trying to delete a key that doesn't exist: If the key is not in the dictionary, attempting to delete it will cause an error.

```python
person = {"name": "Alice", "age": 30}
del person["address"]  # Error! "address" key
doesn't exist
```

4.41 Iterating Over Dictionaries

Iterating over a dictionary means looping through each **key-value pair** in the dictionary. This is useful when you need to process or display all the data stored in the dictionary.

Why does this matter?
When working with dictionaries, you may need to **access all the key-value pairs** at once. For example, if you have a dictionary with user information, you might want to display each user's details.

Syntax

```
for key, value in my_dict.items():
    print(key, value)
```

- `my_dict.items()`: Returns each key-value pair in the dictionary.
- `key`: The key in each key-value pair.
- `value`: The corresponding value for each key.

Syntax Explanation
Here's an example of iterating through a dictionary with information about a person:

```
person = {"name": "Alice", "age": 30, "city": "New York"}
for key, value in person.items():
    print(key, value)
```

- `person.items()`: This retrieves all the key-value pairs in the dictionary.
- `for key, value in person.items()::` This loop goes through each pair, assigning the **key** and **value** to variables you can print or use.

Example:

Here's a simple example that prints each key and value in the `person` dictionary:

```python
person = {"name": "Alice", "age": 30, "city": "New York"}
for key, value in person.items():
    print(key, value)
```

Output:

```
name Alice
age 30
city New York
```

- `for key, value in person.items()`: Loops through the dictionary and prints both the key and the value.

Explanation of the Code

- The loop goes through each **key-value** pair in the dictionary and prints them. For example, it first prints `name` and its value `Alice`, then `age` and `30`, and finally `city` and `New York`.

Common Mistakes

- **Confusing `items()` with `keys()` or `values()`:**
  - `items()`: Retrieves both keys and values.
  - `keys()`: Only retrieves the keys.

`values()`: Only retrieves the values.
```
# Example:
```

```
for key in person.keys():
    print(key)   # Only prints the keys: name, age,
city
for value in person.values():
    print(value)   # Only prints the values: Alice,
30, New York
```

4.42 Formatting Numbers

Formatting numbers means changing how a number looks when printed, such as controlling the number of decimal places or adding commas for large numbers. It's useful for displaying numbers in a more **human-readable** way.

Why does this matter?
When you're displaying data—such as prices, measurements, or large quantities—it's important to show numbers that are easy to read and understand, especially in reports or user interfaces.

Syntax

```
"{:.2f}".format(123.456)
```

- `{:.2f}`: The format specifier. It means to format the number to **2 decimal places**.
- `format(123.456)`: Applies the formatting to the number.

Syntax Explanation
Here's an example of formatting a large number with commas and two decimal places:

```
print("{:,.2f}".format(1234567.891))
```

- `{:,.2f}`: The comma , adds a comma separator for thousands, and `.2f` formats the number to two decimal places.
- The number `1234567.891` is formatted to `"1,234,567.89"`.

Example:
```
print("{:,.2f}".format(1234567.891))  # Output:
1,234,567.89
```

- This formats the large number with commas for thousands and rounds it to two decimal places.

Common Mistakes

- **Using incorrect format specifiers**: For example, using `"%.2f"` instead of `"{:.2f}"`. The correct format is `"{:.2f}"` inside the curly braces.

4.43 Formatting Dates and Times

Formatting dates and times means adjusting how the current date or time is displayed, such as changing the format from numerical (`2024-09-29`) to a more readable form (`Sunday, September 29, 2024`).

Why does this matter?
When displaying dates and times, it's useful to show them in a format that is easy for humans to read or that matches the context (e.g., for logs, reports, or user interfaces).

Syntax

```
import datetime
datetime.datetime.now().strftime("%Y-%m-%d %H:%M:%S")
```

- `strftime()`: Formats the date or time into a specific format.
- `"%Y-%m-%d %H:%M:%S"`: Specifies the format (Year-Month-Day Hour:Minute)

Syntax Explanation

Here's how to format the current date to show it as `"Day, Month Date, Year"`:

```
import datetime
print(datetime.datetime.now().strftime("%A, %B %d, %Y"))
```

- `"%A, %B %d, %Y"`:
  - `%A` shows the full weekday name (e.g., `"Sunday"`).
  - `%B` shows the full month name (e.g., `"September"`).
  - `%d` shows the day of the month with two digits (e.g., `29`).
  - `%Y` shows the four-digit year (e.g., `2024`).

Example:

```
import datetime
print(datetime.datetime.now().strftime("%A, %B %d, %Y"))  # Output:
Sunday, September 29, 2024
```

- This formats the current date as `"Day, Month Date, Year"`.

Common Mistakes

- **Using the wrong format codes**: For example, mixing up `%d` (day) with `%m` (month). Always check the formatting codes carefully.

4.44 Returning More Than One Value

Functions in Python can **return multiple values** as a tuple. This allows a function to send back multiple pieces of data at once.

Why does this matter?
Sometimes a function needs to return **more than one piece of information**. For example, if you want to return both the **x** and **y** coordinates from a function, you can return them together and handle them at once.

Syntax

```
def my_function():
    return value1, value2
```

- `return value1, value2`: This returns two values as a **tuple** (a collection of values).

Syntax Explanation

Here's an example where a function returns two coordinates (x and y):

```python
def get_coordinates():
    return 10, 20
x, y = get_coordinates()
print(x, y)  # Output: 10 20
```

- The function `get_coordinates()` returns two values: 10 and 20.
- The values are **unpacked** into the variables x and y when you call the function.

Example:

```python
def get_coordinates():
    return 10, 20
x, y = get_coordinates()
print(x, y)  # Output: 10 20
```

- The function returns two values, 10 and 20, which are assigned to x and y.

Common Mistakes

Forgetting to unpack the returned values: If you don't unpack the values, you'll only receive a tuple instead of separate values.

```python
result = get_coordinates()  # Output: (10, 20)
```

4.45 Defining a Class

A **class** in Python is a blueprint for creating objects. Objects can have properties (data) and behaviors (functions called methods).

Why does this matter?
Object-Oriented Programming (OOP) allows you to structure your code in a more organized and reusable way. By defining classes, you can create multiple objects that share similar properties and behaviors.

Syntax

```
class MyClass:
    def __init__(self, name):
        self.name = name
```

- `class`: Defines a new class.
- `__init__`: A special method that runs when you create an object. It sets up the object's initial state.
- `self`: Refers to the current object. It allows you to access the object's properties and methods.

Syntax Explanation

Here's an example of a class that defines a **Dog**:

```
class Dog:
    def __init__(self, name, breed):
        self.name = name
        self.breed = breed
```

- `__init__(self, name, breed)`: The `__init__` method initializes the dog's name and breed when an object is created.

- `self.name = name`: Assigns the `name` parameter to the object's `name` property.

Example:

```
class Dog:
    def __init__(self, name, breed):
        self.name = name
        self.breed = breed

my_dog = Dog("Buddy", "Golden Retriever")
print(my_dog.name, my_dog.breed)  # Output: Buddy Golden Retriever
```

- `my_dog = Dog("Buddy", "Golden Retriever")`: Creates a new Dog object with the name `"Buddy"` and breed `"Golden Retriever"`.

Common Mistakes

- **Forgetting the `self` parameter**: Every method in a class (including `__init__`) must have `self` as its first parameter.

4.46 Defining a Method

A **method** is a function that belongs to a class. It defines the **behavior** of an object.

Why does this matter?
Methods allow objects to perform actions. For example, a Dog object can have a method that makes it "bark" or a Car object can have a method that makes it "drive."

Syntax

```
class MyClass:
    def method(self):
        print("Hello")
```

- `def method(self):`: Defines a method for the class. Like functions, methods can have parameters, but the first parameter must always be `self`.

Syntax Explanation

Here's an example of adding a method called **bark** to the Dog class:

```
class Dog:
    def bark(self):
        print(self.name + " is barking!")
```

- `bark(self)`: A method that makes the dog bark by printing the dog's name and a message.

Example:

```
class Dog:
    def __init__(self, name, breed):
        self.name = name
        self.breed = breed

    def bark(self):
        print(self.name + " is barking!")

my_dog = Dog("Buddy", "Golden Retriever")
my_dog.bark()  # Output: Buddy is barking!
```

- `my_dog.bark()`: Calls the `bark` method, which prints `"Buddy is barking!"`.

Common Mistakes

- **Forgetting to include `self`**: If you forget to include `self` in the method definition, Python will raise an error.

4.47 Inheritance

Inheritance allows a class to inherit methods and properties from another class, known as the **parent class**. The new class is called a **child class**.

Why does this matter?
Inheritance allows you to **reuse code** and create specialized versions of existing classes. For example, you can create a generic **Animal** class and then have specific **Dog** and **Cat** classes that inherit from Animal.

Syntax

```
class ChildClass(ParentClass):
    pass
```

- `ParentClass`: The class being inherited from.
- `ChildClass`: The new class that inherits methods and properties from the parent class.

Syntax Explanation

Here's an example where a **Dog** class inherits from an **Animal** class:

```
class Animal:
    def speak(self):
        print("Some sound")
class Dog(Animal):
    def speak(self):
        print("Woof!")
```

- `class Dog(Animal)`: The Dog class inherits from Animal. It **overrides** the speak() method to make a dog-specific sound.

Example:

```
class Animal:
    def speak(self):
        print("Some sound")

class Dog(Animal):
    def speak(self):
        print("Woof!")

my_dog = Dog()
my_dog.speak()   # Output: Woof!
```

- The **Dog** class inherits the speak() method from **Animal**, but it overrides it to print "Woof!".

Common Mistakes

- **Forgetting to call the parent class's __init__()**
  method: If the parent class has an __init__() method, you must explicitly call it in the child class's __init__() method.

4.48 Writing to a File

Writing to a file means saving data (like text or numbers) from your program into a file on your computer. This is useful for storing output, logs, or data that you want to access later.

Why does this matter?
In many projects, you need to **save data** to a file for future use. For example, you might want to store results, logs, or user input in a file that can be accessed after your program finishes running.

Syntax

```
with open("file.txt", "w") as f:
    f.write("Hello, World!")
```

- `open("file.txt", "w")`: Opens the file `file.txt` in **write mode** (`"w"`). If the file doesn't exist, it creates it.
- `f.write()`: Writes the specified text to the file.

Syntax Explanation

Here's an example of writing data to a file:

```
with open("data.txt", "w") as f:
    f.write("This is a test.")
```

- `with open("data.txt", "w") as f:`: Opens `data.txt` in write mode. The file is automatically closed when the `with` block ends.
- `f.write("This is a test.")`: Writes the string `"This is a test."` to the file.

Example:

```
with open("data.txt", "w") as f:
    f.write("This is a test.")
```

- This creates (or opens) the file `data.txt` and writes the text `"This is a test."` to it.

Common Mistakes

- **Forgetting to close the file**: If you don't use the `with` statement, you must close the file manually with `f.close()`. Forgetting this can cause errors.

4.49 Reading from a File

Reading from a file means loading and displaying data from a file in your program. This is useful for retrieving saved data, logs, or configurations.

Why does this matter?
Reading data from a file is essential when you need to **load previously saved data**. For example, if your program stores user settings, it can read them from a file when the program starts.

Syntax

```
with open("file.txt", "r") as f:
    content = f.read()
```

- `open("file.txt", "r")`: Opens the file in **read mode** (`"r"`), allowing you to read its contents.
- `f.read()`: Reads the entire content of the file.

Syntax Explanation

Here's an example of reading from a file:

```
with open("data.txt", "r") as f:
    print(f.read())
```

- `f.read()`: Reads all the content from the file and prints it.

Example:

```
with open("data.txt", "r") as f:
    print(f.read())
```

- This opens the file `data.txt`, reads its contents, and prints it to the screen.

Common Mistakes

Forgetting to handle errors: If the file doesn't exist, Python will raise an error. Use `try-except` to handle missing files gracefully:

```
try:
    with open("missing.txt", "r") as f:
        print(f.read())
except FileNotFoundError:
    print("File not found!")
```

4.50 Handling Exceptions

Exception handling involves using `try` and `except` blocks to catch and manage errors. This prevents your program from crashing when unexpected errors occur.

Why does this matter?
Errors are a normal part of programming, but they can cause your program to stop working. By handling exceptions, you can **manage errors gracefully** and keep your program running smoothly.

Syntax

```
try:
    # code that might raise an error
except Exception as e:
    print(e)
```

- `try`: The code inside the `try` block is executed. If an error occurs, the `except` block is triggered.
- `except`: Catches and handles the error, preventing the program from crashing.

Syntax Explanation
Here's an example of handling a division error:

```
try:
    result = 10 / 0
except ZeroDivisionError:
    print("Cannot divide by zero!")
```

- `ZeroDivisionError`: This error occurs when trying to divide by zero.

- **except ZeroDivisionError::** Catches the error and prints a friendly message instead of crashing.

Example:

```
try:
    result = 10 / 0
except ZeroDivisionError:
    print("Cannot divide by zero!")   # Output: Cannot divide by zero!
```

Common Mistakes
- **Using overly broad exceptions:** It's better to catch specific errors like ZeroDivisionError instead of catching all errors with except :. This helps you know exactly what went wrong.

4.51 Using Modules

A **module** is a file containing Python code, such as functions, that can be imported and used in your program. Using modules extends Python's functionality by providing extra tools and features.

Why does this matter?
Modules make it easy to **reuse code** and access advanced functionality without needing to write everything from scratch. Python has many built-in modules (e.g., math, random), and you can also install third-party modules.

Syntax

```
import math
print(math.sqrt(16))
```

- `import math`: Imports the **math** module.
- `math.sqrt(16)`: Calls the `sqrt` function from the `math` module to compute the square root of `16`.

Syntax Explanation

Here's an example of using the `random` module to generate a random number:

```
import random
print(random.randint(1, 10))
```

- `random.randint(1, 10)`: Generates a random integer between 1 and 10.

Example:

```
import random
print(random.randint(1, 10))  # Output: A random number between 1 and
10
```

Common Mistakes

- **Forgetting to install third-party modules**: If you use a module that isn't built into Python (like `numpy`), you need to install it using `pip install module_name`.

4.52 Random Numbers

Random numbers are generated using Python's `random` module. They are useful in games, simulations, or any application that needs **randomness**.

Why does this matter?

In many programs, you need to **introduce unpredictability**, such as picking a random number for a dice game, selecting a random item from a list, or generating random data for simulations.

Syntax

```
import random
random.randint(1, 10)
```

- `random.randint(1, 10)`: Generates a random integer between 1 and 10, including both 1 and 10.

Syntax Explanation

Here's an example of selecting a random item from a list:

```
import random
print(random.choice(["apple", "banana", "cherry"]))
```

- `random.choice(["apple", "banana", "cherry"])`: Selects a random item from the list.

Example:

```
import random
print(random.choice(["apple", "banana", "cherry"]))  # Output: Randomly
chosen fruit
```

Common Mistakes

- **Forgetting to import the** `random` **module**: You must use `import random` before you can use any functions from the `random` module.

Chapter 5: Exploring Raspberry Pi Hardware

5.0 Introduction

This section introduces the **essential hardware components** and **interfaces** on the Raspberry Pi, such as **GPIO**, **I2C**, and **SPI**. These allow you to connect and control real-world components like **LEDs**, **sensors**, and **motors**.

Why does this matter?
Understanding the hardware interfaces of the Raspberry Pi is important because it helps you interact with physical components and build **interactive projects**. Whether you're creating a simple blinking LED circuit or a more complex robot, knowing how to use these interfaces is essential.

Key Interfaces:

1. **GPIO (General-Purpose Input/Output):**
   - The **GPIO pins** on the Raspberry Pi allow you to send signals to and receive input from external components like LEDs, buttons, and sensors.
   - **Example Use**: Turning an LED on or off using a GPIO pin.
2. **I2C (Inter-Integrated Circuit):**
   - I2C is a communication protocol that allows the Raspberry Pi to communicate with multiple devices

(such as sensors) using only two wires: **SDA** (data) and **SCL** (clock).

- ○ **Example Use**: Reading data from a temperature sensor.

3. **SPI (Serial Peripheral Interface):**
   - ○ SPI is another communication protocol used for high-speed data transfer between the Raspberry Pi and devices like displays or SD cards.
   - ○ **Example Use**: Controlling a display module.

Why These Interfaces Are Important:

- **GPIO**: Lets you control basic components like LEDs, buzzers, or switches.
- **I2C and SPI**: Allow you to connect more advanced components, such as displays, sensors, and other microcontrollers.

Safety First

- **Check Voltage**: The GPIO pins work at 3.3V. Connecting a higher voltage could damage your Raspberry Pi.
- **Avoid Short Circuits**: Always make sure your wiring is correct to avoid damaging components. Double-check connections before powering on.

Tip:

"Don't worry if hardware feels complicated at first! We'll take it **step by step**. Start with simple components like LEDs and buttons, then move on to more complex projects like sensors and displays."

5.1 Finding Your Way Around the GPIO Connector

Introduction to GPIO and Why It Matters

GPIO (General Purpose Input/Output) pins are essential connectors on the Raspberry Pi that let you connect and control hardware components like **LEDs, buttons, motors,** and **sensors**. These pins serve as a bridge between your Raspberry Pi and the real world, enabling you to build interactive projects by sending and receiving electrical signals.

Why It Matters: Learning how to use GPIO pins opens up endless possibilities for interacting with physical components, allowing you to create cool projects like blinking LEDs, controlling motors, and even building home automation systems.

Use Online Tools and Pinout Diagrams

Before starting with GPIO projects, it's important to familiarize yourself with the layout of the GPIO pins on the Raspberry Pi. You can use interactive pinout diagrams like those found on pinout.xyz to help identify which pins are used for **power (5V or 3.3V), GND (ground),** and **data signals (GPIO pins)**. Having a clear reference will prevent miswiring and help you correctly set up your hardware connections.

- **Label your GPIO pins** on your Raspberry Pi case or print out a pinout diagram to make pin identification easier.

Safety Precautions

Working with GPIO pins involves handling low-voltage electronics, but there are still important safety precautions to follow:

1. **Check Voltage**: Always ensure you are connecting components to the appropriate voltage pin (3.3V or 5V). Connecting a 3.3V GPIO pin directly to 5V can **damage your Raspberry Pi**.
2. **Use Resistors**: Always use a current-limiting resistor when connecting an LED to a GPIO pin to prevent damage to both the LED and the Raspberry Pi.
3. **Avoid Short Circuits**: Double-check your wiring to avoid short circuits that could harm your Raspberry Pi.

Project: Light an LED Using GPIO

Goal: Light up an LED using the GPIO pins on your Raspberry Pi.

Components Needed:

- 1 x **LED** (any color)
- 1 x **330Ω resistor**
- 2 x **jumper wires**
- 1 x **breadboard** (optional)

Wiring Instructions:

1. **Identify Pins**: Using your GPIO pinout diagram, identify the following pins:
   - **GPIO Pin**: E.g., GPIO17 (Pin 11)
   - **GND Pin**: E.g., Pin 6
2. **Connect the Components**:

- ○ **LED positive leg (long leg)**: Connect to **GPIO17** (Pin 11).
- ○ **LED negative leg (short leg)**: Connect to **one end of the resistor**.
- ○ Connect the **other end of the resistor** to the **GND Pin** (Pin 6).

Python Script to Control the LED:

```python
import RPi.GPIO as GPIO
import time

GPIO.setmode(GPIO.BCM)  # Use BCM pin numbering (Broadcom)
GPIO.setup(17, GPIO.OUT)  # Set GPIO17 as an output

GPIO.output(17, GPIO.HIGH)  # Turn on the LED
time.sleep(2)               # Keep it on for 2 seconds
GPIO.output(17, GPIO.LOW)   # Turn off the LED

GPIO.cleanup()  # Reset GPIO settings
```

Run the Script:

Save the Python script as `led.py` and run it in your terminal using:

`python3 led.py`

Test Code Incrementally

As you start experimenting with GPIO, always **test your code in small chunks**:

1. Test controlling a single LED before adding more components.
2. Ensure the LED turns on and off as expected before moving on to complex circuits like buttons or sensors.
3. Print debugging statements (e.g., `print("LED ON")`) in your code to trace the progress and check for errors as you develop your project.

Explore Software Tools (gpiozero or RPi.GPIO)

While RPi.GPIO is a good starting point for controlling the GPIO pins, you can also simplify your code with the **gpiozero** library. It's designed for beginners and abstracts away many of the low-level details, making it easier to interact with components.

Example using gpiozero to control the same LED:

```
from gpiozero import LED
from time import sleep
led = LED(17)
while True:
    led.on()
    sleep(2)
    led.off()
    sleep(2)
```

Installation: If you don't already have gpiozero installed, run:
sudo apt-get install python3-gpiozero

The gpiozero library makes it easier to work with components like LEDs, buttons, and motors.

5.2 Keeping Your Raspberry Pi Safe When Using the GPIO

Using the GPIO pins on your Raspberry Pi is exciting, but it's important to follow some safety precautions to protect both your Pi and the components you're connecting. Improper use of the GPIO pins can lead to **hardware damage** or malfunction, so learning the correct safety practices is essential.

Why does this matter?
Incorrect connections, wrong voltages, and short circuits can permanently damage your Raspberry Pi or the external components.

By following simple safety tips, you ensure your Pi and projects stay safe and functional.

---

1. Check the Voltage

- **GPIO pins operate at 3.3V**: The Raspberry Pi GPIO pins use 3.3V for input/output, not 5V. Connecting a 5V power source directly to a 3.3V GPIO pin can **burn out the pin** or damage the Pi permanently.
  - **Tip**: When working with 5V components, use a **level shifter** to convert 5V signals to 3.3V.

2. Use Resistors to Protect Components

- Always use a **current-limiting resistor** (typically 330Ω) when connecting components like LEDs to GPIO pins. This prevents **too much current** from flowing through the LED, which can damage both the LED and the Pi.
  - **Tip**: A 330Ω resistor works well for most small components like LEDs. You can use **Ohm's Law** (V = IR) to calculate the proper resistor for other components.

3. Avoid Short Circuits

- A **short circuit** occurs when current flows in an unintended path, potentially causing serious damage to your Raspberry Pi.
  - **Tip**: Double-check your wiring and connections before powering up. Make sure no wires are accidentally touching or creating a loop between power and ground.

4. Never Use 5V on GPIO Pins

- Some pins provide **5V power**, but GPIO pins themselves should never receive 5V signals. Exposing GPIO pins to higher voltage than 3.3V can **destroy** your Raspberry Pi.
  - **Tip**: If you're using components that require 5V (like some sensors), be sure to use the **5V power pin** instead of connecting it directly to a GPIO pin.

5. Use a Multimeter

- A **multimeter** can help you check voltages and connections before powering up your Raspberry Pi. This is useful for detecting problems in your circuit and avoiding damaging components.
  - **Tip**: Use a multimeter to verify voltages before making connections to ensure you are using the correct power pins and to check for short circuits.

6. Avoid Overloading the GPIO Pins

- Each GPIO pin has a **maximum current limit** (typically 16mA per pin and 50mA total for all pins). Drawing too much current from a GPIO pin can cause overheating or damage to the Raspberry Pi.
  - **Tip**: For high-power devices like motors, always use **external power supplies** and **transistors or relays** to isolate the Raspberry Pi from high currents.

Use Protective Circuits

If you plan on building more advanced projects, you should consider using additional protective components:

- **Diodes**: Prevent current from flowing in the wrong direction, especially when working with motors or other components with inductive loads.

- **Optocouplers**: Provide electrical isolation between your Raspberry Pi and external devices, protecting your Pi from potential spikes or electrical noise.
- **Relays**: Use relays when working with high-current or high-voltage components, ensuring the Raspberry Pi is isolated from high-power circuits.

Using a Breadboard for Testing

- **Breadboards** are ideal for safely prototyping circuits. They allow you to easily test connections without soldering, reducing the chance of errors. You can rearrange wires and components as needed without risk of damaging your Raspberry Pi.

Beware of Static Electricity

- **Static electricity** can harm your Raspberry Pi's sensitive electronics. Avoid touching the GPIO pins directly with your hands, especially in dry environments where static is common.
  - **Tip**: Ground yourself by touching a metal object or use an anti-static wrist strap before working with the Raspberry Pi's GPIO pins.

Always Use the Right Power Supply

- Ensure you are using a **high-quality 5V/2.5A power supply** for your Raspberry Pi. Using an unreliable power source can cause voltage drops, leading to unstable GPIO behavior or random reboots of your Pi.

Backup Your SD Card Regularly

- When experimenting with GPIO, especially in projects that involve sensors or motors, unexpected power issues or mistakes can occur. To avoid losing your work, **back up your SD card** regularly so you can easily restore your Pi to a previous state if something goes wrong.

5.3 Setting Up I2C on Raspberry Pi

I2C (**Inter-Integrated Circuit**) is a communication protocol that allows the Raspberry Pi to talk to multiple devices (like sensors or displays) using just two wires:

- **SDA (Serial Data)**: This is where the data is transferred.
- **SCL (Serial Clock)**: This keeps everything synchronized.

  Don't worry if this sounds a bit technical! Think of it as two people having a conversation: one person talks (SDA) while the other keeps track of time (SCL) to make sure everything is said in order. We'll guide you through the setup step-by-step!

Why Does This Matter?

Once you know how to set up I2C, you'll be able to connect a wide variety of sensors and displays to your Raspberry Pi. This will open up endless possibilities for fun projects, whether it's reading data from a temperature sensor or controlling an LCD screen.

Step 1: Enable I2C on Raspberry Pi

To allow your Raspberry Pi to communicate with I2C devices, we need to enable the I2C interface.

1. **Open the Terminal**:
   - Press Ctrl + Alt + T on your keyboard or find the Terminal app in your applications.
2. **Enter the Raspberry Pi Configuration Menu**:
   - In the Terminal, type the following and press **Enter**:

```
sudo raspi-config
```

3. **Enable I2C**:
   - Using your keyboard arrow keys, navigate to **Interfacing Options** and press **Enter**.
   - Then select **I2C** and press **Enter** again. When prompted, select **Yes** to enable I2C.

Reboot the Raspberry Pi:

```
sudo reboot
```

4. After rebooting, I2C will be ready to use!

Why? By enabling I2C, we're turning on the Raspberry Pi's ability to "talk" to other devices through this specific protocol. This is a crucial step before we can connect any sensors or displays.

Step 2: Install Necessary I2C Tools

Now that I2C is enabled, let's install some tools that will allow you to interact with I2C devices.

Install I2C Tools: In the Terminal, run the following command:

```
sudo apt-get install -y i2c-tools
```

Check If Your I2C Device Is Detected: After connecting your I2C device (we'll get to wiring soon), run the following command:

```
sudo i2cdetect -y 1
```

Why? This command scans your I2C bus and shows the devices that are connected to your Raspberry Pi. If your device is connected properly, you'll see its address listed.

Step 3: Connect Your I2C Device to the Raspberry Pi

Let's wire up your I2C device to the Raspberry Pi! Don't worry—this is simple once you know which pins to use.

1. **Identify the Pins**: You can use a **GPIO pinout diagram** to locate the correct pins on your Raspberry Pi. Visit pinout.xyz for an interactive guide that shows you which pins are SDA, SCL, power, and ground.
   You'll need to find these four important pins:
   - **SDA (Pin 3)**
   - **SCL (Pin 5)**
   - **3.3V Power (Pin 1)** – This will power the device.
   - **GND (Ground, Pin 6)** – This completes the circuit.
2. **Wiring Instructions**:
   - Connect the **SDA** pin of your I2C device to the **SDA (Pin 3)** on the Raspberry Pi.
   - Connect the **SCL** pin of your device to **SCL (Pin 5)**.
   - Connect the **GND** pin to **GND (Pin 6)** on the Pi.
   - Connect the **VCC** (power) pin to **3.3V (Pin 1)** on the Pi.

Why? This wiring allows the Raspberry Pi and the I2C device to communicate using the SDA and SCL pins, while the power and ground pins ensure that the device is powered.

Step 4: Write a Simple Python Script to Read Data

Now that the hardware is set up, let's write a Python script to interact with the I2C device.

Install smbus Library: We'll use a library called smbus to communicate with the I2C device.

```
sudo apt-get install python3-smbus
```

Create a Python Script: In the Terminal, open a text editor (such as Nano or Thonny) and create a Python file:

```
nano i2c_read.py
```

Python Code to Read Data: Here's a simple Python script to read data from an I2C device, such as a temperature sensor:

```python
import smbus
import time

# Initialize the I2C bus
bus = smbus.SMBus(1)
device_address = 0x48  # Replace with your device's address

# Function to read data from the sensor
def read_temperature():
    raw_data = bus.read_byte_data(device_address, 0)
    return raw_data

while True:
    temperature = read_temperature()
    print(f"Temperature: {temperature}°C")
    time.sleep(1)
```

Run the Script: Save the file and run it:

```
python3 i2c_read.py
```

Why? This script lets your Raspberry Pi retrieve data from the I2C device and display it, making it a great starting point for creating more advanced projects.

Common Mistakes (Don't Panic!)

- **Wrong Wiring**: Make sure you've correctly identified the **SDA** and **SCL** pins. Double-check the connections using pinout.xyz for easy reference.
- **Device Not Detected**: If the `i2cdetect` command doesn't show your device, ensure that I2C is enabled and the wiring is correct.

5.4 Using I2C Tools on Raspberry Pi

I2C tools are command-line utilities that help you interact with and troubleshoot I2C devices connected to your Raspberry Pi. These tools allow you to scan, read, and write data to your I2C devices directly from the terminal, which is useful for verifying that your devices are properly connected and functioning.

Why Does This Matter?

Using I2C tools gives you a deeper understanding of how your Raspberry Pi communicates with I2C devices. It also helps troubleshoot any issues you might encounter, such as verifying the correct connection or checking data from a sensor.

Installing I2C Tools

Before using I2C tools, you need to ensure they are installed on your Raspberry Pi.

Install I2C Tools: Open the Terminal and enter the following command:

```
sudo apt-get install -y i2c-tools
```

1. This command installs a set of useful tools that will help you communicate with I2C devices.

Key I2C Tools

Here's a brief overview of the most important I2C tools you'll be using:

1. **i2cdetect**: Scans your I2C bus for connected devices and displays their addresses.
2. **i2cget**: Reads data from a specific I2C device.
3. **i2cset**: Writes data to a specific I2C device.
4. **i2cdump**: Displays all available data from a connected I2C device.

Using I2C Tools

1. Using `i2cdetect` to Scan for Devices

The `i2cdetect` tool helps you identify which I2C devices are connected to your Raspberry Pi.

After wiring your I2C device (like a sensor), run:

```
sudo i2cdetect -y 1
```

1. **What happens**: You'll see a grid with numbers. Each number represents the address of a connected I2C device. For example, if you see $0x48$, it means there is an I2C device at address $0x48$.

Why? This tool is incredibly useful for ensuring your I2C device is properly connected and communicating with the Raspberry Pi.

---

2. Using `i2cget` to Read Data

Once you've detected your device, you can use the `i2cget` tool to read data from it.
Use this command to read a single byte of data from a device:

```
sudo i2cget -y 1 <device_address>
```

Replace `<device_address>` with the actual I2C address of your device (e.g., `0x48`).
Example:
```
sudo i2cget -y 1 0x48
```

1. **What happens**: The command will return the data from that address (usually in hexadecimal format), which you can use in your project or code.

   Why? This tool helps you confirm that your I2C device is returning data correctly, making it easier to debug or monitor sensor readings.

---

3. Using `i2cset` to Write Data

You can also send data to your I2C device using the `i2cset` command.

Use this command to write data to an I2C device:

```
sudo i2cset -y 1 <device_address> <data>
```

Replace `<device_address>` with the address of your I2C device and `<data>` with the value you want to send (in hexadecimal). Example:

```
sudo i2cset -y 1 0x48 0x1F
```

1. **What happens**: This command sends the data `0x1F` to the I2C device at address `0x48`.

    Why? Writing data to a device is useful for controlling I2C components, such as setting a display, adjusting a sensor, or controlling an output device.

---

4. Using `i2cdump` to Dump All Data

`i2cdump` allows you to view all the data available on a connected I2C device.

To view the entire memory map of an I2C device, use this command:

```
sudo i2cdump -y 1 <device_address>
```

Replace `<device_address>` with the address of your I2C device (e.g., `0x48`). Example:

```
sudo i2cdump -y 1 0x48
```

> **What happens**: The command will display a table of data showing all the values stored on your I2C device. This can be useful for debugging and understanding how the device stores its data.
>
> **Why?** If you're unsure what data is being sent or stored on your I2C device, `i2cdump` gives you a full snapshot.

Common Mistakes

1. **Incorrect Device Address**: Always double-check the device address when using `i2cdetect` to make sure you're reading or writing to the correct I2C device.
2. **Wiring Issues**: If `i2cdetect` doesn't show any devices, double-check your wiring, especially the SDA and SCL connections. Use pinout.xyz for an easy-to-follow GPIO pinout reference.
3. **Data Format Confusion**: Remember that I2C tools often return or accept data in hexadecimal. If you're unfamiliar with hex, take a moment to learn how to convert hex to decimal.

5.5 Setting Up SPI on Raspberry Pi

SPI (**Serial Peripheral Interface**) is a high-speed communication protocol used by the Raspberry Pi to talk to devices like displays, sensors, or SD card readers. Unlike I2C, which uses two wires, SPI uses four main lines, providing faster data transfer and allowing for communication with multiple devices simultaneously.

Why Does This Matter?

Learning to use SPI opens up the potential to work with many fast devices that need to transfer large amounts of data. If you're building projects with displays, sensors, or even connecting other microcontrollers, understanding SPI is essential.

Setting Up SPI on Raspberry Pi

Step 1: Enable SPI on the Raspberry Pi

SPI is disabled by default on the Raspberry Pi, so the first step is to enable it.

1. **Open the Terminal**:
   - Press `Ctrl + Alt + T` on your keyboard or find the Terminal in your applications.
2. **Enter the Raspberry Pi Configuration Menu**:
   - In the Terminal, type the following and press **Enter**:
     ```
     sudo raspi-config
     ```
3. **Enable SPI**:
   - Use the arrow keys to navigate to **Interfacing Options** and press **Enter**.
   - Select **SPI**, and when prompted, choose **Yes** to enable SPI.

Reboot Your Raspberry Pi:

```
sudo reboot
```

4. After rebooting, SPI will be enabled and ready for use!

   Why? Enabling SPI turns on the Raspberry Pi's ability to communicate with external devices using this high-speed protocol.

Step 2: Install the SPI Tools

Once SPI is enabled, it's a good idea to install some tools that will help you interact with SPI devices.

Install SPI Tools: In the Terminal, run the following command to install the necessary tools:

```
sudo apt-get install -y python3-spidev
```

Verify SPI Installation: After the reboot, verify that the SPI module is loaded by running:

```
ls /dev/spidev*
```

You should see something like `/dev/spidev0.0` and `/dev/spidev0.1`, which means SPI is correctly set up.

Why? This ensures that SPI is functioning properly and the Raspberry Pi can now communicate with connected SPI devices.

Step 3: Connect Your SPI Device to the Raspberry Pi

SPI uses four main connections, and sometimes a fifth if you're using multiple devices.

1. **Identify the Pins**: You can use a **GPIO pinout diagram** (like the one on pinout.xyz) to find the correct SPI pins. Here are the primary connections you'll need:
   - **MOSI (Pin 19)**: Master Out Slave In – Sends data from the Pi to the device.
   - **MISO (Pin 21)**: Master In Slave Out – Receives data from the device to the Pi.
   - **SCLK (Pin 23)**: Serial Clock – Sends clock pulses to synchronize data.
   - **CE0 (Pin 24)**: Chip Enable 0 – Selects which device the Pi is communicating with (used if you have more than one SPI device).
   - **GND (Pin 6)**: Ground – Provides common ground for the Pi and the device.
   - **3.3V (Pin 1)** or **5V (Pin 2)**: Power for the SPI device (check your device specs).
2. **Wiring Instructions**:
   - Connect the **MOSI** pin on the Raspberry Pi to the **MOSI** pin on your SPI device.
   - Connect the **MISO** pin on the Raspberry Pi to the **MISO** pin on your SPI device.
   - Connect the **SCLK** pin to the **SCLK** pin on your SPI device.

- Connect **CE0** (or **CE1** if you have a second device) to the **CS** pin on your SPI device.
- Connect the **GND** pin to **GND** on the device.
- Connect the power pin (**3.3V** or **5V**) to the appropriate power pin on your SPI device.

Why? These connections allow your Raspberry Pi to send and receive data from the SPI device in sync with the clock signal, making sure data transfer is fast and efficient.

Step 4: Write a Simple Python Script to Communicate with an SPI Device

Now that the hardware is connected, let's write a Python script to send and receive data from the SPI device.

Install the spidev Library: You'll need the `spidev` library to communicate with SPI devices using Python.

```
sudo pip3 install spidev
```

1. **Create a Python Script**: Open a text editor like Nano or Thonny and create a new Python file:

```
nano spi_test.py
```

2. **Python Code to Communicate with SPI Device**: Here's a simple Python script to send and receive data from an SPI device:

```python
import spidev
import time

# Create SPI object
spi = spidev.SpiDev()
spi.open(0, 0)  # Open SPI bus 0, device (CS) 0
spi.max_speed_hz = 1000000  # Set SPI speed to 1 MHz
```

```
# Send data and receive response
def send_receive_data(data):
    response = spi.xfer2([data])
    return response[0]

while True:
    data_to_send = 0x01  # Example data to send
    response = send_receive_data(data_to_send)
    print(f"Received: {response}")
    time.sleep(1)
```

3. **Run the Script**: Save the file and run it in the terminal:

   `python3 spi_test.py`

Why? This script sends a piece of data (0x01 in this case) to the SPI device and receives a response, printing it out on the screen. It demonstrates the basic communication between your Raspberry Pi and the connected SPI device.

Common Mistakes

1. **Wiring Errors**: Double-check your connections, especially **MOSI** and **MISO**. The **MOSI** pin on the Pi must connect to **MOSI** on the device, and the same goes for **MISO**.
2. **Chip Select Confusion**: Ensure you use the correct chip select (CS/CE) pin, especially if you have multiple SPI devices. Use **CE0** for one device and **CE1** for another.
3. **Data Format**: SPI works with hexadecimal data, so make sure to format your data properly when sending and receiving it.

5.6 Installing PySerial for Serial Port Communication on Raspberry Pi

PySerial is a Python library that allows your Raspberry Pi to communicate with devices over a **serial port**. Serial communication is commonly used for communication with devices such as **Arduino boards**, **modems**, **GPS modules**, and other hardware that uses the **UART (Universal Asynchronous Receiver/Transmitter)** protocol.

Why Does This Matter?

Serial communication allows you to send and receive data between the Raspberry Pi and external devices. If you're working on projects that require sending commands or reading sensor data from devices like an Arduino, learning how to use serial communication will be a game-changer.

Installing and Using PySerial on Raspberry Pi

Step 1: Enable the Serial Interface on the Raspberry Pi

Before you can use the serial port, you need to enable it in the Raspberry Pi configuration.

1. **Open the Terminal**:
   - Press `Ctrl + Alt + T` on your keyboard or find the Terminal in your applications.

Enter the Raspberry Pi Configuration Menu: In the Terminal, type the following and press **Enter**:

```
sudo raspi-config
```

2. **Enable Serial**:
   - Use the arrow keys to navigate to **Interfacing Options** and press **Enter**.
   - Select **Serial**, and when prompted:
     - Choose **No** when asked if you want a login shell over the serial interface.
     - Choose **Yes** to enable the serial hardware.

Reboot the Raspberry Pi:

```
sudo reboot
```

Why? Enabling the serial interface allows the Raspberry Pi to communicate with external devices through its UART pins (TX and RX).

Step 2: Install PySerial

Now that the serial interface is enabled, the next step is to install the PySerial library.

Install PySerial: In the Terminal, run the following command to install PySerial:

```
sudo pip3 install pyserial
```

1. **Verify the Installation**: After installation, you can check if PySerial was installed correctly by entering:
   ```
   python3 -m serial.tools.list_ports
   ```
2. This command will list all available serial ports, including any devices connected via USB or the GPIO serial pins (TX/RX).

Why? Installing PySerial allows you to write Python scripts that can send and receive data over the serial port, making communication with external devices easy and reliable.

Step 3: Connect Your Serial Device to the Raspberry Pi

To communicate with an external device over the serial port, you need to connect the device's **TX (transmit)** and **RX (receive)** pins to the Raspberry Pi's **GPIO** pins.

1. **Identify the Pins**:
   - **TX (Pin 8)**: Transmits data from the Raspberry Pi.

- RX (Pin 10): Receives data on the Raspberry Pi.
- GND (Pin 6): Common ground between devices.
2. **Wiring Instructions**:
    - Connect the **TX pin** of your external device to the **RX pin** (Pin 10) on the Raspberry Pi.
    - Connect the **RX pin** of your external device to the **TX pin** (Pin 8) on the Raspberry Pi.
    - Connect the **GND** pin on the device to **GND (Pin 6)** on the Raspberry Pi.

Why? The TX and RX pins allow your Raspberry Pi to send and receive data over a serial connection, while the GND ensures both devices share a common ground.

Step 4: Write a Simple Python Script to Use PySerial

Now that the hardware is connected, let's write a simple Python script to communicate with the serial device using PySerial.

Create a Python Script: Open a text editor (such as Nano or Thonny) and create a new Python file:

```
nano serial_test.py
```

Python Code to Communicate Over Serial: Here's a basic Python script that sends and receives data over the serial port:

```python
import serial
import time

# Open serial port
ser = serial.Serial('/dev/serial0', 9600, timeout=1)
ser.flush()

while True:
    # Send data
    ser.write(b"Hello from Raspberry Pi!\n")
    time.sleep(1)

    # Receive data
    if ser.in_waiting > 0:
        received_data = ser.readline().decode('utf-8').rstrip()
        print(f"Received: {received_data}")
```

Run the Script: Save the file and run the script in the Terminal:
```
python3 serial_test.py
```

Why? This script sends a simple message ("Hello from Raspberry Pi!") to the serial device and waits for a response. If the device sends data back, the Raspberry Pi prints it to the screen. This is a great way to verify that your serial connection is working properly.

Common Mistakes

1. **Incorrect Wiring**: Double-check that you have connected **TX** on your external device to **RX** on the Raspberry Pi, and **RX** on the external device to **TX** on the Raspberry Pi.
2. **Baud Rate Mismatch**: Ensure that the baud rate you set in the Python script matches the baud rate of the external device. A mismatch will result in garbled or incomplete data.

Permissions Issue: If you encounter permission errors when trying to access the serial port, you may need to add your user to the `dialout` group:
```
sudo usermod -a -G dialout pi
```

5.7 Installing Minicom to Test the Serial Port on Raspberry Pi

Minicom is a text-based terminal emulator that allows you to interact with devices connected to the Raspberry Pi via a **serial port**. It is often used to test and debug serial connections by providing an easy-to-use interface for sending and receiving data directly through the UART (Universal Asynchronous Receiver/Transmitter) interface.

Why Does This Matter?

Using Minicom helps you test whether your serial devices (such as GPS modules, Arduino boards, or other UART devices) are communicating properly with your Raspberry Pi. It's a quick and efficient way to verify your serial connection before diving into writing Python scripts.

Installing and Using Minicom on Raspberry Pi

Step 1: Enable the Serial Interface

Before using Minicom, you need to ensure the serial interface on your Raspberry Pi is enabled.

1. **Open the Terminal**:
   - Press `Ctrl + Alt + T` on your keyboard or open the Terminal from your applications.
2. **Enter the Raspberry Pi Configuration Menu**:
   - In the Terminal, type the following and press **Enter**:

```
sudo raspi-config
```

3. **Enable Serial Interface**:
   - Use the arrow keys to navigate to **Interfacing Options** and press **Enter**.
   - Select **Serial**, and when prompted:
     - Choose **No** when asked if you want a login shell over the serial interface.
     - Choose **Yes** to enable the serial hardware.

Reboot the Raspberry Pi:

```
sudo reboot
```

Why? Enabling the serial interface allows the Raspberry Pi to use its TX and RX pins for communication with external devices over UART.

Step 2: Install Minicom

Once the serial interface is enabled, you can install Minicom.

Install Minicom: In the Terminal, run the following command to install Minicom:

```
sudo apt-get install minicom
```

1. **Verify the Installation**: After installation, you can check if Minicom was installed correctly by typing:
   `minicom -h`
2. This should display a help menu, confirming that Minicom is installed and ready to use.

Why? Installing Minicom gives you a simple and powerful tool for testing serial communication with external devices.

Step 3: Set Up and Run Minicom

Before you start using Minicom, you need to configure it to communicate with your serial device.

1. **Identify the Serial Port**:
   - The Raspberry Pi's serial port is typically `/dev/serial0` or `/dev/ttyS0` depending on the Raspberry Pi model. You can verify which one is available by running:
     `ls /dev/serial*`
2. **Run Minicom with Serial Configuration**: To start Minicom and connect to the serial port, run the following command:

```
sudo minicom -b 9600 -o -D /dev/serial0
```

- ○ `-b 9600`: Sets the baud rate to 9600 (make sure this matches your device's baud rate).
- ○ `-D /dev/serial0`: Specifies the device path (adjust if necessary, such as `/dev/ttyS0`).

3. **Testing Communication**:
   - ○ Once Minicom is running, you can start sending data to and receiving data from your connected device through the serial interface.
   - ○ For example, if you have an Arduino or GPS module connected, it will display data in the Minicom terminal.

Why? Minicom allows you to interact directly with your device, making it a great tool for quickly testing serial communication and ensuring your connections and configurations are correct.

Step 4: Exit Minicom

To exit Minicom, press **Ctrl + A**, then **X**, and press **Enter** to confirm.

> **Tip**: If you need to change Minicom's settings (such as baud rate or device path), you can open the configuration menu by pressing **Ctrl + A** followed by **O** (for options) while in Minicom.

Common Mistakes

1. **Incorrect Baud Rate**: Ensure that the baud rate you set in Minicom matches the baud rate of the device you are connecting to. A mismatch will result in no data or garbled data.
2. **Wrong Serial Port**: If you don't see any communication, check that you are using the correct serial port (`/dev/serial0` or `/dev/ttyS0`). Use `ls /dev/serial*` to confirm the correct port.

Permissions Issue: If you encounter permission errors, you may need to run Minicom as `sudo` or add your user to the `dialout` group:

```
sudo usermod -a -G dialout pi
```

5.8 Using a Raspberry Squid (RGB LED) on Raspberry Pi

The **Raspberry Squid** is a special kind of **RGB LED** that can glow in a variety of colors by mixing red, green, and blue light. You can control the brightness of each color using your Raspberry Pi, allowing you to create almost any color you want. It's a perfect project to start learning how to use GPIO pins on the Raspberry Pi.

> **Tip:** Think of the RGB LED as three tiny light bulbs (red, green, and blue) inside one device. By turning them on in different combinations, you can create colors like yellow, purple, or even white!

Why Does This Matter?

Learning to control an RGB LED is a fun way to explore electronics and coding. You'll learn about **GPIO pins**, **PWM (Pulse Width Modulation)**, and how to create cool light effects using Python. Plus, it's a great introduction to controlling physical components with your Raspberry Pi.

Using a Raspberry Squid (RGB LED)

Step 1: Gather Components

To get started, you'll need:

- 1 x **Raspberry Pi** (any model with GPIO pins)

- 1 x **Raspberry Squid RGB LED**
- 3 x **220Ω resistors**
- 3 x **Jumper wires** (Male to Female)
- 1 x **Breadboard** (optional, but makes connections easier)

Step 2: Understand the RGB LED Pins

An RGB LED has four legs:

- **Red leg**: Controls the red color.
- **Green leg**: Controls the green color.
- **Blue leg**: Controls the blue color.
- **Ground (GND) leg**: Common ground for all colors.

Each of these colors can be controlled through a **GPIO pin** on the Raspberry Pi, allowing you to combine them to make different colors.

Step 3: Wiring the Raspberry Squid to the Raspberry Pi

1. **Identify GPIO Pins**: Use a **GPIO pinout diagram** like pinout.xyz to identify the GPIO pins on your Raspberry Pi. You'll need three pins for the red, green, and blue legs.
2. **Wiring Instructions**:
   - **Red leg**: Connect to **GPIO17** (Pin 11) through a **220Ω resistor**.
   - **Green leg**: Connect to **GPIO27** (Pin 13) through a **220Ω resistor**.
   - **Blue leg**: Connect to **GPIO22** (Pin 15) through a **220Ω resistor**.
   - **Ground leg**: Connect to **GND (Pin 6)** on the Raspberry Pi.

   Tip: The resistors limit the current going to each color, preventing the LED from burning out. Never skip this step!

Here's the pin mapping:

- **Red** → GPIO17 (Pin 11)
- **Green** → GPIO27 (Pin 13)
- **Blue** → GPIO22 (Pin 15)
- **GND** → Ground (Pin 6)

Step 4: Install the GPIO Library

Before writing any code, make sure you have the **RPi.GPIO** library installed on your Raspberry Pi.

Install the GPIO Library: Open the Terminal and run:

```
sudo apt-get install python3-rpi.gpio
```

1. **Verify the Installation**: You can check if the library was installed by running a simple Python script to test GPIO functionality.

Step 5: Write Python Code to Control the RGB LED

Now that the hardware is ready, let's write some Python code to control the colors of the LED.

Create a Python Script: Open a text editor (like Nano or Thonny) and create a new Python file:

```
nano rgb_led.py
```

python Code to Control the RGB LED: Here's a simple Python script to control the colors of the RGB LED:

```python
import RPi.GPIO as GPIO
import time
# Set up GPIO mode
GPIO.setmode(GPIO.BCM)
# Set up the GPIO pins for Red, Green, and Blue
red_pin = 17
green_pin = 27
blue_pin = 22
GPIO.setup(red_pin, GPIO.OUT)
GPIO.setup(green_pin, GPIO.OUT)
GPIO.setup(blue_pin, GPIO.OUT)

# Function to turn off all colors
def turn_off():
    GPIO.output(red_pin, GPIO.LOW)
    GPIO.output(green_pin, GPIO.LOW)
    GPIO.output(blue_pin, GPIO.LOW)

# Function to turn on specific color
def set_color(red, green, blue):
    GPIO.output(red_pin, GPIO.HIGH if red else GPIO.LOW)
    GPIO.output(green_pin, GPIO.HIGH if green else GPIO.LOW)
    GPIO.output(blue_pin, GPIO.HIGH if blue else GPIO.LOW)

try:
    while True:
        # Red
        set_color(1, 0, 0)
        time.sleep(1)
        # Green
        set_color(0, 1, 0)
        time.sleep(1)
        # Blue
        set_color(0, 0, 1)
        time.sleep(1)
        # Yellow (Red + Green)
        set_color(1, 1, 0)
        time.sleep(1)
        # Cyan (Green + Blue)
        set_color(0, 1, 1)
        time.sleep(1)
        # Magenta (Red + Blue)
        set_color(1, 0, 1)
        time.sleep(1)
        # White (Red + Green + Blue)
        set_color(1, 1, 1)
        time.sleep(1)
        # Turn off the LED
        turn_off()
        time.sleep(1)

except KeyboardInterrupt:
    turn_off()
    GPIO.cleanup()
```

1. **Run the Script**: Save the file and run it in the Terminal:
   `python3 rgb_led.py`

What does this script do? It cycles through different colors (red, green, blue, yellow, cyan, magenta, and white) by turning the red, green, and blue LEDs on and off in various combinations. You can adjust the timing and colors to create your own effects.

5.9 Using a Raspberry Squid Button on Raspberry Pi

A **Raspberry Squid Button** is a simple push-button component that can be used with the Raspberry Pi to detect button presses. By connecting it to the Raspberry Pi's **GPIO pins**, you can trigger different actions when the button is pressed or released. This allows you to create interactive projects like controlling an LED or triggering other components.

Why Does This Matter?

Using a button introduces an **input** mechanism to your Raspberry Pi projects, giving you the ability to interact with your project in real-time. Whether you're lighting up LEDs or controlling more complex devices, understanding how to work with buttons is a fundamental skill in physical computing.

Using a Raspberry Squid Button on Raspberry Pi

Step 1: Gather Components

You'll need the following components to get started:

- 1 x **Raspberry Pi** (any model with GPIO pins)
- 1 x **Raspberry Squid Button** (or any push-button)
- 1 x **10kΩ resistor** (used as a pull-down resistor)
- 2 x **Jumper wires** (Male to Female)
- 1 x **Breadboard** (optional, but helps make wiring easier)

Step 2: Understand the Button's Functionality

A push-button works as an **input device** that completes a circuit when pressed, allowing current to flow. The Raspberry Pi can detect this change in state (pressed or not pressed) via a **GPIO pin**, and you can use it to trigger different actions in your project.

A **pull-down resistor** ensures the GPIO pin reads a stable signal (LOW) when the button is not pressed.

Step 3: Wiring the Raspberry Squid Button to the Raspberry Pi

1. **Identify GPIO Pins**:
    o   You'll connect one side of the button to a GPIO pin and the other side to **Ground (GND)** on the Raspberry Pi.
2. **Wiring Instructions**:
    o   **One leg of the button**: Connect to **GPIO18** (Pin 12) on the Raspberry Pi.
    o   **Other leg of the button**: Connect to **GND (Pin 6)** on the Raspberry Pi.
    o   **Pull-down resistor (10kΩ)**: Connect one side of the resistor to **GPIO18** and the other side to **GND**.
3. This ensures that when the button is not pressed, the GPIO pin reads **LOW** (ground).

Step 4: Install the GPIO Library (If Needed)

Make sure the **RPi.GPIO** library is installed. You can skip this step if you already have it installed.

Install the GPIO Library: In the Terminal, run:

```
sudo apt-get install python3-rpi.gpio
```

1. **Verify the Installation**: You can check if the library was installed by running a simple Python script to test GPIO functionality.

Step 5: Write Python Code to Detect the Button Press

Now, let's write a Python script to detect when the button is pressed.

Create a Python Script: Open a text editor (like Nano or Thonny) and create a new Python file:

```
nano button_test.py
```

1. **Python Code to Detect Button Press**: Here's a basic Python script to detect when the button is pressed:

```python
import RPi.GPIO as GPIO
import time

# Set up GPIO mode
GPIO.setmode(GPIO.BCM)

# Set up the GPIO pin for the button
button_pin = 18
GPIO.setup(button_pin, GPIO.IN, pull_up_down=GPIO.PUD_DOWN)

try:
    while True:
        # Check if the button is pressed
        if GPIO.input(button_pin) == GPIO.HIGH:
            print("Button Pressed!")
            time.sleep(0.2)  # Debounce delay

except KeyboardInterrupt:
    GPIO.cleanup()
```

2. **Run the Script**: Save the file and run it in the Terminal:

```
python3 button_test.py
```

What happens? When you press the button, the message "Button Pressed!" will appear on the screen. You can modify this script to control other components (like an LED) when the button is pressed.

4.3 Converting 5V Signals to 3.3V with Resistors on Raspberry Pi

The **Raspberry Pi** operates at **3.3V** on its GPIO pins, meaning the maximum voltage it can handle on its input pins is 3.3V. Many external devices, such as Arduino or certain sensors, may output signals at **5V**, which can **damage the Raspberry Pi** if connected directly. To safely interface a 5V device with the Raspberry Pi's 3.3V GPIO pins, you need to **convert the 5V signal to 3.3V**.

The easiest and most cost-effective way to do this is using a **voltage divider** with resistors.

Why Does This Matter?

If you try to connect a **5V signal** directly to a **3.3V GPIO pin**, it can permanently damage your Raspberry Pi by applying more voltage than it can handle. Learning how to safely lower a 5V signal to 3.3V using resistors is an essential skill when working with external devices that operate at higher voltages.

Converting 5V Signals to 3.3V

Step 1: Gather Components

To create a simple **voltage divider** that steps down the 5V signal to 3.3V, you'll need:

- 1 x **5V source** (e.g., output pin from an Arduino or sensor)
- 1 x **Raspberry Pi** (3.3V input on GPIO)
- 1 x **10kΩ resistor**
- 1 x **5.1kΩ resistor**
- 3 x **Jumper wires** (Male to Female)
- 1 x **Breadboard** (optional)

Step 2: Understand the Voltage Divider Concept

A **voltage divider** works by splitting the voltage across two resistors in series. By selecting appropriate resistor values, you can reduce the 5V signal to 3.3V, which is safe for the Raspberry Pi GPIO pins.

Using a **10kΩ resistor** for R1R_1R1 and a **5.1kΩ resistor** for R2R_2R2, we can achieve approximately 3.3V from a 5V signal.

Step 3: Wiring the Voltage Divider

1. **Identify the Pins**:
   - You'll be connecting the **5V signal** (from a sensor, Arduino, or other device) to the Raspberry Pi's GPIO pin, but you'll need to lower it to 3.3V first.
2. **Wiring Instructions**:
   - Connect **one end of the 10kΩ resistor (R1)** to the **5V signal source**.
   - Connect **the other end of the 10kΩ resistor (R1)** to **one end of the 5.1kΩ resistor (R2)**.
   - Connect **the free end of the 5.1kΩ resistor (R2)** to **GND (Ground)**.
   - Connect **the junction between the two resistors** (where R1 meets R2) to the **3.3V input GPIO pin** on the Raspberry Pi.

Here's a summary of the connections:

- 5V signal → 10kΩ resistor → junction point.

- Junction point → 5.1kΩ resistor → Ground (GND).

- Junction point → 3.3V GPIO pin on the Raspberry Pi.

   Tip: You can use a breadboard to make the connections easier and cleaner.

Step 4: Verifying the Voltage Output

Once you've wired the resistors correctly, it's always a good idea to **test the voltage** before connecting it to the Raspberry Pi GPIO pin.

1. **Use a Multimeter**:
   - Set your multimeter to measure **DC voltage**.
   - Place the positive (red) probe on the **junction point** between the resistors.
   - Place the negative (black) probe on **GND**.
   - You should see a voltage close to **3.3V**.

   Why test? Verifying the voltage output ensures that you won't accidentally damage the Raspberry Pi by applying a higher voltage than it can handle.

Step 5: Connect to the Raspberry Pi

Once you've confirmed that the voltage at the junction point is around **3.3V**, you can safely connect it to one of the Raspberry Pi's GPIO input pins. Now your Raspberry Pi can safely read the signal from a 5V device without risk of damage.

   Tip: Be sure to connect the ground from the 5V device to the Raspberry Pi's ground as well. This common ground is necessary for the voltage divider to work properly.

Common Mistakes

1. **Incorrect Resistor Values**:
   - Make sure you are using the correct resistor values (10kΩ and 5.1kΩ). Using the wrong values will result in a voltage output that is either too high (unsafe for

the Pi) or too low (the signal might not be detected correctly).

2. **Floating Ground**:
   - ○ Always ensure that both the 5V device and the Raspberry Pi share a **common ground**. If the grounds are not connected, the voltage divider won't work correctly.

3. **Not Testing the Voltage**:
   - ○ Never skip the step of testing the voltage output with a multimeter before connecting it to your Raspberry Pi. Mistakes in the wiring or resistor values could lead to damaging the GPIO pins if the voltage is higher than 3.3V.

5.10 Using a Level Converter Module with Raspberry Pi

A **Level Converter Module** (or **Logic Level Shifter**) is a device that safely converts voltage levels between different logic systems, such as **5V** (used by some sensors or microcontrollers like Arduino) and **3.3V** (used by the Raspberry Pi). This module allows you to connect **5V devices** to your **3.3V Raspberry Pi GPIO pins** without the risk of damaging the Pi.

Why Does This Matter?

If you connect a **5V signal** directly to one of the Raspberry Pi's **3.3V GPIO pins**, you risk damaging the Pi because it can only safely handle up to **3.3V**. Using a **level converter** ensures that signals from 5V devices are safely converted to 3.3V, and vice versa, protecting your Raspberry Pi while allowing communication between devices with different voltage requirements.

Using a Level Converter Module

Step 1: Gather Components

You'll need the following components to get started:

- 1 x **Raspberry Pi** (any model with GPIO pins)
- 1 x **Level Converter Module** (4-channel or 8-channel)
- 1 x **5V device** (e.g., Arduino, sensor, etc.)
- 4 x **Jumper wires** (Male to Female)
- 1 x **Breadboard** (optional, for easy wiring)

Step 2: Understanding the Level Converter

A **Level Converter Module** typically has four main sections:

1. **High Voltage (HV)**: This is where you connect the **5V side** of the module.
2. **Low Voltage (LV)**: This is where you connect the **3.3V side**, such as your Raspberry Pi.
3. **Ground (GND)**: Both sides must share a common ground.
4. **Data Channels**: These are labeled **TX and RX** (or similar) and allow data to pass between the 5V and 3.3V sides.

The module converts **5V signals** to **3.3V** for the Pi and converts **3.3V signals** to **5V** for the 5V device, allowing safe bidirectional communication.

Step 3: Wiring the Level Converter Module

1. **Identify the Pins on the Level Converter**: You'll need to connect the high voltage (5V), low voltage (3.3V), and ground to the appropriate pins on the Raspberry Pi and the 5V device.
2. **Wiring Instructions**:
   - **High Voltage (HV)**: Connect to the **5V pin** on the 5V device (e.g., Arduino, sensor).
   - **Low Voltage (LV)**: Connect to the **3.3V pin** on the Raspberry Pi (Pin 1).

- Ground (GND): Connect the **GND pin** on the converter to both the Raspberry Pi's **GND (Pin 6)** and the 5V device's **GND**.
- **Data Channels**: Use the labeled **TX** and **RX** channels to pass data between the two devices:
  - For example, if you are sending data from the **Raspberry Pi to a 5V device**, connect the Pi's **GPIO pin** to an **LV** data channel and the corresponding **HV** pin to the 5V device.
  - Similarly, to read data from the **5V device to the Pi**, connect the **HV** data channel to the 5V device and the **LV** pin to the corresponding GPIO pin on the Pi.

Here's a summary of the connections:

- **HV** → 5V on the 5V device (Arduino, sensor, etc.).

- **LV** → 3.3V on the Raspberry Pi (Pin 1).

- **GND** → Ground on both the 5V device and the Raspberry Pi.

- **TX/RX Data Channels** → GPIO pins on the Raspberry Pi and 5V device for data communication.

Step 4: Verifying the Connections

Once the wiring is complete, double-check the following:

1. **Common Ground**: Ensure the Raspberry Pi and the 5V device share a common ground by connecting their **GND pins** to the **GND pin** on the level converter.
2. **Correct Voltage Pins**: Make sure you connected the **5V pin** from the 5V device to the **HV** side and the **3.3V pin** from the Raspberry Pi to the **LV** side.

Tip: It's always good practice to check your connections before powering the devices to avoid damaging components.

Step 5: Testing the Communication

Once the level converter is connected, you can test communication between the Raspberry Pi and the 5V device. Here's how:

1. **Sending Data from the Raspberry Pi to a 5V Device**: You can use the **TX** (transmit) and **RX** (receive) pins on the level converter to safely send and receive signals between the devices.
   - Example: If you're sending a signal from the Raspberry Pi to an Arduino (5V device), connect the Pi's **GPIO pin** (on the LV side) to the **TX** pin, and connect the Arduino's **RX** pin (on the HV side) to the corresponding data channel.
2. **Receiving Data from a 5V Device**: If the 5V device (e.g., sensor or Arduino) is sending data to the Raspberry Pi, use another data channel on the converter:
   - Connect the **5V device's TX** pin to the **HV side** of the converter.
   - Connect the **Raspberry Pi's RX** (GPIO pin) to the **LV side** of the corresponding data channel.

5.11 Powering a Raspberry Pi with Batteries

Why Power the Raspberry Pi with Batteries?

Using batteries to power your **Raspberry Pi** allows you to create portable, untethered projects without the need for a direct connection to a power outlet. This is ideal for projects like **robots**, **IoT devices**, or any setup where the Pi needs to be mobile or deployed in remote areas.

Why Does This Matter?

While the Raspberry Pi typically runs on a **5V power supply**, you can power it with batteries to make it more versatile and mobile. However, you need to ensure that the batteries provide **enough voltage** and **current** to run the Pi safely and without interruptions.

Powering a Raspberry Pi with Batteries

Step 1: Understanding Raspberry Pi Power Requirements

Before connecting batteries, it's important to know the **power requirements** of the Raspberry Pi:

- The Raspberry Pi requires **5V** to operate.
- The amount of **current** (measured in amps) depends on the model and the peripherals connected. On average:
  - Raspberry Pi Zero/Zero W: **~150-300mA**
  - Raspberry Pi 3/4: **~700-1200mA**, or **1.2A to 3A** under heavy load.
  - Additional peripherals (keyboards, cameras, etc.) increase the current demand.

To power your Raspberry Pi from batteries, you'll need a combination of batteries that provide **5V** and can supply sufficient current for your model.

Step 2: Choosing the Right Batteries

There are different battery options for powering a Raspberry Pi. Here are a few common setups:

1. **AA Battery Pack (6 AA Batteries)**:
   - **6 AA batteries** (1.5V each) in series will give you **9V**.

- Use a **5V voltage regulator** or **DC-DC step-down converter** to drop the 9V to 5V. A direct 9V connection will damage the Pi.
- **Current**: Ensure your batteries can provide enough current, especially if you're using peripherals. Alkaline batteries may run out quickly under heavy load, so **rechargeable AA batteries** (NiMH) are a better option.

2. **Li-ion/LiPo Batteries (3.7V)**:
   - A single **Li-ion** or **LiPo battery** typically provides **3.7V**. You will need a **DC-DC step-up converter** to boost this to **5V**.
   - **Capacity**: Look for Li-ion or LiPo batteries with a high capacity (e.g., 2000mAh to 5000mAh) to power your Raspberry Pi for longer periods.
   - **USB Power Bank**: Many Li-ion batteries come in USB power banks that already have a 5V output, which makes them a convenient option.

3. **18650 Li-ion Battery Pack (2-3 Cells)**:
   - **18650 batteries** are a popular choice for powering the Raspberry Pi. Two 18650 batteries in series give about **7.4V**, which can be regulated to **5V** using a **DC-DC step-down converter**.
   - A **3-cell pack** (11.1V) can also be used with a step-down converter.

4. **9V Battery**:
   - A **9V battery** can power the Raspberry Pi, but you will need a **5V regulator** or step-down converter. Note that regular 9V batteries typically have low capacity and may not last long, especially under heavy load.

Step 3: Voltage Regulation and Safety

The Raspberry Pi requires **precisely 5V**, and connecting higher voltages (like 9V from AA batteries or 12V from certain Li-ion packs) can damage the Pi. You'll need a **voltage regulator** or **DC-DC step-down converter** to safely reduce the voltage to **5V**.

1. **DC-DC Step-Down Converter** (Buck Converter):
   - A **DC-DC step-down converter** takes a higher voltage (like 9V or 12V) and lowers it to 5V efficiently.
   - Connect the input of the converter to your battery pack and the output to the Raspberry Pi's **5V pin** or a **USB input**.
2. **DC-DC Step-Up Converter** (Boost Converter):
   - If you're using a **3.7V LiPo battery**, you'll need a **step-up converter** to boost the voltage to 5V.
3. **5V Regulator**:
   - A **5V linear voltage regulator** (like the 7805) can also be used, but it is less efficient than DC-DC converters and can get hot, wasting power in the form of heat.

Safety Tip: Always check the output voltage with a multimeter before connecting to the Raspberry Pi to ensure it's a steady 5V.

Step 4: Wiring the Battery Pack to the Raspberry Pi

1. **Using the 5V Pin on the GPIO Header**:
   - If you're using a **DC-DC converter** or **voltage regulator** to provide 5V, you can power the Raspberry Pi directly through the **5V pin** on the GPIO header (Pin 2 or Pin 4).
   - Connect the **+5V output** of the converter to the **5V pin** on the Raspberry Pi and connect the **Ground (GND)** to a **GND pin** (Pin 6 or Pin 14).
2. **Using the Micro-USB/USB-C Power Port**:
   - If you're using a **USB power bank** or have a **5V USB output** from a LiPo battery pack, you can simply plug the USB output into the Raspberry Pi's **Micro-USB**

(Raspberry Pi 3 or earlier) or **USB-C** (Raspberry Pi 4) power input.

Tip: The **5V GPIO pins** are unprotected, meaning there's no over-voltage or under-voltage protection. It's safer to use the **USB port** when possible, as it includes built-in protection.

Step 5: Testing the Setup

1. **Check the Voltage**:
   o Before powering up the Raspberry Pi, use a multimeter to check that your voltage output is steady at **5V**.
2. **Power On the Raspberry Pi**:
   o Once everything is connected, turn on the power from the battery pack or power bank. Your Raspberry Pi should boot up normally.
3. **Monitor Power Consumption**:
   o Keep an eye on how long your battery pack lasts. Heavier loads (more peripherals, higher processing demands) will drain the battery faster. Consider using **power monitoring software** or a **multimeter** to track current usage.

Chapter 6: Controlling Devices with Raspberry Pi

6.1 Connecting an LED to Raspberry Pi

An **LED (Light Emitting Diode)** is a small electronic component that lights up when current flows through it. LEDs are commonly used in electronics projects to provide visual feedback, such as indicating when something is on or off.

Why Does This Matter?

Learning to connect and control an LED with your **Raspberry Pi** is a great starting point for exploring **GPIO (General Purpose Input/Output)** functionality. You'll be able to turn the LED on and off using Python code, giving you hands-on experience with physical computing.

Connecting an LED to Raspberry Pi

Step 1: Gather Components

To get started, you'll need the following components:

- 1 x **Raspberry Pi** (any model with GPIO pins)
- 1 x **LED** (any color)
- 1 x **330Ω resistor** (to limit current and protect the LED)
- 2 x **Jumper wires** (Male to Female)
- 1 x **Breadboard** (optional, but helpful for easy connections)

Step 2: Understand LED Polarity

An LED has **two legs**:

- **Anode (positive, longer leg)**: This leg needs to be connected to a GPIO pin to receive voltage.
- **Cathode (negative, shorter leg)**: This leg needs to be connected to **Ground (GND)** to complete the circuit.

Step 3: Wiring the LED to the Raspberry Pi

1. **Identify the GPIO Pins**: Use a **GPIO pinout diagram** like pinout.xyz to help you identify the correct pins on your

Raspberry Pi. You will use a **GPIO pin** to control the LED and a **GND pin** to complete the circuit.

2. **Wiring Instructions**:
   - **Anode (longer leg)**: Connect to **GPIO17** (Pin 11) through a **330Ω resistor**.
   - **Cathode (shorter leg)**: Connect directly to a **GND pin** (Pin 6) on the Raspberry Pi.

Here's a summary of the connections:

- **GPIO17 (Pin 11)** → Resistor → **Anode (longer leg)** of the LED.
- **GND (Pin 6)** → **Cathode (shorter leg)** of the LED.

  Tip: The resistor limits the current flowing through the LED, preventing it from burning out. The 330Ω value is a good choice for most standard LEDs.

Step 4: Install the GPIO Library (If Needed)

Make sure the **RPi.GPIO** library is installed on your Raspberry Pi to control the GPIO pins via Python.

Install the GPIO Library: In the Terminal, run:

```
sudo apt-get install python3-rpi.gpio
```

1. **Verify the Installation**: You can check if the library was installed by running a simple Python script to test GPIO functionality.

Step 5: Write Python Code to Control the LED

Now that your LED is wired to the Raspberry Pi, let's write a simple Python script to turn it on and off.

Create a Python Script: Open a text editor (like Nano or Thonny) and create a new Python file:

```
nano led_control.py
```

Python Code to Control the LED: Here's a basic Python script that turns the LED on and off with a 1-second delay:

```python
import RPi.GPIO as GPIO
import time

# Set up GPIO mode
GPIO.setmode(GPIO.BCM)

# Set up the GPIO pin for the LED
led_pin = 17
GPIO.setup(led_pin, GPIO.OUT)

try:
    while True:
        GPIO.output(led_pin, GPIO.HIGH)  # Turn on the LED
        print("LED ON")
        time.sleep(1)  # Wait for 1 second

        GPIO.output(led_pin, GPIO.LOW)   # Turn off the LED
        print("LED OFF")
        time.sleep(1)  # Wait for 1 second

except KeyboardInterrupt:
    GPIO.cleanup()  # Clean up GPIO when the script is stopped
```

Run the Script: Save the file and run it in the Terminal:

```
python3 led_control.py
```

What happens? The LED will blink on and off with a 1-second delay between each blink. You can modify the `time.sleep()` values to change the speed of the blinking.

Step 6: Experiment with the Code

Now that you've successfully connected and controlled the LED, here are some ideas to modify and expand the project:

- **Change the Blink Rate**: Adjust the `time.sleep()` values to make the LED blink faster or slower.
- **Turn on the LED for a Longer Period**: Change the timing to have the LED stay on for 2 seconds and off for 1 second, or vice versa.
- **Control Multiple LEDs**: Add more LEDs to different GPIO pins and modify the script to control them individually.

6.2 Leaving the GPIO Pins in a Safe State

What Does It Mean to Leave GPIO Pins in a Safe State?

When working with the **GPIO pins** on your Raspberry Pi, it's important to make sure they are left in a **safe state** when your program ends or the Raspberry Pi is powered off. If the pins are not properly managed, they can remain in a **high (on)** state, potentially causing **unintended behavior** or even **damage** to the components connected to them.

Why Does This Matter?

Leaving the GPIO pins in an unsafe state can lead to problems such as:

- **Components staying powered** (e.g., LEDs staying on when they shouldn't).
- **Short circuits** or **electrical noise** that can damage the Raspberry Pi or attached devices.
- **Wasted power** if components like motors or LEDs remain active after your program finishes.

By ensuring the GPIO pins are properly reset and powered down after use, you protect both your Raspberry Pi and your connected devices.

Leaving GPIO Pins in a Safe State

Step 1: Why Use GPIO.cleanup()

When you run a program that controls the GPIO pins, you need to reset the pins when the program finishes. This can be done using the GPIO.cleanup() function from the **RPi.GPIO** library.

- GPIO.cleanup() ensures that all GPIO pins are reset to their default state, which is **input mode**. This disconnects the pins from any active output and prevents electrical noise or stray signals.

  Tip: Always use GPIO.cleanup() at the end of your scripts to ensure safe shutdown of the GPIO pins.

Step 2: Adding GPIO.cleanup() to Your Code

Let's modify the previous LED script to include GPIO.cleanup() so the GPIO pins are left in a safe state after the program ends.

Create a Python Script: Open a text editor (like Nano or Thonny) and create a new Python file:

```
nano safe_gpio_led.py
```

Python Code with GPIO.cleanup(): Here's the modified script to safely manage the GPIO pins:

```python
import RPi.GPIO as GPIO
import time
# Set up GPIO mode
GPIO.setmode(GPIO.BCM)
# Set up the GPIO pin for the LED
led_pin = 17
GPIO.setup(led_pin, GPIO.OUT)

try:
    while True:
        GPIO.output(led_pin, GPIO.HIGH)  # Turn on the LED
        print("LED ON")
        time.sleep(1)  # Wait for 1 second

        GPIO.output(led_pin, GPIO.LOW)   # Turn off the LED
        print("LED OFF")
        time.sleep(1)  # Wait for 1 second

except KeyboardInterrupt:
    # Safely clean up the GPIO pins
    print("Exiting... Cleaning up GPIO.")
    GPIO.cleanup()
```

Run the Script: Save the file and run it in the Terminal:

```
python3 safe_gpio_led.py
```

Step 3: Using `GPIO.cleanup()` in Different Scenarios

When You Use Multiple GPIO Pins: If your project uses multiple GPIO pins, `GPIO.cleanup()` will reset all of them to their default state (input mode), preventing any potential issues.
Example:

```
GPIO.cleanup()  # This will clean up all GPIO
pins that were used
```

Cleaning Up Specific Pins: If you want to clean up only certain GPIO pins and leave others active, you can pass a list of pins to `GPIO.cleanup()`:
Example:

```
GPIO.cleanup([17, 18])  # This will clean up
only GPIO17 and GPIO18
```

Why Use `try` and `except`? Using the `try` block allows your program to keep running indefinitely (for example, blinking an LED), and the `except` block catches the **KeyboardInterrupt** error when the user presses `Ctrl + C` to stop the program. This ensures the GPIO pins are cleaned up properly when the program ends unexpectedly.

Step 4: Setting Up GPIO Defaults for Power-On/Off

By default, all GPIO pins are set as **inputs** when the Raspberry Pi boots up or shuts down. This is generally safe, but for certain projects (like motors or relays), it's important to configure the **default state** of GPIO pins at startup to prevent unwanted behavior (e.g., motors starting when they shouldn't).

1. **Use Pull-Up/Down Resistors**: If your project requires a specific state at startup (e.g., an LED should be off), you can use **pull-up** or **pull-down resistors** to ensure the GPIO pin defaults to a known state.
   - **Pull-down resistor**: Ensures the pin starts in a **LOW** state.
   - **Pull-up resistor**: Ensures the pin starts in a **HIGH** state.

Example:
```
GPIO.setup(17, GPIO.OUT, initial=GPIO.LOW)  #
Sets the LED to start off (LOW)
```

2. **Persistent GPIO Settings**: For more advanced setups, you can configure GPIO states at boot using **device tree overlays** or scripts in `/boot/config.txt` to ensure certain pins default to high or low when the Pi powers on.

6.3 Controlling the Brightness of an LED (Using PWM)

PWM (Pulse Width Modulation) is a technique used to simulate an analog output by rapidly turning a digital pin on and off at a certain frequency. By adjusting the proportion of time the signal is on (called the **duty cycle**), you can control the brightness of an **LED** or the speed of a motor.

Why Does This Matter?
PWM allows you to control the brightness of an LED, rather than just turning it on or off. By using PWM, you can make the LED dim or brighten gradually, giving you more control over your project.

Controlling the Brightness of an LED Using PWM

Step 1: Gather Components
You'll need the following components to get started:

- 1 x **Raspberry Pi** (any model with GPIO pins)
- 1 x **LED** (any color)
- 1 x **330Ω resistor** (to limit current)
- 2 x **Jumper wires** (Male to Female)

- 1 x **Breadboard** (optional)

Step 2: Wiring the LED to the Raspberry Pi

1. **Identify GPIO Pins**: Use a **GPIO pinout diagram** like pinout.xyz to help identify the GPIO pins. We'll use **GPIO18** (Pin 12) because it supports PWM.
2. **Wiring Instructions**:
   - **Anode (longer leg)** of the LED: Connect to **GPIO18 (Pin 12)** through a **330Ω resistor**.
   - **Cathode (shorter leg)**: Connect directly to **GND (Pin 6)**.

Here's a summary of the connections:

- **GPIO18 (Pin 12)** → Resistor → **Anode (longer leg)** of the LED.
- **GND (Pin 6)** → **Cathode (shorter leg)** of the LED.

   Tip: The resistor limits the current through the LED, protecting both the LED and your Raspberry Pi.

Step 3: Install the GPIO Library (If Needed)

Before you can control the brightness of the LED, ensure that the **RPi.GPIO** library is installed. This library allows you to control the GPIO pins and use PWM.

Install the GPIO Library: In the Terminal, run:

```
sudo apt-get install python3-rpi.gpio
```

1. **Verify the Installation**: You can check if the library was installed by running a simple Python script to test GPIO functionality.

Step 4: Write Python Code to Control the Brightness Using PWM

Now that the LED is wired to your Raspberry Pi, let's write a Python script to control its brightness using **PWM**.

Create a Python Script: Open a text editor (like Nano or Thonny) and create a new Python file:

```
nano pwm_led_control.py
```

Python Code to Control LED Brightness: Here's a Python script that gradually increases and decreases the brightness of the LED using PWM:

```python
import RPi.GPIO as GPIO
import time

# Set up GPIO mode
GPIO.setmode(GPIO.BCM)

# Set up the GPIO pin for the LED
led_pin = 18
GPIO.setup(led_pin, GPIO.OUT)

# Set up PWM on the LED pin at 100Hz
pwm = GPIO.PWM(led_pin, 100)  # 100Hz frequency
pwm.start(0)  # Start PWM with 0% duty cycle (off)

try:
    while True:
        # Increase brightness
        for duty_cycle in range(0, 101, 5):  # Duty cycle from 0 to
100%
            pwm.ChangeDutyCycle(duty_cycle)
            time.sleep(0.05)  # Short delay to see the change

        # Decrease brightness
        for duty_cycle in range(100, -1, -5):  # Duty cycle from 100%
to 0%
            pwm.ChangeDutyCycle(duty_cycle)
            time.sleep(0.05)

except KeyboardInterrupt:
    # Safely clean up the GPIO pins
    pwm.stop()  # Stop PWM
    GPIO.cleanup()
```

- pwm = GPIO.PWM(led_pin, 100): Initializes PWM on GPIO18 with a frequency of 100Hz.
- pwm.start(0): Starts PWM with a **0% duty cycle**, meaning the LED is initially off.
- ChangeDutyCycle(): Adjusts the brightness of the LED by changing the duty cycle (0% = off, 100% = fully on).
- The script gradually increases and decreases the brightness of the LED.

Run the Script: Save the file and run it in the Terminal:

```
python3 pwm_led_control.py
```

What happens? The LED will gradually get brighter and then dimmer in a smooth, repeating cycle. You can modify the **frequency** and **duty cycle** values to control how fast the LED changes brightness.

Step 5: Experiment with PWM Settings

Now that you've successfully controlled the LED brightness, you can experiment with different settings to see how PWM works:

Change the Frequency: Adjust the PWM frequency to see how it affects the LED. For example:

```
pwm = GPIO.PWM(led_pin, 50)  # Try 50Hz frequency
```

- Lower frequencies may cause flickering, while higher frequencies will result in smoother control.
- **Modify the Duty Cycle Range**: Experiment with different duty cycle ranges to see how the LED responds:

Use smaller increments, such as:

```
for duty_cycle in range(0, 101, 1):  # Increase by 1%
```

- **Add User Input**: Create a script that allows the user to control the brightness by entering a value for the duty cycle.

6.4 Changing the Color of an RGB LED

An **RGB LED** is a single LED that contains three separate LEDs inside: **Red**, **Green**, and **Blue**. By adjusting the brightness of each of these colors, you can create a wide range of colors. This makes the RGB LED a versatile component for projects that require customizable lighting.

Why Does This Matter?

Learning to control the individual **Red**, **Green**, and **Blue** LEDs allows you to create different colors by mixing them. You can use your **Raspberry Pi** to control the brightness of each color using **Pulse Width Modulation (PWM)**, giving you the ability to create virtually any color.

Changing the Color of an RGB LED

Step 1: Gather Components

You'll need the following components to get started:

- 1 x **Raspberry Pi** (any model with GPIO pins)
- 1 x **RGB LED** (common anode or common cathode)
- 3 x **330Ω resistors** (to limit current for each color)
- 4 x **Jumper wires** (Male to Female)
- 1 x **Breadboard** (optional, but helpful for easy wiring)

Step 2: Understand the RGB LED Pins

An **RGB LED** has four legs:

1. **Red**: Controls the red color.

2. **Green**: Controls the green color.
3. **Blue**: Controls the blue color.
4. **Common Anode or Cathode**:
   ○ If it's a **common anode** RGB LED, the **longest leg** is connected to **3.3V**.
   ○ If it's a **common cathode** RGB LED, the **longest leg** is connected to **GND**.

Tip: Check your RGB LED type (common anode or common cathode) before wiring, as this affects how you control the colors.

Step 3: Wiring the RGB LED to the Raspberry Pi

1. **Identify GPIO Pins**: Use a **GPIO pinout diagram** like pinout.xyz to identify the GPIO pins on the Raspberry Pi. We'll use three GPIO pins that support **PWM** to control the brightness of each color:
   ○ **GPIO17 (Pin 11)** for the **Red** LED.
   ○ **GPIO27 (Pin 13)** for the **Green** LED.
   ○ **GPIO22 (Pin 15)** for the **Blue** LED.
2. **Wiring Instructions**:
   ○ **Common Anode LED**: Connect the **longest leg** (common anode) to **3.3V (Pin 1)**.
   ○ **Common Cathode LED**: Connect the **longest leg** (common cathode) to **GND (Pin 6)**.
   ○ **Red leg**: Connect to **GPIO17 (Pin 11)** through a **330Ω resistor**.
   ○ **Green leg**: Connect to **GPIO27 (Pin 13)** through a **330Ω resistor**.
   ○ **Blue leg**: Connect to **GPIO22 (Pin 15)** through a **330Ω resistor**.

Tip: The resistors limit the current for each color, protecting the LED and the Raspberry Pi.

Here's a summary of the connections:

- **Common Anode**: Longest leg → 3.3V (Pin 1).

- **Common Cathode**: Longest leg → GND (Pin 6).

- **Red**: GPIO17 (Pin 11) → Resistor → Red leg.

- **Green**: GPIO27 (Pin 13) → Resistor → Green leg.

- **Blue**: GPIO22 (Pin 15) → Resistor → Blue leg.

Step 4: Install the GPIO Library (If Needed)

Make sure the **RPi.GPIO** library is installed on your Raspberry Pi to control the GPIO pins via Python.

Install the GPIO Library: In the Terminal, run:

```
sudo apt-get install python3-rpi.gpio
```

1. **Verify the Installation**: You can check if the library was installed by running a simple Python script to test GPIO functionality.

Step 5: Write Python Code to Change the Color of the RGB LED

Now that your RGB LED is wired to the Raspberry Pi, let's write a Python script to change its color by controlling the brightness of the Red, Green, and Blue LEDs using **PWM**.

Create a Python Script: Open a text editor (like Nano or Thonny) and create a new Python file:

```
nano rgb_led_control.py
```

Python Code to Control the RGB LED: Here's a Python script that uses **PWM** to mix Red, Green, and Blue to create different colors:

```
import RPi.GPIO as GPIO
import time
```

```python
# Set up GPIO mode
GPIO.setmode(GPIO.BCM)

# Set up the GPIO pins for the RGB LED
red_pin = 17
green_pin = 27
blue_pin = 22

GPIO.setup(red_pin, GPIO.OUT)
GPIO.setup(green_pin, GPIO.OUT)
GPIO.setup(blue_pin, GPIO.OUT)

# Set up PWM for each color with a frequency of 100Hz
pwm_red = GPIO.PWM(red_pin, 100)
pwm_green = GPIO.PWM(green_pin, 100)
pwm_blue = GPIO.PWM(blue_pin, 100)

# Start PWM with 0% duty cycle (off)
pwm_red.start(0)
pwm_green.start(0)
pwm_blue.start(0)
# Function to change the color
def set_color(red, green, blue):
    pwm_red.ChangeDutyCycle(red)     # Set Red brightness (0-100%)
    pwm_green.ChangeDutyCycle(green)  # Set Green brightness (0-100%)
    pwm_blue.ChangeDutyCycle(blue)   # Set Blue brightness (0-100%)

try:
    while True:
        # Red
        set_color(100, 0, 0)
        time.sleep(1)

        # Green
        set_color(0, 100, 0)
        time.sleep(1)

        # Blue
        set_color(0, 0, 100)
        time.sleep(1)

        # Yellow (Red + Green)
        set_color(100, 100, 0)
        time.sleep(1)

        # Cyan (Green + Blue)
        set_color(0, 100, 100)
        time.sleep(1)
                # Magenta (Red + Blue)
        set_color(100, 0, 100)
        time.sleep(1)
          # White (Red + Green + Blue)
        set_color(100, 100, 100)
        time.sleep(1)
except KeyboardInterrupt:
    # Safely clean up the GPIO pins
```

```
        pwm_red.stop()
        pwm_green.stop()
        pwm_blue.stop()
        GPIO.cleanup()
```

Run the Script: Save the file and run it in the Terminal:

```
python3 rgb_led_control.py
```

What happens? The RGB LED will cycle through different colors (red, green, blue, yellow, cyan, magenta, and white) by adjusting the brightness of the red, green, and blue LEDs.

Step 6: Experiment with Custom Colors

Now that you have control over each color channel, you can experiment by mixing different amounts of red, green, and blue to create your own custom colors.

Try different values for red, green, and blue in the `set_color()` function to create new colors:

```
set_color(50, 0, 50)   # Purple
set_color(25, 75, 0)   # Orange
```

Create smooth transitions between colors by adjusting the duty cycle in smaller increments:

```
for red in range(0, 101, 5):
    set_color(red, 0, 100 - red)   # Transition
from blue to red
    time.sleep(0.1)
```

Common Mistakes

1. **Incorrect Wiring**:
   o Double-check that the **common anode or cathode** is connected correctly to **3.3V** (for common anode) or **GND** (for common cathode).
   o Ensure that the **red, green, and blue legs** are connected to the correct GPIO pins with resistors.
2. **Wrong GPIO Pin Number**:

- o Ensure that you are using the correct GPIO pin numbers in the Python code. For example, **GPIO17**, **GPIO27**, and **GPIO22** are used in the example script.

3. **No Resistor**:
   - o Always include **330Ω resistors** for each color to prevent too much current from flowing through the RGB LED, which could damage the LED or the Raspberry Pi.

Troubleshooting Tips

1. **RGB LED Won't Light Up**:
   - o **Check wiring**: Ensure that the common anode or cathode is connected to the correct power source (3.3V for common anode, GND for common cathode).
   - o **Verify GPIO pins**: Make sure you are using the correct GPIO pins in both the wiring and the code.

2. **Colors Are Incorrect**:
   - o **Check the code**: Ensure you are setting the correct duty cycle for each color. For example, if the red LED is too bright or doesn't turn on, make sure you are adjusting the **red** channel in set_color() correctly.

3. **LED Flickers**:

Try increasing the **PWM frequency** to reduce flickering. For example, use **200Hz** instead of 100Hz:

```
pwm_red = GPIO.PWM(red_pin, 200)   # Higher
frequency
```

Expansion Ideas

Once you've mastered controlling an RGB LED, here are some fun projects to try:

1. **Interactive RGB LED Control**:

- Add buttons or sliders to manually adjust the brightness of each color, allowing you to create colors interactively.

2. **Music-Synced Light Show**:
   - Use the RGB LED to create a light show that changes colors based on sound or music input.
3. **Automatic Color Transitions**:
   - Program the RGB LED to transition smoothly between colors, creating an ambient lighting effect.
4. **IoT-Controlled Lighting**:
   - Combine the RGB LED with a web server or IoT platform to control the colors remotely through a web interface or smartphone app.

Tip: Start by experimenting with basic colors and duty cycles. Once you're comfortable, explore more advanced control by creating interactive projects or adding sensors.

6.5 Switching a High-Power DC Device Using a Transistor

A **transistor** is a tiny electronic switch that can control the flow of electricity through a circuit. You can use a small signal from your **Raspberry Pi's GPIO pin** to turn on and off much larger electrical devices, like **motors**, **fans**, or **high-power LEDs**.

Why Does This Matter?

The Raspberry Pi's GPIO pins can only handle small currents (about **16mA per pin**, with a total of **50mA** across all pins), which isn't enough to power **high-power DC devices**. Using a **transistor** allows you to safely control devices that require more power than the GPIO pins can provide.

Step 1: Gather Components

To get started, you'll need the following components:

- 1 x **Raspberry Pi** (any model with GPIO pins)
- 1 x **NPN Transistor** (e.g., **2N2222** or **BC547**)
- 1 x **High-power DC device** (e.g., a motor, fan, or high-power LED)
- 1 x **1kΩ resistor** (for the transistor's base)
- 1 x **Diode** (e.g., 1N4007, if you are controlling a motor or other inductive load)
- 1 x **External power supply** (e.g., 9V or 12V for the high-power device)
- Jumper wires (Male to Female)
- **Breadboard** (optional, for easier connections)

Step 2: Understand How the Transistor Works

You'll be using an **NPN transistor** to control the high-power device. The transistor has **three legs**:

1. **Base**: This is where you send a small current from the Raspberry Pi to turn the transistor on.
2. **Collector**: This is where the high-power device (like a motor) is connected.
3. **Emitter**: This connects to **Ground (GND)**.

When the **GPIO pin** sends a signal to the **base** of the transistor, it allows a much larger current to flow between the **collector** and the **emitter**, powering the high-power device.

Step 3: Wiring the Transistor to the Raspberry Pi and the High-Power Device

1. **Identify the GPIO Pins**: Use a **GPIO pinout diagram** like pinout.xyz to identify the correct pins on your Raspberry Pi.

We'll use **GPIO17 (Pin 11)** for this example to control the transistor.

2. **Wiring Instructions**:
    ○ **Base of the Transistor**: Connect to **GPIO17 (Pin 11)** through a **1kΩ resistor**.
    ○ **Collector of the Transistor**: Connect to the **negative terminal of the high-power device**.
    ○ **Emitter of the Transistor**: Connect to **GND (Pin 6)** on the Raspberry Pi and the **negative side of the power supply**.
    ○ **Positive terminal of the high-power device**: Connect to the **positive side of the external power supply** (e.g., 9V or 12V).

If you're using a **motor or inductive load**, you'll also need to add a **diode** to protect the transistor from voltage spikes:

● **Diode**: Connect the **anode** (non-striped side) to the **collector** and the **cathode** (striped side) to the **positive terminal** of the power supply.

Step 4: Install the GPIO Library (If Needed)

Make sure the **RPi.GPIO** library is installed on your Raspberry Pi. This will allow you to control the GPIO pins via Python.

Install the GPIO Library: In the Terminal, run:

```
sudo apt-get install python3-rpi.gpio
```

1. **Verify the Installation**: You can check if the library was installed by running a simple Python script to test GPIO functionality.

Step 5: Write Python Code to Control the High-Power Device

Now that everything is wired up, let's write a Python script to turn the high-power device on and off using the **transistor**.

Create a Python Script: Open a text editor (like Nano or Thonny) and create a new Python file:

```
nano transistor_control.py
```

Python Code to Control the Transistor: Here's a simple Python script to switch the high-power device on and off:

```python
import RPi.GPIO as GPIO
import time

# Set up GPIO mode
GPIO.setmode(GPIO.BCM)

# Set up the GPIO pin to control the transistor
transistor_pin = 17
GPIO.setup(transistor_pin, GPIO.OUT)

try:
    while True:
        GPIO.output(transistor_pin, GPIO.HIGH)  # Turn on the high-
power device
        print("Device ON")
        time.sleep(2)  # Keep it on for 2 seconds

        GPIO.output(transistor_pin, GPIO.LOW)   # Turn off the high-
power device
        print("Device OFF")
        time.sleep(2)  # Keep it off for 2 seconds

except KeyboardInterrupt:
    GPIO.cleanup()  # Clean up GPIO when the script is stopped
```

Run the Script: Save the file and run it in the Terminal:

```
python3 transistor_control.py
```

What happens? The high-power device (e.g., motor, fan, or LED) will turn on for 2 seconds and then turn off for 2 seconds, repeating this cycle.

Step 6: Test and Experiment

Now that the transistor is controlling the high-power device, you can experiment with the timing or even control the device based on user input or sensor data.

- **Change the Timing**: Modify the `time.sleep()` values to change how long the device stays on or off.
- **Use a Button or Sensor**: Add a button or sensor to control when the high-power device is switched on.

6.6 Switching a High-Power Device Using a Relay

A **relay** is an electrically operated switch that allows you to control a high-power device (like a motor, fan, or household appliance) using a low-power signal from your **Raspberry Pi**. Relays are often used to control devices that require more current or voltage than the Raspberry Pi can handle directly.

Why Does This Matter?

The **GPIO pins** on the Raspberry Pi can only handle small amounts of current (about **16mA per pin**, with a total of **50mA** across all pins), which isn't enough to control high-power devices like motors, lights, or appliances. A **relay** safely isolates the Raspberry Pi from these high-power devices, allowing you to control them without damaging your Pi.

Switching a High-Power Device Using a Relay

Step 1: Gather Components

You'll need the following components to get started:

- 1 x **Raspberry Pi** (any model with GPIO pins)
- 1 x **Relay module** (5V relay, typically used for DC or AC loads)
- 1 x **High-power device** (e.g., motor, fan, light, or household appliance)

- 1 x **External power supply** (if needed for the high-power device)
- **Jumper wires** (Male to Female)
- **Breadboard** (optional, for easier wiring)

Tip: Ensure that you use a **relay module** that is rated for the voltage and current of your high-power device. Common relay modules are rated for **5V control** and can switch **AC or DC devices**.

Step 2: Understand How the Relay Works

A **relay module** typically has:

1. **Control Pins**:
    - ○ **VCC**: Connects to 5V on the Raspberry Pi.
    - ○ **GND**: Connects to ground (GND) on the Raspberry Pi.
    - ○ **IN**: Receives the control signal from the Raspberry Pi's GPIO pin.
2. **Switching Terminals**:
    - ○ **Common (COM)**: This is the common terminal, which is connected to your high-power device.
    - ○ **Normally Open (NO)**: The terminal where the device is connected when the relay is **inactive**. The device turns on when the relay is activated.
    - ○ **Normally Closed (NC)**: The terminal where the device is connected when the relay is **active**. The device turns off when the relay is activated (less commonly used).

When you send a signal from the Raspberry Pi to the **IN pin** of the relay, it switches the connection between the **COM** and **NO** terminals, allowing the high-power device to turn on.

Step 3: Wiring the Relay to the Raspberry Pi and High-Power Device

1. **Identify GPIO Pins**: Use a **GPIO pinout diagram** like pinout.xyz to identify the correct pins on your Raspberry Pi. We'll use **GPIO17 (Pin 11)** to control the relay.
2. **Wiring Instructions**:
    - **VCC** of the relay: Connect to **5V (Pin 2)** on the Raspberry Pi.
    - **GND** of the relay: Connect to **GND (Pin 6)** on the Raspberry Pi.
    - **IN** of the relay: Connect to **GPIO17 (Pin 11)** on the Raspberry Pi.
3. **Connecting the High-Power Device**:
    - **COM terminal**: Connect to one terminal of the high-power device (e.g., motor, light, fan).
    - **NO terminal**: Connect to the positive terminal of the external power supply for the high-power device.
    - **Negative terminal of the power supply**: Connect to the negative side of the high-power device.

Step 4: Install the GPIO Library (If Needed)

Make sure the **RPi.GPIO** library is installed on your Raspberry Pi. This library allows you to control the GPIO pins via Python.

Install the GPIO Library: In the Terminal, run:

```
sudo apt-get install python3-rpi.gpio
```

1. **Verify the Installation**: You can check if the library was installed by running a simple Python script to test GPIO functionality.

Step 5: Write Python Code to Control the Relay

Now that everything is wired up, let's write a Python script to turn the high-power device on and off using the relay.

Create a Python Script: Open a text editor (like Nano or Thonny) and create a new Python file:

```
nano relay_control.py
```

Python Code to Control the Relay: Here's a simple Python script to switch the high-power device on and off using the relay:

```python
import RPi.GPIO as GPIO
import time

# Set up GPIO mode
GPIO.setmode(GPIO.BCM)

# Set up the GPIO pin to control the relay
relay_pin = 17
GPIO.setup(relay_pin, GPIO.OUT)

try:
    while True:
        GPIO.output(relay_pin, GPIO.HIGH)  # Activate the relay (turn
on the high-power device)
        print("Device ON")
        time.sleep(2)  # Keep it on for 2 seconds

        GPIO.output(relay_pin, GPIO.LOW)   # Deactivate the relay (turn
off the high-power device)
        print("Device OFF")
        time.sleep(2)  # Keep it off for 2 seconds

except KeyboardInterrupt:
    GPIO.cleanup()  # Clean up GPIO when the script is stopped
```

Run the Script: Save the file and run it in the Terminal:

```
python3 relay_control.py
```

What happens? The relay will switch the high-power device (e.g., motor, fan, or light) on and off in a cycle, controlled by the Raspberry Pi.

Step 6: Test and Experiment

Now that the relay is controlling the high-power device, you can experiment with the timing or even control the device based on user input or sensor data.

- **Change the Timing**: Modify the `time.sleep()` values to change how long the device stays on or off.
- **Use a Button or Sensor**: Add a button or sensor to control when the relay is activated.

6.7 Controlling Hardware with Android and Bluetooth

Bluetooth is a wireless technology that allows devices to communicate with each other over short distances. By using Bluetooth, you can control hardware (like LEDs, motors, or relays) on your **Raspberry Pi** using an **Android smartphone**. This makes it easy to control devices remotely without needing a wired connection.

Why Does This Matter?

Using **Bluetooth** to control your Raspberry Pi with an **Android device** allows for **wireless communication**, which is essential in projects where mobility and remote control are important. Whether you're controlling an LED, a motor, or other components, Bluetooth makes it possible to interact with your hardware from a distance.

Step 1: Gather Components

You'll need the following components:

- 1 x **Raspberry Pi** (any model with built-in Bluetooth, like the Pi 3, 4, or Zero W)

- 1 x **Android smartphone** (with Bluetooth capabilities)
- 1 x **LED** (or another device to control)
- 1 x **330Ω resistor** (if using an LED)
- 2 x **Jumper wires** (Male to Female)
- **Breadboard** (optional, for easier connections)

Note: The example will use an **LED** as the controlled hardware, but this method can be expanded to other devices (like motors or relays).

Step 2: Set Up Bluetooth on the Raspberry Pi

1. **Turn on Bluetooth**:

Open a terminal on your Raspberry Pi and type the following command to enable Bluetooth:

```
sudo systemctl enable hciuart
sudo systemctl start hciuart
```

2. **Install Bluetooth Tools**:

Install Bluetooth-related utilities to manage Bluetooth connections:

```
sudo apt-get install bluetooth bluez python3-bluez
```

3. **Check Bluetooth Status**:

Ensure that Bluetooth is running by typing:

```
sudo systemctl status bluetooth
```

- The status should show that Bluetooth is **active**.

4. **Pair Your Android Device with the Raspberry Pi**:

- On your Android device, go to **Settings > Bluetooth** and enable Bluetooth.
- Search for your Raspberry Pi and pair with it (it should show up as "**raspberrypi**").
- You may be asked for a PIN; by default, it's usually 0000 or 1234.

Step 3: Wiring the LED to the Raspberry Pi

1. **Identify GPIO Pins**: Use a **GPIO pinout diagram** like pinout.xyz to identify the GPIO pins on your Raspberry Pi. We'll use **GPIO17 (Pin 11)** to control the LED.
2. **Wiring Instructions**:
   - **Anode (longer leg)** of the LED: Connect to **GPIO17 (Pin 11)** through a **330Ω resistor**.
   - **Cathode (shorter leg)** of the LED: Connect directly to **GND (Pin 6)** on the Raspberry Pi.

   Tip: The resistor limits the current through the LED, protecting both the LED and your Raspberry Pi.

Step 4: Set Up a Bluetooth Server on the Raspberry Pi

1. **Install PyBluez**:

Install **PyBluez**, a Python library for Bluetooth communication:

```
sudo apt-get install python3-bluez
```

2. **Write a Python Script to Control the LED via Bluetooth**:
   - Create a Python script that listens for Bluetooth commands from the Android device and controls the LED accordingly.

Create the Python Script: Open a text editor (like Nano or Thonny) and create a new Python file:

```
nano bluetooth_control.py
```

Python Code for Bluetooth Control: Here's a basic Python script that listens for commands to turn the LED on or off:

```python
import RPi.GPIO as GPIO
import bluetooth

# Set up GPIO mode and LED pin
GPIO.setmode(GPIO.BCM)
led_pin = 17
GPIO.setup(led_pin, GPIO.OUT)

# Start with the LED off
GPIO.output(led_pin, GPIO.LOW)

# Set up Bluetooth server
server_socket = bluetooth.BluetoothSocket(bluetooth.RFCOMM)
server_socket.bind(("", bluetooth.PORT_ANY))
server_socket.listen(1)

# Wait for connection from client (Android device)
print("Waiting for connection...")
client_socket, address = server_socket.accept()
print(f"Connected to {address}")

try:
    while True:
        # Receive data from Android device
        data = client_socket.recv(1024).decode("utf-8").strip()
        print(f"Received: {data}")

        # Control the LED based on received data
        if data == "on":
            GPIO.output(led_pin, GPIO.HIGH)  # Turn on the LED
            print("LED ON")
        elif data == "off":
            GPIO.output(led_pin, GPIO.LOW)  # Turn off the LED
            print("LED OFF")

except KeyboardInterrupt:
    # Clean up GPIO and Bluetooth socket
    GPIO.cleanup()
    client_socket.close()
    server_socket.close()
```

Run the Script: Save the file and run it in the Terminal:
`python3 bluetooth_control.py`

What happens? The script waits for Bluetooth commands from your Android device to control the LED.

Step 5: Set Up the Android Device for Bluetooth Control

1. **Download a Bluetooth Terminal App**:
   - On your Android smartphone, download a **Bluetooth terminal app** from the Google Play Store (e.g., **Bluetooth Terminal** or **Serial Bluetooth Terminal**).
2. **Connect to the Raspberry Pi**:
   - Open the Bluetooth terminal app on your Android device.
   - Select the **paired Raspberry Pi** from the list of devices.
   - Once connected, you can send commands to the Raspberry Pi.
3. **Control the LED**:
   - In the Bluetooth terminal, type `on` and press **Send** to turn on the LED.
   - Type `off` and press **Send** to turn off the LED.

   Tip: You can expand this to control other devices like motors or relays by adjusting the Python code.

6.8 Making a User Interface to Turn Things On and Off

A **User Interface (UI)** is a way for people to interact with a system or device. By creating a simple graphical interface on your **Raspberry Pi**, you can make it easier to control devices like LEDs, motors, or other components using buttons, sliders, or text inputs. This makes your Raspberry Pi projects more accessible and user-friendly.

Why Does This Matter?

Instead of typing commands in a terminal, a **graphical UI** allows you to control your Raspberry Pi's hardware with a few clicks, making it more intuitive for users. Whether you want to turn on an LED, start a motor, or control a fan, a simple UI will make your project more interactive and fun.

Making a User Interface to Turn Things On and Off

Step 1: Gather Components

You'll need the following components to get started:

- 1 x **Raspberry Pi** (any model with GPIO pins)
- 1 x **LED** (or another device to control)
- 1 x **330Ω resistor** (for the LED)
- 2 x **Jumper wires** (Male to Female)
- **Breadboard** (optional, for easier connections)

    Note: The example uses an LED, but this method can be expanded to control other devices (like motors or relays).

Step 2: Install Tkinter for GUI Development

Tkinter is a Python library that makes it easy to create **graphical user interfaces (GUIs)**. It's included by default on most Raspberry Pi setups, but if it's not installed, you can install it manually.

Check if Tkinter is installed: In the terminal, run the following command:

```
python3 -m tkinter
```

1. If a window opens, Tkinter is already installed. If not, proceed with the next step.

Install Tkinter: Install the Tkinter library using the following command:

```
sudo apt-get install python3-tk
```

Step 3: Wiring the LED to the Raspberry Pi

1. **Identify GPIO Pins**: Use a **GPIO pinout diagram** like pinout.xyz to identify the GPIO pins on your Raspberry Pi. We'll use **GPIO17 (Pin 11)** to control the LED.
2. **Wiring Instructions**:
   - **Anode (longer leg)** of the LED: Connect to **GPIO17 (Pin 11)** through a **330Ω resistor**.
   - **Cathode (shorter leg)** of the LED: Connect directly to **GND (Pin 6)** on the Raspberry Pi.

   Tip: The resistor limits the current through the LED, protecting both the LED and your Raspberry Pi.

Step 4: Write the Python Script for the UI

Now that everything is wired up, let's create a simple UI to control the LED using **Tkinter**.

Create a Python Script: Open a text editor (like Nano or Thonny) and create a new Python file:

```
nano led_ui_control.py
```

Python Code for the GUI: Here's a basic Python script that creates a graphical interface with two buttons to turn the LED on and off:

```python
import tkinter as tk
import RPi.GPIO as GPIO

# Set up GPIO mode and LED pin
GPIO.setmode(GPIO.BCM)
led_pin = 17
GPIO.setup(led_pin, GPIO.OUT)

# Start with the LED off
GPIO.output(led_pin, GPIO.LOW)

# Define functions to control the LED
def led_on():
    GPIO.output(led_pin, GPIO.HIGH)
    status_label.config(text="LED is ON")

def led_off():
    GPIO.output(led_pin, GPIO.LOW)
    status_label.config(text="LED is OFF")

# Create the main window
window = tk.Tk()
window.title("LED Control")

# Create buttons to turn the LED on and off
on_button = tk.Button(window, text="Turn LED ON", command=led_on)
on_button.pack(pady=10)

off_button = tk.Button(window, text="Turn LED OFF", command=led_off)
off_button.pack(pady=10)

# Status label to show LED status
status_label = tk.Label(window, text="LED is OFF")
status_label.pack(pady=10)

# Run the main loop
window.mainloop()

# Clean up GPIO when the window is closed
GPIO.cleanup()
```

Run the Script: Save the file and run it in the Terminal:

```
python3 led_ui_control.py
```

What happens? A window will open with two buttons: **Turn LED ON** and **Turn LED OFF**. Clicking the buttons will control the LED.

Step 5: Customize the UI

Now that you have a basic UI working, you can customize it by adding more controls, text, or images.

Add More Buttons: You can add more buttons to control additional devices (e.g., motors or relays) by modifying the code:

```python
# Additional device example
def motor_on():
    GPIO.output(motor_pin, GPIO.HIGH)
    status_label.config(text="Motor is ON")

motor_on_button = tk.Button(window, text="Turn Motor ON",
command=motor_on)
motor_on_button.pack(pady=10)
```

Use Sliders: You can also add sliders to control the brightness of the LED using **PWM**:

```python
def change_brightness(value):
    pwm_led.ChangeDutyCycle(int(value))

# Create a slider to control brightness
brightness_slider = tk.Scale(window, from_=0, to=100,
orient=tk.HORIZONTAL, command=change_brightness)
brightness_slider.pack(pady=10)
```

1. **Improve the Design**:
   - Add more labels or images to make the interface more user-friendly.
   - Change the button colors or styles for a more professional look.

6.9 Making a User Interface to Control PWM Power for LEDs and Motors

Pulse Width Modulation (PWM) is a technique used to control the brightness of an LED or the speed of a motor by adjusting the amount of power delivered to the device. Instead of sending a constant voltage, PWM rapidly turns the power on and off. The ratio of on-time to off-time is called the **duty cycle**, and it determines how much power the device receives.

Why Does This Matter?

Using **PWM** allows you to have more control over your hardware. For example, instead of just turning an LED on or off, you can **dim the LED** or **control the speed of a motor**. By creating a **graphical user interface (UI)**, you can easily adjust the PWM settings with sliders, making the control of these devices more intuitive.

Making a User Interface to Control PWM for LEDs and Motors

Step 1: Gather Components

You'll need the following components:

- 1 x **Raspberry Pi** (any model with GPIO pins)
- 1 x **LED** (or motor)
- 1 x **330Ω resistor** (for the LED)
- 2 x **Jumper wires** (Male to Female)
- **Breadboard** (optional, for easier connections)

  Note: This example will use an **LED**, but the method can be applied to motors or other devices that can be controlled with PWM.

Step 2: Install Tkinter for GUI Development

Tkinter is a Python library that makes it easy to create **graphical user interfaces (GUIs)**. It is included by default on most Raspberry Pi setups, but if it's not installed, you can install it manually.

Check if Tkinter is installed: In the terminal, run the following command:

```
python3 -m tkinter
```

1. If a window opens, Tkinter is already installed. If not, proceed to the next step.

Install Tkinter: Install the Tkinter library using the following command:

```
sudo apt-get install python3-tk
```

Step 3: Wiring the LED (or Motor) to the Raspberry Pi

1. **Identify GPIO Pins**: Use a **GPIO pinout diagram** like pinout.xyz to identify the GPIO pins on your Raspberry Pi. We'll use **GPIO18 (Pin 12)** to control the LED with PWM.
2. **Wiring Instructions**:
   ○ **Anode (longer leg)** of the LED: Connect to **GPIO18 (Pin 12)** through a **330Ω resistor**.
   ○ **Cathode (shorter leg)** of the LED: Connect directly to **GND (Pin 6)** on the Raspberry Pi.

   Note: If you're using a motor instead of an LED, you would wire the motor in place of the LED. Ensure that you're using a transistor or motor driver to safely control the motor.

Step 4: Set Up the Python Environment for PWM

Install the RPi.GPIO Library: Make sure the **RPi.GPIO** library is installed. This library allows you to control the Raspberry Pi's GPIO pins and use PWM.

In the terminal, run the following command:

```
sudo apt-get install python3-rpi.gpio
```

1. **Set Up PWM on GPIO18 (Pin 12)**: We'll use **PWM** on **GPIO18** to control the brightness of the LED or the speed of a motor.

Step 5: Write the Python Script for the GUI with PWM Control

Now that everything is wired up and set up, let's create a simple UI using **Tkinter** that will allow you to control the PWM signal with a slider.

Create a Python Script: Open a text editor (like Nano or Thonny) and create a new Python file:

```
nano pwm_ui_control.py
```

Python Code for the GUI with PWM: Here's a basic Python script that creates a graphical interface with a slider to control the brightness of the LED (or the speed of a motor) using PWM:

```python
import tkinter as tk
import RPi.GPIO as GPIO

# Set up GPIO mode and PWM pin
GPIO.setmode(GPIO.BCM)
pwm_pin = 18
GPIO.setup(pwm_pin, GPIO.OUT)
```

```
# Set up PWM on GPIO18 with a frequency of 100Hz
pwm = GPIO.PWM(pwm_pin, 100)
pwm.start(0)  # Start with a duty cycle of 0% (off)

# Define function to change the duty cycle based on slider value
def change_duty_cycle(value):
    pwm.ChangeDutyCycle(int(value))
    status_label.config(text=f"PWM Duty Cycle: {value}%")

# Create the main window
window = tk.Tk()
window.title("PWM Control")

# Create a slider to adjust PWM duty cycle
slider = tk.Scale(window, from_=0, to=100, orient=tk.HORIZONTAL,
command=change_duty_cycle)
slider.pack(pady=10)

# Create a status label to show the current PWM duty cycle
status_label = tk.Label(window, text="PWM Duty Cycle: 0%")
status_label.pack(pady=10)

# Run the main loop
window.mainloop()

# Clean up GPIO when the window is closed
GPIO.cleanup()
```

Run the Script: Save the file and run it in the terminal:

```
python3 pwm_ui_control.py
```

What happens? A window will open with a slider that adjusts the PWM duty cycle. As you move the slider, the brightness of the LED will change (or the speed of the motor if you're using one).

Step 6: Customize the UI

Now that you have a working UI, you can customize it by adding more controls, buttons, or labels.

Add More Devices: You can add more sliders or buttons to control multiple LEDs or motors by modifying the code. For example:

```
def change_motor_speed(value):
    pwm_motor.ChangeDutyCycle(int(value))
    motor_status_label.config(text=f"Motor Speed: {value}%")
```

```
motor_slider = tk.Scale(window, from_=0, to=100, orient=tk.HORIZONTAL,
command=change_motor_speed)
motor_slider.pack(pady=10)
motor_status_label = tk.Label(window, text="Motor Speed: 0%")
motor_status_label.pack(pady=10)
```

Use Buttons for On/Off Control: You can also add buttons to turn
devices on or off while still using the slider for PWM control:

```
def led_on():
    pwm.ChangeDutyCycle(100)  # Set duty cycle to 100% (fully on)
    status_label.config(text="LED ON (100%)")

def led_off():
    pwm.ChangeDutyCycle(0)  # Set duty cycle to 0% (off)
    status_label.config(text="LED OFF (0%)")

on_button = tk.Button(window, text="Turn LED ON", command=led_on)
on_button.pack(pady=5)

off_button = tk.Button(window, text="Turn LED OFF", command=led_off)
off_button.pack(pady=5)
```

Change the Design: You can improve the UI by adjusting button
colors, fonts, or the overall layout:

```
window.geometry("400x200")  # Set window size
on_button.config(bg="green", fg="white", font=("Arial", 12))
off_button.config(bg="red", fg="white", font=("Arial", 12))
```

Chapter 7: Basic Motor Control with Raspberry Pi

7.1 Controlling the Speed of a DC Motor

A **DC motor** is a type of electric motor that runs on direct current
(DC) power. These motors are commonly used in robotics and
electronics projects to drive wheels, fans, or other mechanical parts.
Controlling the speed of a **DC motor** with a **Raspberry Pi** allows
you to adjust how fast the motor spins, which is useful in many
projects like robots, vehicles, or fans.

Why Does This Matter?

By controlling the speed of a **DC motor**, you can make your project more dynamic and responsive. Whether you're building a robot or a fan, being able to **increase or decrease the motor's speed** gives you more flexibility. You can use **Pulse Width Modulation (PWM)** to control the motor's speed with the Raspberry Pi.

Controlling the Speed of a DC Motor

Step 1: Gather Components

To get started, you'll need the following components:

- 1 x **Raspberry Pi** (any model with GPIO pins)
- 1 x **DC motor** (a simple, small 5V-12V DC motor)
- 1 x **NPN transistor** (e.g., **2N2222** or **BC547**) or an **H-bridge motor driver** (e.g., L298N or L293D for more complex control)
- 1 x **Diode** (e.g., 1N4007) to prevent voltage spikes
- 1 x **1kΩ resistor** (for the transistor's base)
- External **power supply** (e.g., a 9V battery or a 5V-12V DC adapter for the motor)
- Jumper wires (Male to Female)
- Breadboard (optional, for easier connections)

Step 2: Understand the Circuit

To control the motor's speed, you'll use **PWM** from a Raspberry Pi GPIO pin. You can use an **NPN transistor** as a switch to turn the motor on and off rapidly, varying the **duty cycle** to control the motor speed. The transistor acts as a bridge between the low-power GPIO signal and the higher-power motor circuit.

Step 3: Wiring the DC Motor to the Raspberry Pi

1. **Identify GPIO Pins**: Use a **GPIO pinout diagram** like pinout.xyz to identify the GPIO pins on your Raspberry Pi. We'll use **GPIO18 (Pin 12)** to control the motor speed using PWM.
2. **Wiring Instructions**:
   - **Motor Power**:
     - The **positive terminal** of the motor connects to the **positive terminal of the external power supply**.
     - The **negative terminal** of the motor connects to the **collector** of the transistor.
   - **Transistor Wiring**:
     - **Base** of the transistor: Connect to **GPIO18 (Pin 12)** through a **1kΩ resistor**.
     - **Emitter** of the transistor: Connect to **GND (Pin 6)** on the Raspberry Pi.
   - **Diode**: Place the **diode** across the motor terminals, with the **anode** (non-striped side) connected to the negative terminal of the motor and the **cathode** (striped side) connected to the positive terminal of the motor. This protects the transistor from voltage spikes when the motor turns off.

Here's a summary of the connections:

- **GPIO18 (Pin 12) → 1kΩ resistor → Base of transistor**.
- **Collector of transistor → Negative terminal of motor**.
- **Emitter of transistor → GND (Pin 6)**.
- **Diode**: Anode to **negative motor terminal**, cathode to **positive motor terminal**.
- **External power supply** (e.g., 9V or 12V): **Positive terminal** to **positive motor terminal, negative terminal to GND (Pin 6)**.

Tip: The **transistor** is essential to safely switch and control the motor's speed without overloading the Raspberry Pi's GPIO pins.

Step 4: Set Up the Python Environment for PWM

Install the RPi.GPIO Library: The **RPi.GPIO** library allows you to control the Raspberry Pi's GPIO pins and use **PWM**. Make sure it's installed by running:

```
sudo apt-get install python3-rpi.gpio
```

1. **Set Up PWM on GPIO18 (Pin 12)**: You'll use PWM on **GPIO18** to control the motor's speed. PWM lets you vary the amount of power sent to the motor, which adjusts its speed.

Step 5: Write the Python Script to Control Motor Speed

Now that everything is wired up, let's write a simple Python script to control the motor's speed using PWM.

Create a Python Script: Open a text editor (like Nano or Thonny) and create a new Python file:

```
nano motor_speed_control.py
```

Python Code to Control Motor Speed: Here's a basic Python script to adjust the motor speed using a PWM signal:

```python
import RPi.GPIO as GPIO
import time

# Set up GPIO mode and motor pin
GPIO.setmode(GPIO.BCM)
motor_pin = 18
GPIO.setup(motor_pin, GPIO.OUT)

# Set up PWM on GPIO18 with a frequency of 100Hz
pwm = GPIO.PWM(motor_pin, 100)
pwm.start(0)  # Start PWM with 0% duty cycle (motor off)
```

```
try:
    while True:
        # Gradually increase the motor speed
        for speed in range(0, 101, 5):  # Speed from 0% to 100%
            pwm.ChangeDutyCycle(speed)
            print(f"Motor Speed: {speed}%")
            time.sleep(0.1)

        # Gradually decrease the motor speed
        for speed in range(100, -1, -5):  # Speed from 100% to 0%
            pwm.ChangeDutyCycle(speed)
            print(f"Motor Speed: {speed}%")
            time.sleep(0.1)

except KeyboardInterrupt:
    pwm.stop()  # Stop PWM
    GPIO.cleanup()  # Clean up GPIO when the script is stopped
```

Run the Script: Save the file and run it in the terminal:

```
python3 motor_speed_control.py
```

What happens? The motor will gradually speed up to full speed and then slow down again in a loop. You can adjust the **duty cycle** to control how fast the motor runs.

Step 6: Customize the Motor Control

Now that you have a basic motor speed control, you can modify the script to add more features.

Add User Input: You can let the user input the desired speed using the keyboard:

```
while True:
    speed = int(input("Enter motor speed (0-100): "))
    if 0 <= speed <= 100:
        pwm.ChangeDutyCycle(speed)
        print(f"Motor Speed: {speed}%")
    else:
        print("Please enter a value between 0 and 100")
```

1. **Create a PWM Slider UI**: Use **Tkinter** to create a graphical user interface (GUI) with a slider to control the motor speed

(similar to the previous section about controlling LEDs with PWM).

7.2 Controlling the Direction of a DC Motor

Controlling the **direction** of a DC motor means being able to rotate it **clockwise** and **counterclockwise**. This is important in projects like **robots**, **vehicles**, or **automated systems**, where you may need the motor to spin in both directions. By using an **H-Bridge motor driver**, you can control both the speed and direction of a DC motor.

Why Does This Matter?

Being able to control the **speed** and **direction** of a motor makes your project much more versatile. For example, if you're building a **robot car**, you'll need the ability to drive the motors **forward** and **backward**. An **H-Bridge motor driver** allows you to change the direction by switching the polarity of the voltage supplied to the motor.

Controlling the Direction of a DC Motor

Step 1: Gather Components

You'll need the following components:

- 1 x **Raspberry Pi** (any model with GPIO pins)
- 1 x **DC motor** (a simple, small 5V-12V DC motor)
- 1 x **H-Bridge motor driver** (e.g., **L298N** or **L293D**)
- External **power supply** (e.g., a 9V battery or a 5V-12V DC adapter for the motor)
- Jumper wires (Male to Female)
- Breadboard (optional, for easier connections)

    Tip: The **L298N** and **L293D** are common H-Bridge motor drivers that allow you to control the **direction** and

speed of DC motors. They also protect your Raspberry Pi from the high current needed to run the motors.

Step 2: Understand How the H-Bridge Works

An **H-Bridge motor driver** allows you to control the direction of a motor by switching the polarity of the voltage supplied to it. By activating different pins on the H-Bridge, you can make the motor spin **clockwise** or **counterclockwise**.

The H-Bridge typically has:

- **Two inputs**: These are used to control the direction of the motor.
- **Two enable pins**: These are used to control the speed of the motor using **PWM**.
- **Power input**: To power the motor (e.g., 9V or 12V).
- **Motor outputs**: Connect the DC motor to these terminals.

Step 3: Wiring the H-Bridge and DC Motor to the Raspberry Pi

1. **Identify GPIO Pins**: Use a **GPIO pinout diagram** like pinout.xyz to identify the GPIO pins on your Raspberry Pi. We'll use **GPIO17 (Pin 11)** and **GPIO27 (Pin 13)** to control the motor direction, and **GPIO18 (Pin 12)** to control the speed using **PWM**.
2. **Wiring Instructions for the L298N or L293D**:
   - **IN1 and IN2 (Input Pins)**: These control the motor direction:
     - **IN1** connected to **GPIO17 (Pin 11)**.
     - **IN2** connected to **GPIO27 (Pin 13)**.
   - **Enable Pin (EN)**: This controls the motor speed using **PWM**:
     - **EN** connected to **GPIO18 (Pin 12)**.
   - **Motor Outputs (Out1 and Out2)**:

- Connect the **positive terminal of the motor** to **Out1**.
- Connect the **negative terminal of the motor** to **Out2**.
  - **Power Supply**:
    - **VCC** connected to the **positive terminal** of the external power supply (e.g., 9V or 12V).
    - **GND** connected to **GND (Pin 6)** on the Raspberry Pi and the **negative terminal** of the external power supply.

Here's a summary of the connections:

- **GPIO17 (Pin 11)** → **IN1** on the H-Bridge.

- **GPIO27 (Pin 13)** → **IN2** on the H-Bridge.

- **GPIO18 (Pin 12)** → **Enable pin** (EN) on the H-Bridge.

- **Out1** → **positive motor terminal**.

- **Out2** → **negative motor terminal**.

- **VCC** (on H-Bridge) → **positive terminal of external power supply**.

- **GND** (on H-Bridge) → **GND (Pin 6)** and **negative terminal of external power supply**.

  Tip: Make sure to use an external power supply to power the motor, as the Raspberry Pi cannot provide enough current to run the motor directly.

Step 4: Write the Python Script to Control Motor Direction and Speed

Now that everything is wired up, let's write a Python script to control both the **speed** and **direction** of the motor using the **H-Bridge**.

Create a Python Script: Open a text editor (like Nano or Thonny) and create a new Python file:

```
nano motor_direction_control.py
```

Python Code to Control Motor Speed and Direction: Here's a Python script to control the direction of the motor using **GPIO17** and **GPIO27**, and the speed using **PWM** on **GPIO18**:

```python
import RPi.GPIO as GPIO
import time
# Set up GPIO mode
GPIO.setmode(GPIO.BCM)

# Set up the GPIO pins for motor control
in1_pin = 17
in2_pin = 27
en_pin = 18
GPIO.setup(in1_pin, GPIO.OUT)
GPIO.setup(in2_pin, GPIO.OUT)
GPIO.setup(en_pin, GPIO.OUT)
# Set up PWM on the enable pin
pwm = GPIO.PWM(en_pin, 100)  # 100Hz frequency
pwm.start(0)  # Start with 0% duty cycle (motor off)

# Function to set motor direction
def set_motor_direction(direction):
    if direction == "forward":
        GPIO.output(in1_pin, GPIO.HIGH)
        GPIO.output(in2_pin, GPIO.LOW)
        print("Motor running forward")
    elif direction == "backward":
        GPIO.output(in1_pin, GPIO.LOW)
        GPIO.output(in2_pin, GPIO.HIGH)
        print("Motor running backward")
try:
    while True:
        # Set motor direction to forward and increase speed
        set_motor_direction("forward")
        for speed in range(0, 101, 5):  # Speed from 0% to 100%
            pwm.ChangeDutyCycle(speed)
            print(f"Motor Speed: {speed}%")
            time.sleep(0.1)
        # Set motor direction to backward and decrease speed
        set_motor_direction("backward")
        for speed in range(100, -1, -5):  # Speed from 100% to 0%
            pwm.ChangeDutyCycle(speed)
            print(f"Motor Speed: {speed}%")
            time.sleep(0.1)
except KeyboardInterrupt:
    pwm.stop()  # Stop PWM
    GPIO.cleanup()  # Clean up GPIO when the script is stopped
```

Run the Script: Save the file and run it in the terminal:

```
python3 motor_direction_control.py
```

What happens? The motor will start running **forward** (clockwise) at increasing speed, then switch to **backward** (counterclockwise) at decreasing speed.

Step 5: Customize the Motor Direction and Speed Control

Now that you have basic motor control, you can modify the script to add more functionality.

Add User Input: You can let the user control the motor direction and speed with keyboard input:

```python
while True:
    direction = input("Enter direction (forward/backward): ")
    speed = int(input("Enter motor speed (0-100): "))
    if 0 <= speed <= 100:
        set_motor_direction(direction)
        pwm.ChangeDutyCycle(speed)
    else:
        print("Please enter a speed between 0 and 100")
```

1. **Use a UI for Control**: You can create a **Tkinter** GUI with buttons to control the motor direction and speed with a slider (similar to previous sections on controlling devices with PWM).

7.3 Controlling Servo Motors

A **servo motor** is a special type of motor that allows for precise control of **angular position**. Unlike DC motors, which rotate continuously, servo motors rotate to a specific angle between **0 and 180 degrees** (or more in some cases). This makes them ideal for projects that require precise movement, such as **robotic arms**, **steering systems**, or **pan-tilt mechanisms**.

Why Does This Matter?

Servo motors are commonly used in robotics, drones, and other projects where you need precise control over position and movement. By learning how to control a servo motor, you can create more advanced and precise mechanical systems with your **Raspberry Pi**.

Controlling a Servo Motor

Step 1: Gather Components

You'll need the following components:

- 1 x **Raspberry Pi** (any model with GPIO pins)
- 1 x **Servo motor** (a small hobby servo like the SG90 or MG996R)
- External **5V power supply** (if using a larger servo motor)
- Jumper wires (Male to Female)
- **Breadboard** (optional, for easier connections)

    Note: Small servos like the **SG90** can be powered directly from the Raspberry Pi's **5V pin**, but larger servos (like the **MG996R**) will require an external power supply.

Step 2: Understand How a Servo Motor Works

A **servo motor** has three wires:

- **Ground (GND)**: Connects to ground.
- **Power (VCC)**: Provides power, usually 5V.
- **Signal**: Receives a **PWM signal** from the Raspberry Pi to control the position of the servo.

The position of the servo is controlled by sending it a **PWM signal** with a specific **duty cycle**. The duty cycle corresponds to a specific angle:

- **0% duty cycle** moves the servo to 0 degrees.
- **50% duty cycle** moves the servo to 90 degrees.
- **100% duty cycle** moves the servo to 180 degrees.

Step 3: Wiring the Servo Motor to the Raspberry Pi

1. **Identify GPIO Pins**: Use a **GPIO pinout diagram** like pinout.xyz to identify the GPIO pins on your Raspberry Pi. We'll use **GPIO18 (Pin 12)** to control the servo motor using **PWM**.
2. **Wiring Instructions**:
   - **GND (Ground)**: Connect the **GND wire** of the servo to **GND (Pin 6)** on the Raspberry Pi.
   - **VCC (Power)**: Connect the **VCC wire** of the servo to **5V (Pin 2)** on the Raspberry Pi.
   - **Signal**: Connect the **signal wire** of the servo to **GPIO18 (Pin 12)** on the Raspberry Pi.

If you're using a **larger servo motor** (like the MG996R), connect the **VCC** wire to an **external 5V power supply** instead of the Raspberry Pi's 5V pin.

Here's a summary of the connections:

- **GND (Pin 6)** → **GND of servo**.

- **5V (Pin 2)** → **VCC of servo**.

- **GPIO18 (Pin 12)** → **Signal of servo**.

   Tip: Always use a **separate power supply** if you're powering more than one servo or if your servo requires a lot of current.

Step 4: Set Up the Python Environment for PWM

Install the RPi.GPIO Library: Make sure the **RPi.GPIO** library is installed on your Raspberry Pi. This library allows you to control the GPIO pins and use **PWM**. To install it, run:

```
sudo apt-get install python3-rpi.gpio
```

1. **Set Up PWM on GPIO18 (Pin 12)**: You'll use **PWM** on **GPIO18** to control the angle of the servo. The servo moves to different angles depending on the duty cycle of the PWM signal.

Step 5: Write the Python Script to Control the Servo Motor

Now that everything is wired up, let's write a Python script to control the **position** of the servo motor using PWM.

Create a Python Script: Open a text editor (like Nano or Thonny) and create a new Python file:

```
nano servo_control.py
```

Python Code to Control the Servo Motor: Here's a basic Python script to control the position of the servo motor:

```python
import RPi.GPIO as GPIO
import time

# Set up GPIO mode and servo pin
GPIO.setmode(GPIO.BCM)
servo_pin = 18
GPIO.setup(servo_pin, GPIO.OUT)

# Set up PWM on GPIO18 with a frequency of 50Hz (standard for servos)
pwm = GPIO.PWM(servo_pin, 50)
pwm.start(0)  # Start PWM with 0% duty cycle

# Function to set servo angle
def set_servo_angle(angle):
    duty = 2 + (angle / 18)  # Calculate duty cycle for angle
    GPIO.output(servo_pin, True)
    pwm.ChangeDutyCycle(duty)
    time.sleep(0.5)
    GPIO.output(servo_pin, False)
    pwm.ChangeDutyCycle(0)
```

```
try:
    while True:
        # Move servo to 0 degrees
        set_servo_angle(0)
        print("Servo at 0 degrees")
        time.sleep(2)

        # Move servo to 90 degrees
        set_servo_angle(90)
        print("Servo at 90 degrees")
        time.sleep(2)

        # Move servo to 180 degrees
        set_servo_angle(180)
        print("Servo at 180 degrees")
        time.sleep(2)

except KeyboardInterrupt:
    pwm.stop()  # Stop PWM
    GPIO.cleanup()  # Clean up GPIO when the script is stopped
```

Run the Script: Save the file and run it in the terminal:

```
python3 servo_control.py
```

What happens? The servo will rotate to **0 degrees**, **90 degrees**, and **180 degrees** in sequence, with a pause between each movement.

Step 6: Customize the Servo Motor Control

Now that you have basic servo control, you can modify the script to add more functionality.

Add User Input: You can let the user input the desired angle to move the servo using the keyboard:

```
while True:
    angle = int(input("Enter servo angle (0-180): "))
    if 0 <= angle <= 180:
        set_servo_angle(angle)
        print(f"Servo moved to {angle} degrees")
    else:
        print("Please enter a valid angle between 0 and 180")
```

1. **Use a GUI for Control**: You can create a **Tkinter** graphical user interface (GUI) with sliders to control the servo position interactively (similar to previous sections).

7.4 Controlling Servo Motors Precisely

Precise control of a **servo motor** means being able to move the motor to **specific angles** with accuracy, such as rotating to **45°, 90°, 135°, or any other angle** in a controlled manner. This is useful in projects like **robot arms**, **pan-tilt cameras**, and other mechanical systems where exact positioning is required.

Why Does This Matter?

In many projects, you need more than just moving a servo to **0°, 90°, or 180°**. For example, in a **robotic arm**, you may need to move each joint to a specific angle with high accuracy. Being able to fine-tune the angle of a servo motor gives you more control over your project, making it much more functional and versatile.

Controlling Servo Motors Precisely

Step 1: Gather Components

You'll need the following components:

- 1 x **Raspberry Pi** (any model with GPIO pins)
- 1 x **Servo motor** (a small hobby servo like the SG90 or MG996R)
- External **5V power supply** (if using a larger servo motor)
- Jumper wires (Male to Female)
- **Breadboard** (optional, for easier connections)

Step 2: Recap on How a Servo Motor Works

A **servo motor** has three wires:

- **GND (Ground)**: Connects to the ground.
- **VCC (Power)**: Provides power, usually 5V.
- **Signal**: Receives a **PWM signal** from the Raspberry Pi to control the position of the servo.

The position of the servo motor is controlled by a **PWM signal** with a specific **duty cycle**. The duty cycle determines the angle of the servo:

- **2% duty cycle** usually corresponds to **0°**.
- **7.5% duty cycle** corresponds to **90°**.
- **12% duty cycle** corresponds to **180°**.

However, these values may vary slightly between different servos, so you may need to fine-tune them for precise control.

Step 3: Wiring the Servo Motor to the Raspberry Pi

1. **Identify GPIO Pins**: Use a **GPIO pinout diagram** like pinout.xyz to identify the GPIO pins on your Raspberry Pi. We'll use **GPIO18 (Pin 12)** to control the servo motor using **PWM**.
2. **Wiring Instructions**:
   - **GND (Ground)**: Connect the **GND wire** of the servo to **GND (Pin 6)** on the Raspberry Pi.
   - **VCC (Power)**: Connect the **VCC wire** of the servo to **5V (Pin 2)** on the Raspberry Pi.
   - **Signal**: Connect the **signal wire** of the servo to **GPIO18 (Pin 12)** on the Raspberry Pi.

Here's a summary of the connections:

- **GND (Pin 6)** → **GND of servo**.
- **5V (Pin 2)** → **VCC of servo**.
- **GPIO18 (Pin 12)** → **Signal of servo**.

   Tip: For **larger servos**, use an **external power supply** to provide enough current.

Step 4: Install the Required Libraries for PWM

Install the RPi.GPIO Library: Make sure the **RPi.GPIO** library is installed on your Raspberry Pi. This library allows you to control the GPIO pins and use **PWM**. To install it, run:

```
sudo apt-get install python3-rpi.gpio
```

1. **Set Up PWM on GPIO18 (Pin 12)**: You'll use **PWM** on **GPIO18** to control the angle of the servo motor. The PWM signal will be used to precisely move the servo to specific angles.

Step 5: Write the Python Script for Precise Servo Control

Now that everything is wired up, let's write a Python script to control the **angle** of the servo motor precisely using **PWM**.

Create a Python Script: Open a text editor (like Nano or Thonny) and create a new Python file:

```
nano precise_servo_control.py
```

Python Code for Precise Servo Control: Here's a Python script to move the servo to precise angles based on user input:

```python
import RPi.GPIO as GPIO
import time

# Set up GPIO mode and servo pin
GPIO.setmode(GPIO.BCM)
servo_pin = 18
GPIO.setup(servo_pin, GPIO.OUT)

# Set up PWM on GPIO18 with a frequency of 50Hz
pwm = GPIO.PWM(servo_pin, 50)  # Standard frequency for servos
pwm.start(0)  # Start with 0% duty cycle

# Function to set servo angle with precise control
def set_servo_angle(angle):
    duty = 2 + (angle / 18)  # Convert angle to duty cycle (for 0° to
180°)
    GPIO.output(servo_pin, True)
    pwm.ChangeDutyCycle(duty)
    time.sleep(0.5)  # Allow the servo to move
    GPIO.output(servo_pin, False)
```

```
    pwm.ChangeDutyCycle(0)  # Stop sending PWM signal after moving

try:
    while True:
        # Get user input for servo angle
        angle = int(input("Enter servo angle (0-180): "))
        if 0 <= angle <= 180:
            set_servo_angle(angle)
            print(f"Servo moved to {angle} degrees")
        else:
            print("Please enter a valid angle between 0 and 180")

except KeyboardInterrupt:
    pwm.stop()  # Stop PWM
    GPIO.cleanup()  # Clean up GPIO when the script is stopped
```

Run the Script: Save the file and run it in the terminal:

```
python3 precise_servo_control.py
```

What happens? The script will prompt you to enter a servo angle (between 0° and 180°), and the servo will move to that angle.

Step 6: Fine-Tuning for More Precision

Every servo motor may have slight variations, so you may need to **fine-tune the duty cycle** to achieve more precise control. You can adjust the values in the `set_servo_angle()` function if needed:

- If the servo doesn't reach exactly 0° or 180°, try adjusting the **2** in `duty = 2 + (angle / 18)` slightly higher or lower.

Customizing the Servo Control for Greater Precision

Control a Smaller Range of Angles: If you only need to control a smaller range of angles (e.g., 30° to 150°), you can adjust the script to limit the input and fine-tune for that specific range:

```
def set_servo_angle(angle):
    # Adjust duty cycle range for more precision within smaller angles
    duty = 2 + (angle / 18)  # Adjust as necessary
```

Use Timed Movements for Smooth Motion: For applications like **robot arms**, smooth and precise motion is important. You can break down larger movements into smaller increments for a smoother transition:

```python
def smooth_move(start_angle, end_angle, step=1):
    if start_angle < end_angle:
        for angle in range(start_angle, end_angle + 1, step):
            set_servo_angle(angle)
            time.sleep(0.05)  # Delay for smoother movement
    else:
        for angle in range(start_angle, end_angle - 1, -step):
            set_servo_angle(angle)
            time.sleep(0.05)
```

7.5 Controlling Multiple Servo Motors Precisely

Controlling **multiple servo motors** means using the **Raspberry Pi** to move several servos independently. This is useful in projects like **robotic arms**, **pan-tilt cameras**, **walking robots**, or any project requiring several precise movements.

Why Does This Matter?

Understanding how to control multiple servos allows you to create more complex and functional projects. For example, in a **robotic arm**, each joint could be controlled by a separate servo. With **precise control**, you can make the servos move in sync or independently, allowing for complex movement patterns.

Controlling Multiple Servo Motors

Step 1: Gather Components

You'll need the following components:

- 1 x **Raspberry Pi** (any model with GPIO pins)
- **2 or more servo motors** (small hobby servos like SG90 or MG996R)
- External **5V power supply** (for powering multiple servos)

- Jumper wires (Male to Female)
- **Breadboard** (optional, for easier connections)

Note: For controlling multiple servos, using an **external 5V power supply** is recommended, especially for larger servos like MG996R, as the Raspberry Pi's **5V pin** cannot provide enough current for more than one small servo.

Step 2: Understand How to Control Multiple Servos

Each **servo motor** has three wires:

- **Ground (GND)**: Connects to the ground.
- **Power (VCC)**: Provides power, usually 5V.
- **Signal**: Receives a **PWM signal** from the Raspberry Pi to control the position of the servo.

You will assign a **separate GPIO pin** for each servo motor to control their individual movements.

Step 3: Wiring Multiple Servo Motors to the Raspberry Pi

1. **Identify GPIO Pins**: Use a **GPIO pinout diagram** like pinout.xyz to identify the GPIO pins on your Raspberry Pi. We'll use **GPIO18 (Pin 12)** and **GPIO19 (Pin 35)** to control two servos as an example.
2. **Wiring Instructions for Two Servos**:
   - **GND (Ground)**: Connect the **GND wire** of both servos to **GND (Pin 6)** on the Raspberry Pi.
   - **VCC (Power)**: Connect the **VCC wire** of both servos to **5V (Pin 2)** on the Raspberry Pi or an **external 5V power supply**.
   - **Signal (Servo 1)**: Connect the **signal wire** of the first servo to **GPIO18 (Pin 12)**.

- Signal (Servo 2): Connect the **signal wire** of the second servo to **GPIO19 (Pin 35)**.

Here's a summary of the connections:

- **GND (Pin 6) → GND of both servos**.
- **5V (Pin 2) → VCC of both servos** (or use an external power supply).
- **GPIO18 (Pin 12) → Signal of Servo 1**.
- **GPIO19 (Pin 35) → Signal of Servo 2**.

   Tip: If using more than two servos, simply connect additional servos' **signal wires** to available GPIO pins and adjust the code accordingly.

Step 4: Install the Required Libraries for PWM

Install the RPi.GPIO Library: Make sure the **RPi.GPIO** library is installed on your Raspberry Pi. To install it, run:

```
sudo apt-get install python3-rpi.gpio
```

1. **Set Up PWM on Multiple GPIO Pins**: You will set up **PWM** on each GPIO pin controlling a separate servo. In this case, **GPIO18** will control **Servo 1**, and **GPIO19** will control **Servo 2**.

Step 5: Write the Python Script to Control Multiple Servos

Now that everything is wired up, let's write a Python script to control **multiple servos**.

Create a Python Script: Open a text editor (like Nano or Thonny) and create a new Python file:

```
nano multi_servo_control.py
```

Python Code to Control Multiple Servos: Here's a Python script to move **two servo motors** independently to different angles:

```python
import RPi.GPIO as GPIO
import time

# Set up GPIO mode and servo pins
GPIO.setmode(GPIO.BCM)
servo1_pin = 18
servo2_pin = 19
GPIO.setup(servo1_pin, GPIO.OUT)
GPIO.setup(servo2_pin, GPIO.OUT)

# Set up PWM on GPIO18 and GPIO19 with a frequency of 50Hz
pwm1 = GPIO.PWM(servo1_pin, 50)
pwm2 = GPIO.PWM(servo2_pin, 50)
pwm1.start(0)
pwm2.start(0)

# Function to set the angle of a servo
def set_servo_angle(pwm, angle):
    duty = 2 + (angle / 18)  # Convert angle to duty cycle
    GPIO.output(servo1_pin, True)
    pwm.ChangeDutyCycle(duty)
    time.sleep(0.5)
    GPIO.output(servo1_pin, False)
    pwm.ChangeDutyCycle(0)

try:
    while True:
        # Move Servo 1 to 0 degrees
        set_servo_angle(pwm1, 0)
        print("Servo 1 at 0 degrees")
        time.sleep(2)

        # Move Servo 2 to 90 degrees
        set_servo_angle(pwm2, 90)
        print("Servo 2 at 90 degrees")
        time.sleep(2)

        # Move Servo 1 to 180 degrees
        set_servo_angle(pwm1, 180)
        print("Servo 1 at 180 degrees")
        time.sleep(2)
        # Move Servo 2 to 45 degrees
        set_servo_angle(pwm2, 45)
        print("Servo 2 at 45 degrees")
        time.sleep(2)
except KeyboardInterrupt:
    pwm1.stop()  # Stop PWM for Servo 1
    pwm2.stop()  # Stop PWM for Servo 2
    GPIO.cleanup()  # Clean up GPIO when the script is stopped
```

Run the Script: Save the file and run it in the terminal:

```
python3 multi_servo_control.py
```

What happens? The two servos will move independently to different angles as specified in the code.

Step 6: Customize the Multi-Servo Control

Now that you have basic multi-servo control, you can customize the script further.

Add More Servos: If you want to control more than two servos, add more GPIO pins to the script and set up additional **PWM** instances for each new servo. For example:

```
servo3_pin = 20
GPIO.setup(servo3_pin, GPIO.OUT)
pwm3 = GPIO.PWM(servo3_pin, 50)
pwm3.start(0)
```

Use Smooth Movements: You can create smoother movements by gradually increasing or decreasing the angles of the servos over time. For example:

```
def smooth_move(pwm, start_angle, end_angle, step=1):
    if start_angle < end_angle:
        for angle in range(start_angle, end_angle + 1, step):
            set_servo_angle(pwm, angle)
            time.sleep(0.05)
    else:
        for angle in range(start_angle, end_angle - 1, -step):
            set_servo_angle(pwm, angle)
            time.sleep(0.05)
```

Add User Input for Multiple Servos: You can ask the user to control the angle of each servo via keyboard input:

```
while True:
    angle1 = int(input("Enter angle for Servo 1 (0-180): "))
    angle2 = int(input("Enter angle for Servo 2 (0-180): "))
    set_servo_angle(pwm1, angle1)
    set_servo_angle(pwm2, angle2)
```

7.6 Using a Unipolar Stepper Motor

A **unipolar stepper motor** is a type of motor that moves in precise steps rather than rotating continuously like a **DC motor** or moving to specific angles like a **servo motor**. Stepper motors are commonly used in projects that require precise control of position, such as **CNC machines**, **3D printers**, and **robotic arms**.

Why Does This Matter?

Stepper motors allow for very precise control of rotation, which is essential for applications where accuracy is important. Unlike DC or servo motors, stepper motors can be rotated to exact positions with repeatability, making them ideal for projects like **automated mechanisms** or **camera sliders**.

Using a Unipolar Stepper Motor

Step 1: Gather Components

You'll need the following components:

- 1 x **Raspberry Pi** (any model with GPIO pins)
- 1 x **Unipolar stepper motor** (e.g., **28BYJ-48**)
- 1 x **ULN2003 stepper motor driver board** (commonly used with 28BYJ-48 motors)
- External **5V power supply** (for the stepper motor)
- Jumper wires (Male to Female)
- **Breadboard** (optional, for easier connections)

    Note: The **ULN2003** is a driver board designed to control unipolar stepper motors like the **28BYJ-48**, making it easier to interface with the Raspberry Pi.

Step 2: Understand How a Unipolar Stepper Motor Works

A **unipolar stepper motor** has **multiple coils** inside that are energized in a specific sequence to rotate the motor in precise steps. The **28BYJ-48** motor typically has **4 phases** that are controlled in sequence by a **driver board** (like the **ULN2003**). Each pulse sent to the motor moves it by one **step**. Combining these steps allows you to move the motor by a specific number of degrees.

- **Steps per Revolution**: The **28BYJ-48** has **64 steps per revolution**, and with the internal gearbox, it typically requires **2048 steps** to complete one full rotation (360 degrees).

Step 3: Wiring the Stepper Motor to the Raspberry Pi

1. **Identify GPIO Pins**: Use a **GPIO pinout diagram** like pinout.xyz to identify the GPIO pins on your Raspberry Pi. We'll use **four GPIO pins** to control the stepper motor, specifically **GPIO17 (Pin 11)**, **GPIO18 (Pin 12)**, **GPIO27 (Pin 13)**, and **GPIO22 (Pin 15)**.
2. **Wiring Instructions**:
   - **ULN2003 IN1**: Connect to **GPIO17 (Pin 11)**.
   - **ULN2003 IN2**: Connect to **GPIO18 (Pin 12)**.
   - **ULN2003 IN3**: Connect to **GPIO27 (Pin 13)**.
   - **ULN2003 IN4**: Connect to **GPIO22 (Pin 15)**.
   - **GND (Ground)**: Connect the **GND pin** on the ULN2003 driver board to **GND (Pin 6)** on the Raspberry Pi.
   - **VCC (Power)**: Connect the **5V pin** on the ULN2003 driver board to **5V (Pin 2)** on the Raspberry Pi (or use an external **5V power supply** for the stepper motor if needed).

Here's a summary of the connections:

- **GPIO17 (Pin 11) → IN1 on ULN2003.**
- **GPIO18 (Pin 12) → IN2 on ULN2003.**
- **GPIO27 (Pin 13) → IN3 on ULN2003.**
- **GPIO22 (Pin 15) → IN4 on ULN2003.**
- **GND (Pin 6) → GND on ULN2003.**
- **5V (Pin 2) → VCC on ULN2003** (or external power supply).

> **Tip**: Use an external **5V power supply** if your stepper motor requires more current than the Raspberry Pi's **5V pin** can provide.

Step 4: Install the Required Libraries

You'll use the **RPi.GPIO** library to control the GPIO pins and step the motor in sequence.

Install the RPi.GPIO Library: In the terminal, install the **RPi.GPIO** library if it's not already installed:

```
sudo apt-get install python3-rpi.gpio
```

Step 5: Write the Python Script to Control the Stepper Motor

Now that everything is wired up, let's write a Python script to control the **unipolar stepper motor**.

Create a Python Script: Open a text editor (like Nano or Thonny) and create a new Python file:

```
nano stepper_control.py
```

Python Code to Control the Stepper Motor: Here's a Python
script to rotate the stepper motor:

```python
import RPi.GPIO as GPIO
import time

# Set up GPIO mode
GPIO.setmode(GPIO.BCM)

# Define GPIO pins for the stepper motor
IN1 = 17
IN2 = 18
IN3 = 27
IN4 = 22

# Set up the GPIO pins as outputs
GPIO.setup(IN1, GPIO.OUT)
GPIO.setup(IN2, GPIO.OUT)
GPIO.setup(IN3, GPIO.OUT)
GPIO.setup(IN4, GPIO.OUT)

# Define the sequence of steps for the stepper motor (full-step
sequence)
step_sequence = [
    [1, 0, 0, 0],
    [0, 1, 0, 0],
    [0, 0, 1, 0],
    [0, 0, 0, 1]
]

# Function to turn the motor a certain number of steps
def step_motor(steps, delay=0.01):
    for _ in range(steps):
        for step in step_sequence:
            GPIO.output(IN1, step[0])
            GPIO.output(IN2, step[1])
            GPIO.output(IN3, step[2])
            GPIO.output(IN4, step[3])
            time.sleep(delay)

try:
    while True:
        # Rotate the motor 2048 steps (one full revolution)
        print("Rotating motor 1 revolution clockwise...")
        step_motor(2048)  # Full revolution (2048 steps)
        time.sleep(2)  # Pause for 2 seconds

        # Rotate the motor 2048 steps in the opposite direction
        print("Rotating motor 1 revolution counterclockwise...")
        step_motor(-2048)  # Reverse direction (2048 steps)

        time.sleep(2)  # Pause for 2 seconds

except KeyboardInterrupt:
    GPIO.cleanup()  # Clean up GPIO when the script is stopped
```

Run the Script: Save the file and run it in the terminal:

```
python3 stepper_control.py
```

What happens? The stepper motor will rotate **one full revolution** clockwise, pause for 2 seconds, and then rotate **one full revolution** counterclockwise.

Step 6: Customize the Stepper Motor Control

Now that you have basic stepper motor control, you can customize the script further.

Adjust the Speed: You can control the speed of the stepper motor by changing the **delay** between steps:

```
step_motor(2048, delay=0.005)  # Faster rotation
step_motor(2048, delay=0.02)   # Slower rotation
```

1. **Control a Specific Angle**: Since the **28BYJ-48** requires **2048 steps** for one full revolution (360 degrees), you can control a specific angle by calculating the number of steps:
   - **90 degrees**: (2048 / 360) * 90 = 512 steps
   - **180 degrees**: (2048 / 360) * 180 = 1024 steps

```
# Rotate the motor 90 degrees
print("Rotating motor 90 degrees clockwise...")
step_motor(512)

time.sleep(2)

# Rotate the motor 180 degrees counterclockwise
print("Rotating motor 180 degrees counterclockwise...")
step_motor(-1024)
```

7.7 Using a Bipolar Stepper Motor

A **bipolar stepper motor** is a type of motor that uses two coils (or windings) and requires a **reversing current** to change the magnetic field direction, making it more powerful and efficient than a **unipolar stepper motor**. Bipolar stepper motors are commonly used in applications that require **higher torque** and **precise control**, such as **3D printers**, **CNC machines**, and **robotics**.

Why Does This Matter?

Bipolar stepper motors allow for **precise control of position** and **higher torque** compared to unipolar stepper motors. They require an **H-Bridge driver** (such as an **L298N** or **A4988**) to reverse the current through the coils. This makes them more complex to control, but they are more efficient in terms of torque and size, which is useful in demanding applications.

Using a Bipolar Stepper Motor

Step 1: Gather Components

You'll need the following components:

- 1 x **Raspberry Pi** (any model with GPIO pins)
- 1 x **Bipolar stepper motor** (e.g., **NEMA 17**)
- 1 x **H-Bridge motor driver** (e.g., **L298N**, **L293D**, or **A4988 stepper driver**)
- External **12V power supply** (for the stepper motor)
- Jumper wires (Male to Female)
- **Breadboard** (optional, for easier connections)

    Note: A **bipolar stepper motor** like the **NEMA 17** typically requires more current than a unipolar stepper motor, so using an external power supply is essential.

Step 2: Understand How a Bipolar Stepper Motor Works

A **bipolar stepper motor** has **two coils** (A and B). The current direction in each coil needs to be reversed to create the stepping motion. Each **step** moves the motor by a specific angle, and controlling the order and direction of current through the coils makes the motor rotate.

- **Steps per Revolution**: Common bipolar stepper motors like the **NEMA 17** have **200 steps per revolution**, meaning each step moves the motor **1.8 degrees**.

To control the **bipolar stepper motor**, you need an **H-Bridge driver** (such as **L298N**, **L293D**, or **A4988**) to switch the direction of current through the coils.

Step 3: Wiring the Bipolar Stepper Motor to the Raspberry Pi

1. **Identify GPIO Pins**: Use a **GPIO pinout diagram** like pinout.xyz to identify the GPIO pins on your Raspberry Pi. We'll use **four GPIO pins** to control the H-Bridge driver: **GPIO17 (Pin 11)**, **GPIO18 (Pin 12)**, **GPIO27 (Pin 13)**, and **GPIO22 (Pin 15)**.
2. **Wiring Instructions for the L298N H-Bridge**:
   - **IN1 (Input Pin 1 on L298N)**: Connect to **GPIO17 (Pin 11)**.
   - **IN2 (Input Pin 2 on L298N)**: Connect to **GPIO18 (Pin 12)**.
   - **IN3 (Input Pin 3 on L298N)**: Connect to **GPIO27 (Pin 13)**.
   - **IN4 (Input Pin 4 on L298N)**: Connect to **GPIO22 (Pin 15)**.
   - **Motor Output 1 (OUT1)**: Connect to one wire of **Coil A** on the stepper motor.
   - **Motor Output 2 (OUT2)**: Connect to the other wire of **Coil A**.

- **Motor Output 3 (OUT3)**: Connect to one wire of **Coil B** on the stepper motor.
- **Motor Output 4 (OUT4)**: Connect to the other wire of **Coil B**.
- **GND (Ground)**: Connect the **GND** pin on the L298N to **GND (Pin 6)** on the Raspberry Pi.
- **VCC**: Connect the **12V power supply** to the **VCC** pin on the L298N.

Here's a summary of the connections:

- **GPIO17 (Pin 11)** → **IN1 on L298N**.

- **GPIO18 (Pin 12)** → **IN2 on L298N**.

- **GPIO27 (Pin 13)** → **IN3 on L298N**.

- **GPIO22 (Pin 15)** → **IN4 on L298N**.

- **OUT1** → **Coil A** (one wire).

- **OUT2** → **Coil A** (other wire).

- **OUT3** → **Coil B** (one wire).

- **OUT4** → **Coil B** (other wire).

- **12V power supply** → **VCC on L298N**.

- **GND (Pin 6)** → **GND on L298N**.

Tip: Make sure to correctly identify the wires for **Coil A** and **Coil B** on your bipolar stepper motor. You can use a multimeter to test for continuity between wires to determine which belong to each coil.

Step 4: Install the Required Libraries

You'll use the **RPi.GPIO** library to control the GPIO pins and switch the H-Bridge driver to move the motor in the correct step sequence.

Install the RPi.GPIO Library: In the terminal, install the **RPi.GPIO** library if it's not already installed:

```
sudo apt-get install python3-rpi.gpio
```

Step 5: Write the Python Script to Control the Bipolar Stepper Motor

Now that everything is wired up, let's write a Python script to control the **bipolar stepper motor**.

Create a Python Script: Open a text editor (like Nano or Thonny) and create a new Python file:

```
nano bipolar_stepper_control.py
```

Python Code to Control the Bipolar Stepper Motor: Here's a Python script to rotate the bipolar stepper motor:

```python
import RPi.GPIO as GPIO
import time

# Set up GPIO mode
GPIO.setmode(GPIO.BCM)

# Define GPIO pins for the stepper motor
IN1 = 17
IN2 = 18
IN3 = 27
IN4 = 22

# Set up the GPIO pins as outputs
GPIO.setup(IN1, GPIO.OUT)
GPIO.setup(IN2, GPIO.OUT)
GPIO.setup(IN3, GPIO.OUT)
GPIO.setup(IN4, GPIO.OUT)

# Define the step sequence for the bipolar stepper motor (half-step
sequence)
step_sequence = [
    [1, 0, 0, 0],
    [1, 1, 0, 0],
    [0, 1, 0, 0],
    [0, 1, 1, 0],
    [0, 0, 1, 0],
    [0, 0, 1, 1],
    [0, 0, 0, 1],
    [1, 0, 0, 1]
]

# Function to turn the motor a certain number of steps
def step_motor(steps, delay=0.01):
```

```
    for _ in range(steps):
        for step in step_sequence:
            GPIO.output(IN1, step[0])
            GPIO.output(IN2, step[1])
            GPIO.output(IN3, step[2])
            GPIO.output(IN4, step[3])
            time.sleep(delay)

try:
    while True:
        # Rotate the motor 400 steps (2 full revolutions)
        print("Rotating motor 2 revolutions clockwise...")
        step_motor(400)

        time.sleep(2)  # Pause for 2 seconds

        # Rotate the motor 400 steps in the opposite direction
        print("Rotating motor 2 revolutions counterclockwise...")
        step_motor(-400)

        time.sleep(2)  # Pause for 2 seconds

except KeyboardInterrupt:
    GPIO.cleanup()  # Clean up GPIO when the script is stopped
```

Run the Script: Save the file and run it in the terminal:

```
python3 bipolar_stepper_control.py
```

What happens? The stepper motor will rotate **two full revolutions** clockwise, pause for 2 seconds, and then rotate **two full revolutions** counterclockwise.

Step 6: Customize the Bipolar Stepper Motor Control

Now that you have basic stepper motor control, you can customize the script further.

Adjust the Speed: You can control the speed of the stepper motor by changing the **delay** between steps:

```
step_motor(400, delay=0.005)  # Faster rotation
step_motor(400, delay=0.02)   # Slower rotation
```

1. **Control a Specific Angle**: Since the **NEMA 17** requires **200 steps** for one full revolution (360 degrees), you can control a specific angle by calculating the number of steps:
   - **90 degrees**: (200 / 360) * 90 = 50 steps
   - **180 degrees**: (200 / 360) * 180 = 100 steps

```
# Rotate the motor 90 degrees
print("Rotating motor 90 degrees clockwise...")
step_motor(50)
time.sleep(2)

# Rotate the motor 180 degrees counterclockwise
print("Rotating motor 180 degrees counterclockwise...")
step_motor(-100)
```

Chapter 8: Working with Switches and Buttons

8.1 Connecting a Push Switch

A **push switch** (also called a **push button**) is a simple mechanical device that allows or interrupts the flow of electricity when pressed. It is often used as a control input in electronics projects to trigger actions, such as turning on an LED, starting a motor, or sending a signal to a **Raspberry Pi**.

Why Does This Matter?

Push switches are fundamental components in many projects, allowing you to create user inputs for controlling other components, like motors or LEDs. By connecting a push switch to your **Raspberry Pi**, you can trigger specific events like turning on a light or initiating a program. This is a great way to add physical interaction to your project.

Connecting a Push Switch

Step 1: Gather Components

You'll need the following components:

- 1 x **Raspberry Pi** (any model with GPIO pins)
- 1 x **Push button** (standard momentary push button)
- 1 x **10kΩ resistor** (for pull-down or pull-up resistance)
- Jumper wires (Male to Female)
- **Breadboard** (optional, for easier connections)

Step 2: Understand the Basics of a Push Switch

A **push switch** has two states:

- **Pressed**: When the button is pressed, it completes a circuit, allowing current to flow.
- **Released**: When the button is released, the circuit is broken, and no current flows.

To avoid unpredictable signals when the button is not pressed, we use a **pull-down resistor** to keep the GPIO pin at a low state (0V). When the button is pressed, the GPIO pin goes high (3.3V), which we can detect in our code.

Step 3: Wiring the Push Switch to the Raspberry Pi

1. **Identify GPIO Pins**: Use a **GPIO pinout diagram** like pinout.xyz to identify the GPIO pins on your Raspberry Pi. We'll use **GPIO17 (Pin 11)** to read the state of the button.
2. **Wiring Instructions**:
     - **One leg of the push button**: Connect to **GPIO17 (Pin 11)**.

- o **Other leg of the push button**: Connect to **GND (Pin 6)**.
- o **10kΩ pull-down resistor**: Connect between **GPIO17 (Pin 11)** and **GND (Pin 6)**.

Here's a summary of the connections:

- **GPIO17 (Pin 11)** → **One leg of the push button**.
- **GND (Pin 6)** → **Other leg of the push button** and **one leg of the 10kΩ resistor**.
- **GPIO17 (Pin 11)** → **Other leg of the 10kΩ resistor**.

This setup ensures that when the button is **not pressed**, the GPIO pin reads **LOW** (0V), and when the button is **pressed**, the GPIO pin reads **HIGH** (3.3V).

Step 4: Install the Required Libraries

You'll use the **RPi.GPIO** library to read the button press from the GPIO pin.

Install the RPi.GPIO Library: In the terminal, install the **RPi.GPIO** library if it's not already installed:

```
sudo apt-get install python3-rpi.gpio
```

Step 5: Write the Python Script to Read the Push Button

Now that everything is wired up, let's write a Python script to detect when the button is pressed.

Create a Python Script: Open a text editor (like Nano or Thonny) and create a new Python file:

```
nano button_control.py
```

Python Code to Detect a Button Press: Here's a basic Python script that detects when the button is pressed and prints a message to the terminal:

```python
import RPi.GPIO as GPIO
import time

# Set up GPIO mode
GPIO.setmode(GPIO.BCM)

# Define the GPIO pin for the button
button_pin = 17

# Set up the GPIO pin as an input with a pull-down resistor
GPIO.setup(button_pin, GPIO.IN, pull_up_down=GPIO.PUD_DOWN)

try:
    while True:
        # Check if the button is pressed
        if GPIO.input(button_pin) == GPIO.HIGH:
            print("Button pressed!")
        else:
            print("Button not pressed.")

        time.sleep(0.1)  # Small delay to avoid bouncing

except KeyboardInterrupt:
    GPIO.cleanup()  # Clean up GPIO when the script is stopped
```

Run the Script: Save the file and run it in the terminal:
```
python3 button_control.py
```

What happens? The script will continuously check the button's state. When the button is pressed, it prints "Button pressed!" to the terminal, and when the button is not pressed, it prints "Button not pressed."

Step 6: Customize the Button Behavior

Now that you can detect a button press, you can customize the script to trigger specific actions.

Toggle an LED with a Button Press: You can modify the script to toggle an **LED** each time the button is pressed:

```
import RPi.GPIO as GPIO
import time

# Set up GPIO mode
GPIO.setmode(GPIO.BCM)

# Define the GPIO pins for the button and LED
button_pin = 17
led_pin = 18

# Set up the GPIO pins
GPIO.setup(button_pin, GPIO.IN, pull_up_down=GPIO.PUD_DOWN)
GPIO.setup(led_pin, GPIO.OUT)

# Variable to keep track of LED state
led_on = False

try:
    while True:
        # Check if the button is pressed
        if GPIO.input(button_pin) == GPIO.HIGH:
            led_on = not led_on  # Toggle the LED state
            GPIO.output(led_pin, led_on)
            time.sleep(0.5)  # Debounce delay

except KeyboardInterrupt:
    GPIO.cleanup()  # Clean up GPIO when the script is stopped
```

Trigger a Python Function: You can trigger a custom function when the button is pressed:

```
def button_action():
    print("Button pressed! Action triggered!")
try:
    while True:
        if GPIO.input(button_pin) == GPIO.HIGH:
            button_action()
            time.sleep(0.5)  # Debounce delay
except KeyboardInterrupt:
    GPIO.cleanup()
```

8.2 Toggling with a Push Switch

Toggling refers to the action of changing a state between two values, typically **on** and **off** (or **high** and **low**). When using a **push switch** with a **Raspberry Pi**, you can toggle the state of an output (such as an **LED** or **motor**) every time the button is pressed. This is commonly used in projects where you want to control components like lights or devices with a single button press.

Why Does This Matter?

Toggling with a push switch allows you to control components more interactively. Instead of holding the button down to keep a component active, you can press the button once to turn something **on**, and press it again to turn it **off**. This functionality is widely used in simple electronics projects to control things like **LEDs**, **motors**, or **relays**.

Toggling with a Push Switch

Step 1: Gather Components

You'll need the following components:

- 1 x **Raspberry Pi** (any model with GPIO pins)
- 1 x **Push button** (standard momentary push button)
- 1 x **10kΩ resistor** (for pull-down resistance)
- 1 x **LED** (or another output to toggle)
- 1 x **330Ω resistor** (for the LED)
- Jumper wires (Male to Female)
- **Breadboard** (optional, for easier connections)

Step 2: Understand the Toggling Mechanism

Toggling means changing the state of a device between **on** and **off** with each press of a button. In our case:

- The **push button** will toggle the state of the **LED**.
- Each time the button is pressed, the LED will switch between **on** (lit) and **off** (unlit).

The push button will be wired to a **GPIO input**, and the **LED** will be wired to a **GPIO output**.

Step 3: Wiring the Push Switch and LED to the Raspberry Pi

1. **Identify GPIO Pins**: Use a **GPIO pinout diagram** like
   pinout.xyz to identify the GPIO pins on your Raspberry Pi.
   We'll use **GPIO17 (Pin 11)** to read the state of the button,
   and **GPIO18 (Pin 12)** to control the LED.
2. **Wiring Instructions**:
   - **One leg of the push button**: Connect to **GPIO17
     (Pin 11)**.
   - **Other leg of the push button**: Connect to **GND (Pin
     6)**.
   - **10kΩ pull-down resistor**: Connect between **GPIO17
     (Pin 11)** and **GND (Pin 6)**.
   - **Long leg of the LED**: Connect to **GPIO18 (Pin 12)**.
   - **Short leg of the LED**: Connect to **one side of the
     330Ω resistor**.
   - **Other side of the 330Ω resistor**: Connect to **GND
     (Pin 6)**.

Here's a summary of the connections:

- **GPIO17 (Pin 11) → One leg of the push button**.

- **GND (Pin 6) → Other leg of the push button** and **one leg
  of the 10kΩ resistor**.

- **GPIO18 (Pin 12) → Long leg of the LED**.

- **GND (Pin 6) → Other side of the 330Ω resistor**.

This setup ensures that when the button is **not pressed**, the GPIO
pin reads **LOW** (0V), and when the button is **pressed**, the GPIO pin
reads **HIGH** (3.3V). The LED will toggle between **on** and **off** based
on the button press.

Step 4: Install the Required Libraries

You'll use the **RPi.GPIO** library to read the button press and control the LED.

Install the RPi.GPIO Library: In the terminal, install the **RPi.GPIO** library if it's not already installed:

```
sudo apt-get install python3-rpi.gpio
```

Step 5: Write the Python Script to Toggle the LED

Now that everything is wired up, let's write a Python script to toggle the **LED** with the **push switch**.

Create a Python Script: Open a text editor (like Nano or Thonny) and create a new Python file:

```
nano toggle_button.py
```

Python Code to Toggle an LED: Here's a basic Python script that toggles the state of an LED each time the button is pressed:

```python
import RPi.GPIO as GPIO
import time

# Set up GPIO mode
GPIO.setmode(GPIO.BCM)

# Define the GPIO pins for the button and LED
button_pin = 17
led_pin = 18

# Set up the GPIO pins
GPIO.setup(button_pin, GPIO.IN, pull_up_down=GPIO.PUD_DOWN)
GPIO.setup(led_pin, GPIO.OUT)

# Variable to keep track of the LED state
led_on = False

try:
    while True:
        # Check if the button is pressed
        if GPIO.input(button_pin) == GPIO.HIGH:
            # Toggle the LED state
            led_on = not led_on
            GPIO.output(led_pin, led_on)
            print(f"LED {'on' if led_on else 'off'}")
            time.sleep(0.5)  # Debounce delay

except KeyboardInterrupt:
    GPIO.cleanup()  # Clean up GPIO when the script is stopped
```

Run the Script: Save the file and run it in the terminal:

```
python3 toggle_button.py
```

What happens? The LED will toggle between **on** and **off** each time you press the button. The script uses a small **debounce delay** to avoid multiple detections from a single press due to button bouncing.

Step 6: Customize the Toggling Behavior

You can customize the script to control different components or add more functionality.

Toggle Multiple LEDs: You can modify the script to toggle multiple LEDs using different buttons:

```python
led2_pin = 23
GPIO.setup(led2_pin, GPIO.OUT)
# Variable to keep track of the second LED state
led2_on = False

try:
    while True:
        if GPIO.input(button_pin) == GPIO.HIGH:
            led_on = not led_on
            GPIO.output(led_pin, led_on)
            print(f"LED 1 {'on' if led_on else 'off'}")
            time.sleep(0.5)  # Debounce delay

            led2_on = not led2_on
            GPIO.output(led2_pin, led2_on)
            print(f"LED 2 {'on' if led2_on else 'off'}")
            time.sleep(0.5)  # Debounce delay
```

Use a Button Press to Control Another Device: Instead of toggling an LED, you can use the button press to control a **motor, relay,** or another device:

```python
motor_pin = 23
GPIO.setup(motor_pin, GPIO.OUT)

# Toggle the motor state
motor_on = False

try:
    while True:
        if GPIO.input(button_pin) == GPIO.HIGH:
            motor_on = not motor_on
            GPIO.output(motor_pin, motor_on)
            print(f"Motor {'on' if motor_on else 'off'}")
            time.sleep(0.5)  # Debounce delay
```

8.3 Using a Two-Position Toggle or Slide Switch

A **two-position toggle switch** or **slide switch** is a mechanical switch that can toggle between two states: **on** or **off** (sometimes referred to as **high** or **low**). Unlike a momentary push button, which only stays active while pressed, a toggle or slide switch maintains its state until physically flipped or slid to the other position. These switches are often used in electronics projects to control devices like **LEDs**, **motors**, or **relays**.

Why Does This Matter?

Using a **toggle** or **slide switch** allows you to control a component by permanently switching it on or off without the need for continuous pressing. This is ideal for projects where you want to maintain a state, such as turning an LED on until the switch is flipped off. It's simple and user-friendly for controlling electronics in a stable way.

Using a Two-Position Toggle or Slide Switch

Step 1: Gather Components

You'll need the following components:

- 1 x **Raspberry Pi** (any model with GPIO pins)
- 1 x **Two-position toggle switch** or **slide switch**
- 1 x **10kΩ resistor** (for pull-down resistance)
- 1 x **LED** (or another output to control)
- 1 x **330Ω resistor** (for the LED)
- Jumper wires (Male to Female)
- **Breadboard** (optional, for easier connections)

Step 2: Understand How a Toggle or Slide Switch Works

A **two-position switch** works by connecting or disconnecting a circuit. In one position, it completes the circuit and allows current to flow (typically **on** or **high**). In the other position, the circuit is disconnected, and no current flows (typically **off** or **low**).

We will wire the **toggle switch** to a **GPIO input pin** on the Raspberry Pi to detect whether the switch is in the **on** or **off** position, and use this to control an **LED** or another component.

Step 3: Wiring the Toggle Switch and LED to the Raspberry Pi

1. **Identify GPIO Pins**: Use a **GPIO pinout diagram** like pinout.xyz to identify the GPIO pins on your Raspberry Pi. We'll use **GPIO17 (Pin 11)** to read the state of the switch, and **GPIO18 (Pin 12)** to control the LED.
2. **Wiring Instructions**:
   - **One leg of the toggle switch**: Connect to **GPIO17 (Pin 11)**.
   - **Other leg of the toggle switch**: Connect to **GND (Pin 6)**.
   - **10kΩ pull-down resistor**: Connect between **GPIO17 (Pin 11)** and **GND (Pin 6)**.
   - **Long leg of the LED**: Connect to **GPIO18 (Pin 12)**.
   - **Short leg of the LED**: Connect to **one side of the 330Ω resistor**.
   - **Other side of the 330Ω resistor**: Connect to **GND (Pin 6)**.

Here's a summary of the connections:

- **GPIO17 (Pin 11) → One leg of the toggle switch.**
- **GND (Pin 6) → Other leg of the toggle switch and one leg of the 10kΩ resistor.**
- **GPIO18 (Pin 12) → Long leg of the LED.**
- **GND (Pin 6) → Other side of the 330Ω resistor.**

This setup ensures that when the switch is **in one position**, the GPIO pin reads **HIGH** (3.3V), and when the switch is **in the other position**, it reads **LOW** (0V).

Step 4: Install the Required Libraries

You'll use the **RPi.GPIO** library to read the switch's state and control the LED.

Install the RPi.GPIO Library: In the terminal, install the **RPi.GPIO** library if it's not already installed:

```
sudo apt-get install python3-rpi.gpio
```

Step 5: Write the Python Script to Control the LED with the Switch

Now that everything is wired up, let's write a Python script to toggle the **LED** based on the position of the **switch**.

Create a Python Script: Open a text editor (like Nano or Thonny) and create a new Python file:

```
nano toggle_switch.py
```

Python Code to Control the LED: Here's a simple Python script that reads the state of the switch and turns the LED **on** or **off** based on the position of the switch:

```python
import RPi.GPIO as GPIO
import time
# Set up GPIO mode
GPIO.setmode(GPIO.BCM)
# Define the GPIO pins for the switch and LED
switch_pin = 17
led_pin = 18

# Set up the GPIO pins
GPIO.setup(switch_pin, GPIO.IN, pull_up_down=GPIO.PUD_DOWN)
GPIO.setup(led_pin, GPIO.OUT)

try:
    while True:
        # Read the state of the switch
        if GPIO.input(switch_pin) == GPIO.HIGH:
            GPIO.output(led_pin, True)  # Turn on the LED
            print("Switch is ON, LED is ON")
        else:
            GPIO.output(led_pin, False)  # Turn off the LED
            print("Switch is OFF, LED is OFF")
        time.sleep(0.1)  # Small delay to avoid bouncing
except KeyboardInterrupt:
    GPIO.cleanup()  # Clean up GPIO when the script is stopped
```

Run the Script: Save the file and run it in the terminal:

```
python3 toggle_switch.py
```

What happens? The LED will turn on when the switch is in the **on** position and turn off when the switch is in the **off** position.

Step 6: Customize the Switch Control

Now that you can detect the switch's state, you can customize the script to control different components.

Control a Motor or Another Device: Instead of controlling an LED, you can use the switch to control a **motor** or another device:

```python
motor_pin = 23
GPIO.setup(motor_pin, GPIO.OUT)

try:
    while True:
        if GPIO.input(switch_pin) == GPIO.HIGH:
            GPIO.output(motor_pin, True)  # Turn on the motor
            print("Switch is ON, Motor is ON")
        else:
            GPIO.output(motor_pin, False)  # Turn off the motor
            print("Switch is OFF, Motor is OFF")

        time.sleep(0.1)
```

Trigger a Python Function: You can trigger a specific Python function when the switch is turned on or off:

```python
def switch_action():
    print("Switch toggled! Performing action...")

try:
    while True:
        if GPIO.input(switch_pin) == GPIO.HIGH:
            switch_action()  # Call the function when the switch is on
            time.sleep(0.1)

except KeyboardInterrupt:
    GPIO.cleanup()
```

8.4 Using a Center-Off Toggle or Slide Switch

A **center-off toggle switch** (also called a **three-position switch**) is a type of switch that has three positions: **on**, **off**, and **on**. The center position is **off**, while the two outer positions connect two separate circuits. This type of switch is commonly used when you need to switch between two devices or two states, with the ability to turn both off in the middle position.

Why Does This Matter?

A **center-off toggle switch** gives you more control than a standard two-position switch because it allows you to toggle between two different actions or devices while also providing an **off** state. This is useful for projects where you need to control multiple outputs, like running a motor in forward or reverse, or switching between different components.

Using a Center-Off Toggle or Slide Switch

Step 1: Gather Components

You'll need the following components:

- 1 x **Raspberry Pi** (any model with GPIO pins)
- 1 x **Center-off toggle switch** or **slide switch** (3-position switch)
- 2 x **10kΩ resistors** (for pull-down resistance)
- 1 x **LED** (or other output devices to control)
- 1 x **330Ω resistor** (for the LED)
- Jumper wires (Male to Female)
- **Breadboard** (optional, for easier connections)

Step 2: Understand How a Center-Off Switch Works

A **center-off switch** has three states:

1. **On (Position 1)**: This connects the circuit and can activate one output (e.g., turn an LED on).
2. **Off (Middle position)**: This disconnects the circuit and turns everything off.
3. **On (Position 2)**: This connects a different circuit and can activate a second output (e.g., turn another LED or device on).

You can wire the two **"on"** positions of the switch to two separate GPIO pins on the Raspberry Pi and use them to control different devices or outputs.

Step 3: Wiring the Center-Off Toggle Switch and LED to the Raspberry Pi

1. **Identify GPIO Pins**: Use a **GPIO pinout diagram** like pinout.xyz to identify the GPIO pins on your Raspberry Pi. We'll use **GPIO17 (Pin 11)** and **GPIO27 (Pin 13)** to detect the two **on** positions of the switch, and **GPIO18 (Pin 12)** to control the LED.
2. **Wiring Instructions**:
   - **One side of the toggle switch (Position 1)**: Connect to **GPIO17 (Pin 11)**.
   - **Other side of the toggle switch (Position 2)**: Connect to **GPIO27 (Pin 13)**.
   - **Middle pin of the switch**: Connect to **GND (Pin 6)**.
   - **10kΩ resistor**: Connect between **GPIO17 (Pin 11)** and **GND (Pin 6)** (pull-down resistor for Position 1).
   - **Another 10kΩ resistor**: Connect between **GPIO27 (Pin 13)** and **GND (Pin 6)** (pull-down resistor for Position 2).
   - **Long leg of the LED**: Connect to **GPIO18 (Pin 12)**.
   - **Short leg of the LED**: Connect to **one side of the 330Ω resistor**.
   - **Other side of the 330Ω resistor**: Connect to **GND (Pin 6)**.

Here's a summary of the connections:

- **GPIO17 (Pin 11)** → **One side of the toggle switch (Position 1).**
- **GPIO27 (Pin 13)** → **Other side of the toggle switch (Position 2).**
- **Middle pin of the switch** → **GND (Pin 6).**
- **GND (Pin 6)** → **One side of the 10kΩ resistor** and **one side of the 330Ω resistor.**
- **GPIO18 (Pin 12)** → **Long leg of the LED.**

This setup ensures that when the switch is in **Position 1**, GPIO17 reads **HIGH** (3.3V), and when the switch is in **Position 2**, GPIO27 reads **HIGH**. In the **center (off) position**, both GPIO pins read **LOW**.

Step 4: Install the Required Libraries

You'll use the **RPi.GPIO** library to read the state of the switch and control the LED.

Install the RPi.GPIO Library: In the terminal, install the **RPi.GPIO** library if it's not already installed:

```
sudo apt-get install python3-rpi.gpio
```

Step 5: Write the Python Script to Control the LED with the Switch

Now that everything is wired up, let's write a Python script to toggle the **LED** based on the position of the **center-off toggle switch**.

Create a Python Script: Open a text editor (like Nano or Thonny) and create a new Python file:

```
nano center_off_switch.py
```

Python Code to Control the LED: Here's a basic Python script that reads the state of the switch and turns the LED **on** or **off** depending on the switch's position:

```python
import RPi.GPIO as GPIO
import time

# Set up GPIO mode
GPIO.setmode(GPIO.BCM)

# Define the GPIO pins for the switch and LED
switch_pin1 = 17  # Position 1
switch_pin2 = 27  # Position 2
led_pin = 18

# Set up the GPIO pins
GPIO.setup(switch_pin1, GPIO.IN, pull_up_down=GPIO.PUD_DOWN)
GPIO.setup(switch_pin2, GPIO.IN, pull_up_down=GPIO.PUD_DOWN)
GPIO.setup(led_pin, GPIO.OUT)

try:
    while True:
        if GPIO.input(switch_pin1) == GPIO.HIGH:
            GPIO.output(led_pin, True)  # Turn on the LED
            print("Switch in Position 1: LED ON")
        elif GPIO.input(switch_pin2) == GPIO.HIGH:
            GPIO.output(led_pin, True)  # Turn on the LED
            print("Switch in Position 2: LED ON")
        else:
            GPIO.output(led_pin, False)  # Turn off the LED
            print("Switch in Center: LED OFF")

        time.sleep(0.1)  # Small delay to avoid bouncing

except KeyboardInterrupt:
    GPIO.cleanup()  # Clean up GPIO when the script is stopped
```

Run the Script: Save the file and run it in the terminal:

```
python3 center_off_switch.py
```

What happens? The LED will turn on when the switch is in either **Position 1** or **Position 2**, and will turn off when the switch is in the **center (off) position**.

Step 6: Customize the Switch Control

Now that you can detect the switch's position, you can customize the script to control different components.

Control Multiple LEDs or Devices: Instead of controlling a single LED, you can use each position of the switch to control different outputs (like different LEDs, motors, or relays):

```python
led1_pin = 18
led2_pin = 23
GPIO.setup(led1_pin, GPIO.OUT)
GPIO.setup(led2_pin, GPIO.OUT)

try:
    while True:
        if GPIO.input(switch_pin1) == GPIO.HIGH:
            GPIO.output(led1_pin, True)   # Turn on LED 1
            GPIO.output(led2_pin, False)  # Turn off LED 2
            print("Switch in Position 1: LED 1 ON, LED 2 OFF")
        elif GPIO.input(switch_pin2) == GPIO.HIGH:
            GPIO.output(led1_pin, False)  # Turn off LED 1
            GPIO.output(led2_pin, True)   # Turn on LED 2
            print("Switch in Position 2: LED 1 OFF, LED 2 ON")
        else:
            GPIO.output(led1_pin, False)  # Turn off LED 1
            GPIO.output(led2_pin, False)  # Turn off LED 2
            print("Switch in Center: Both LEDs OFF")

        time.sleep(0.1)
```

Trigger Different Actions Based on the Switch Position: You can use the switch to trigger different actions, like running different Python functions:

```python
def action_one():
    print("Switch in Position 1: Action One triggered!")
def action_two():
    print("Switch in Position 2: Action Two triggered!")
try:
    while True:
        if GPIO.input(switch_pin1) == GPIO.HIGH:
            action_one()
        elif GPIO.input(switch_pin2) == GPIO.HIGH:
            action_two()
        else:
            print("Switch in Center: No action")

        time.sleep(0.1)
```

8.5 Debouncing a Button Press

Debouncing is a technique used to ensure that a button press is registered accurately by eliminating multiple signals caused by mechanical vibrations inside the switch. When a button is pressed, it doesn't just open or close cleanly — the contacts can bounce several times in quick succession, causing multiple signals to be sent to the Raspberry Pi. Without debouncing, this could lead to erratic behavior, such as a button press being detected multiple times when it was only pressed once.

Why Does This Matter?

Debouncing is essential for reliable button input. If you don't debounce a button press, the Raspberry Pi could mistakenly detect multiple presses or trigger multiple actions from a single press. This is particularly important in projects where buttons are used to trigger actions like toggling an LED, controlling a motor, or selecting an option in a menu.

Debouncing a Button Press

Step 1: Gather Components

You'll need the following components:

- 1 x **Raspberry Pi** (any model with GPIO pins)
- 1 x **Push button**
- 1 x **10kΩ resistor** (for pull-down resistance)
- 1 x **LED** (optional, for testing button press)
- 1 x **330Ω resistor** (for the LED)
- Jumper wires (Male to Female)
- **Breadboard** (optional, for easier connections)

Step 2: Understand Button Debouncing

When a button is pressed, the mechanical contacts can bounce and create several rapid, unintended signals. This bouncing can happen over a very short time period (a few milliseconds). Debouncing ensures that the Raspberry Pi reads only **one clean press** by ignoring the small fluctuations caused by bouncing.

There are two common methods for debouncing:

1. **Software Debouncing**: Handled by adding a delay in your Python code to ignore rapid fluctuations.
2. **Hardware Debouncing**: Uses a capacitor and resistor to filter out bouncing signals (this guide will focus on software debouncing as it's simpler for beginners).

Step 3: Wiring the Button to the Raspberry Pi

1. **Identify GPIO Pins**: Use a **GPIO pinout diagram** like pinout.xyz to identify the GPIO pins on your Raspberry Pi. We'll use **GPIO17 (Pin 11)** to read the state of the button, and **GPIO18 (Pin 12)** to control an optional LED.
2. **Wiring Instructions**:
   - **One leg of the push button**: Connect to **GPIO17 (Pin 11)**.
   - **Other leg of the push button**: Connect to **GND (Pin 6)**.
   - **10kΩ pull-down resistor**: Connect between **GPIO17 (Pin 11)** and **GND (Pin 6)**.
   - **Optional: Long leg of the LED**: Connect to **GPIO18 (Pin 12)**.
   - **Optional: Short leg of the LED**: Connect to **one side of the 330Ω resistor**.
   - **Other side of the 330Ω resistor**: Connect to **GND (Pin 6)**.

Here's a summary of the connections:

- **GPIO17 (Pin 11)** → **One leg of the push button**.
- **GND (Pin 6)** → **Other leg of the push button** and **one side of the 10kΩ resistor**.
- **GPIO18 (Pin 12)** → **Optional long leg of the LED**.

This setup ensures that when the button is **not pressed**, the GPIO pin reads **LOW** (0V), and when the button is **pressed**, the GPIO pin reads **HIGH** (3.3V).

Step 4: Install the Required Libraries

You'll use the **RPi.GPIO** library to read the button press and implement software debouncing.

Install the RPi.GPIO Library: In the terminal, install the **RPi.GPIO** library if it's not already installed:

```
sudo apt-get install python3-rpi.gpio
```

Step 5: Write the Python Script with Debouncing

Now that everything is wired up, let's write a Python script to detect the button press and apply **software debouncing**.

Create a Python Script: Open a text editor (like Nano or Thonny) and create a new Python file:

```
nano debounce_button.py
```

Python Code to Debounce a Button: Here's a simple Python script that reads the button press and debounces it using a small delay:

```
import RPi.GPIO as GPIO
import time

# Set up GPIO mode
GPIO.setmode(GPIO.BCM)

# Define the GPIO pin for the button
button_pin = 17
led_pin = 18   # Optional, for testing

# Set up the GPIO pins
GPIO.setup(button_pin, GPIO.IN, pull_up_down=GPIO.PUD_DOWN)
GPIO.setup(led_pin, GPIO.OUT)  # Optional, for testing

# Function to debounce a button press
def button_pressed(channel):
    print("Button pressed!")
    GPIO.output(led_pin, not GPIO.input(led_pin))  # Toggle the LED

# Set up an event detection with debounce
GPIO.add_event_detect(button_pin, GPIO.RISING, callback=button_pressed,
bouncetime=300)

try:
    while True:
        time.sleep(1)  # Keep the program running

except KeyboardInterrupt:
    GPIO.cleanup()  # Clean up GPIO when the script is stopped
```

Run the Script: Save the file and run it in the terminal:

```
python3 debounce_button.py
```

What happens? When the button is pressed, the script will print "Button pressed!" and, if connected, toggle the LED on or off. The debouncing ensures that even if the button contacts bounce, only one press is registered.

Step 6: Customize the Debouncing Behavior

You can customize the debounce time and the actions triggered by the button press.

Adjust the Debounce Time: If you notice that your button is still registering multiple presses, you can increase the debounce time.

Conversely, if the response feels too slow, you can reduce the debounce time:

```
GPIO.add_event_detect(button_pin, GPIO.RISING, callback=button_pressed,
bouncetime=100)  # 100ms debounce
```

Trigger Different Actions: You can modify the button_pressed() function to perform different actions when the button is pressed, such as toggling a motor or sending data to a server:

```
def button_pressed(channel):
    print("Button pressed! Toggling device.")
    # Perform other actions here, like controlling a motor or sending
data
```

8.6 Using an External Pull-Up Resistor

A **pull-up resistor** is a resistor used to ensure a stable **HIGH** (3.3V) signal on a GPIO pin when no other signal is being applied. It "pulls" the voltage up to a **HIGH** level when the button or switch connected to the GPIO pin is **open** (not pressed or activated). When the button is pressed, the pin is pulled **LOW** (0V) because the circuit is closed to ground (GND). An **external pull-up resistor** is placed between the GPIO pin and the 3.3V pin to ensure this behavior.

Why Does This Matter?

Using an external pull-up resistor ensures that a GPIO pin reads a stable **HIGH** signal when not connected to ground, avoiding floating states that can lead to unpredictable behavior. This is important in situations where you want to detect when a button is pressed and need to avoid erratic readings on the GPIO pin when the button is not pressed.

Step 1: Gather Components

You'll need the following components:

- 1 x **Raspberry Pi** (any model with GPIO pins)
- 1 x **Push button**
- 1 x **10kΩ resistor** (for the external pull-up resistor)
- 1 x **LED** (optional, for testing)
- 1 x **330Ω resistor** (for the LED)
- Jumper wires (Male to Female)
- **Breadboard** (optional, for easier connections)

Step 2: Understand How a Pull-Up Resistor Works

In a normal button setup without a pull-up resistor, the GPIO pin could "float" between **HIGH** and **LOW** when the button is not pressed, leading to unreliable readings. By adding a **pull-up resistor**, we ensure that the GPIO pin is pulled to **HIGH** when the button is open (not pressed). When the button is pressed, it connects the GPIO pin to **GND** and pulls the pin to **LOW**.

How the Circuit Works:

- **Button Not Pressed**: The pull-up resistor pulls the GPIO pin to **HIGH** (3.3V).
- **Button Pressed**: The circuit connects the GPIO pin to **GND**, and the pin reads **LOW** (0V).

Step 3: Wiring the Button with an External Pull-Up Resistor

1. **Identify GPIO Pins**: Use a **GPIO pinout diagram** like pinout.xyz to identify the GPIO pins on your Raspberry Pi. We'll use **GPIO17 (Pin 11)** to read the state of the button, and **GPIO18 (Pin 12)** to control an optional LED.

2. **Wiring Instructions**:
    o **One leg of the push button**: Connect to **GND (Pin 6)**.
    o **Other leg of the push button**: Connect to **GPIO17 (Pin 11)**.
    o **10kΩ pull-up resistor**: Connect between **GPIO17 (Pin 11) and 3.3V (Pin 1)**.
    o **Optional: Long leg of the LED**: Connect to **GPIO18 (Pin 12)**.
    o **Optional: Short leg of the LED**: Connect to **one side of the 330Ω resistor**.
    o **Other side of the 330Ω resistor**: Connect to **GND (Pin 6)**.

Here's a summary of the connections:

- **GPIO17 (Pin 11) → One leg of the push button.**

- **GND (Pin 6) → Other leg of the push button.**

- **3.3V (Pin 1) → One side of the 10kΩ resistor.**

- **GPIO17 (Pin 11) → Other side of the 10kΩ resistor.**

- **Optional: GPIO18 (Pin 12) → Long leg of the LED.**

This setup ensures that when the button is **not pressed**, the GPIO pin reads **HIGH** (3.3V), and when the button is **pressed**, the GPIO pin reads **LOW** (0V).

Step 4: Install the Required Libraries

You'll use the **RPi.GPIO** library to read the button press and apply the external pull-up resistor logic.

Install the RPi.GPIO Library: In the terminal, install the **RPi.GPIO** library if it's not already installed:

```
sudo apt-get install python3-rpi.gpio
```

Step 5: Write the Python Script for the External Pull-Up Resistor

Now that everything is wired up, let's write a Python script to detect when the button is pressed and use the external pull-up resistor.

Create a Python Script: Open a text editor (like Nano or Thonny) and create a new Python file:

nano external_pullup_button.py

Python Code to Detect a Button Press: Here's a simple Python script that reads the button press and toggles an LED (or prints a message) using the external pull-up resistor:

```python
import RPi.GPIO as GPIO
import time

# Set up GPIO mode
GPIO.setmode(GPIO.BCM)

# Define the GPIO pin for the button and LED
button_pin = 17
led_pin = 18  # Optional, for testing

# Set up the GPIO pins
GPIO.setup(button_pin, GPIO.IN)  # External pull-up is used, so no need
for pull_up_down
GPIO.setup(led_pin, GPIO.OUT)    # Optional, for testing

try:
    while True:
        if GPIO.input(button_pin) == GPIO.LOW:  # Button pressed
            GPIO.output(led_pin, True)  # Turn on the LED
            print("Button pressed!")
        else:
            GPIO.output(led_pin, False)  # Turn off the LED
            print("Button not pressed.")

        time.sleep(0.1)  # Small delay to avoid bouncing

except KeyboardInterrupt:
    GPIO.cleanup()  # Clean up GPIO when the script is stopped
```

Run the Script: Save the file and run it in the terminal:

python3 external_pullup_button.py

What happens? The LED will turn on (or the message "Button pressed!" will print) when the button is pressed, and the LED will turn off (or "Button not pressed" will print) when the button is released.

Step 6: Customize the Behavior of the Button

You can customize the behavior to trigger different actions when the button is pressed or released.

Toggle the State of an LED: Instead of just turning the LED on and off, you can toggle its state with each button press:

```python
led_state = False
def button_pressed():
    global led_state
    led_state = not led_state  # Toggle the LED state
    GPIO.output(led_pin, led_state)
    print(f"LED {'on' if led_state else 'off'}")

try:
    while True:
        if GPIO.input(button_pin) == GPIO.LOW:
            button_pressed()
            time.sleep(0.3)  # Debounce delay
```

Trigger Different Functions: You can modify the script to call different functions based on the button press:

```python
def start_action():
    print("Action started!")

def stop_action():
    print("Action stopped!")

try:
    while True:
        if GPIO.input(button_pin) == GPIO.LOW:
            start_action()
            time.sleep(0.3)  # Debounce delay
        else:
            stop_action()
```

8.7 Using a Rotary (Quadrature) Encoder

A **rotary encoder** (also known as a **quadrature encoder**) is a type of sensor that converts the rotational position of a shaft into digital signals. It can be used to track the position, direction, and speed of rotation. Rotary encoders are commonly used in electronics projects for controlling volume knobs, tracking the position of motors, and navigating menus on a display.

Unlike a potentiometer, which only tracks the angle within a set range (e.g., 0-270 degrees), a rotary encoder can rotate infinitely, making it useful for precise position tracking.

Why Does This Matter?

A **quadrature encoder** generates two digital signals, **A** and **B**, which are 90 degrees out of phase. By reading these two signals, you can determine the **direction** of rotation (clockwise or counterclockwise) and the **number of steps** (the encoder's resolution). This gives you a more flexible and accurate way to track rotation in your project.

Using a Rotary (Quadrature) Encoder

Step 1: Gather Components

You'll need the following components:

- 1 x **Raspberry Pi** (any model with GPIO pins)
- 1 x **Rotary (quadrature) encoder** (e.g., KY-040)
- 1 x **10kΩ resistor** (optional, for pull-up resistance)
- 1 x **LED** (optional, for testing rotation or direction)
- 1 x **330Ω resistor** (for the LED)
- Jumper wires (Male to Female)
- **Breadboard** (optional, for easier connections)

Step 2: Understand How a Rotary Encoder Works

A **rotary encoder** has two outputs, **A** and **B**, which produce square wave signals. These signals are **90 degrees out of phase** with each other, meaning they don't rise and fall at the same time. This phase difference allows you to detect the **direction** of rotation:

- If **A** leads **B**, the encoder is rotating **clockwise**.
- If **B** leads **A**, the encoder is rotating **counterclockwise**.

There is usually an additional pin for a **push button** on the encoder, which can be used to trigger actions (like selecting a menu item).

Step 3: Wiring the Rotary Encoder to the Raspberry Pi

1. **Identify GPIO Pins**: Use a **GPIO pinout diagram** like pinout.xyz to identify the GPIO pins on your Raspberry Pi. We'll use **GPIO17 (Pin 11)** and **GPIO18 (Pin 12)** for the encoder's **A** and **B** outputs, and **GPIO27 (Pin 13)** for the optional push button.
2. **Wiring Instructions**:
   - **A pin of the encoder**: Connect to **GPIO17 (Pin 11)**.
   - **B pin of the encoder**: Connect to **GPIO18 (Pin 12)**.
   - **GND pin of the encoder**: Connect to **GND (Pin 6)**.
   - **VCC pin of the encoder**: Connect to **3.3V (Pin 1)**.
   - **Optional: Push button pin**: Connect to **GPIO27 (Pin 13)**.
   - **Optional: Long leg of the LED**: Connect to **GPIO22 (Pin 15)**.
   - **Short leg of the LED**: Connect to **one side of the 330Ω resistor**.
   - **Other side of the 330Ω resistor**: Connect to **GND (Pin 6)**.

Here's a summary of the connections:

- **GPIO17 (Pin 11)** → **A pin** of the rotary encoder.

- **GPIO18 (Pin 12)** → **B pin** of the rotary encoder.

- **GPIO27 (Pin 13)** → **Push button pin** of the encoder (optional).

- **GND (Pin 6)** → **GND pin** of the rotary encoder.

- **3.3V (Pin 1)** → **VCC pin** of the rotary encoder.

Step 4: Install the Required Libraries

You'll use the **RPi.GPIO** library to read the rotary encoder's signals.

Install the RPi.GPIO Library: In the terminal, install the **RPi.GPIO** library if it's not already installed:

```
sudo apt-get install python3-rpi.gpio
```

Step 5: Write the Python Script to Read the Rotary Encoder

Now that everything is wired up, let's write a Python script to detect the rotary encoder's movement.

Create a Python Script: Open a text editor (like Nano or Thonny) and create a new Python file:

```
nano rotary_encoder.py
```

Python Code to Track Rotary Encoder Movement: Here's a simple Python script to track the rotation and direction of the rotary encoder:

```python
import RPi.GPIO as GPIO
import time

# Set up GPIO mode
GPIO.setmode(GPIO.BCM)

# Define GPIO pins for the encoder and LED
clk = 17   # A pin
dt = 18    # B pin
led_pin = 22  # Optional, for direction indication

GPIO.setup(clk, GPIO.IN, pull_up_down=GPIO.PUD_UP)
GPIO.setup(dt, GPIO.IN, pull_up_down=GPIO.PUD_UP)
GPIO.setup(led_pin, GPIO.OUT)

counter = 0
clkLastState = GPIO.input(clk)

try:
```

```
    while True:
        clkState = GPIO.input(clk)
        dtState = GPIO.input(dt)

        # If the A pin changes state, check direction
        if clkState != clkLastState:
            if dtState != clkState:
                counter += 1  # Clockwise
                GPIO.output(led_pin, True)  # Turn on the LED (for
testing)
                print("Rotating clockwise, Counter:", counter)
            else:
                counter -= 1  # Counterclockwise
                GPIO.output(led_pin, False)  # Turn off the LED (for
testing)
                print("Rotating counterclockwise, Counter:", counter)

            clkLastState = clkState

        time.sleep(0.01)  # Small delay to debounce the encoder signals

except KeyboardInterrupt:
    GPIO.cleanup()  # Clean up GPIO when the script is stopped
```

Run the Script: Save the file and run it in the terminal:

```
python3 rotary_encoder.py
```

What happens? When you rotate the encoder, the script will print whether the encoder is rotating **clockwise** or **counterclockwise**, and display the updated counter value. If you connected an LED, it will light up when turning clockwise and turn off when rotating counterclockwise.

Step 6: Customize the Rotary Encoder Behavior

You can customize the behavior to trigger different actions based on the rotation.

Use the Rotary Encoder to Adjust a Value: You can use the encoder to adjust a value (e.g., volume or brightness) based on the number of steps:

```
volume = 50  # Initial volume level
def adjust_volume(change):
    global volume
    volume += change
    volume = max(0, min(100, volume))  # Clamp between 0 and 100
```

```
        print(f"Volume level: {volume}%")

try:
    while True:
        clkState = GPIO.input(clk)
        dtState = GPIO.input(dt)

        if clkState != clkLastState:
            if dtState != clkState:
                adjust_volume(1)   # Increase volume
            else:
                adjust_volume(-1)   # Decrease volume

            clkLastState = clkState
        time.sleep(0.01)
```

Use the Encoder to Navigate a Menu: You can use the encoder to scroll through menu items and the push button to select an option:

```
menu = ["Option 1", "Option 2", "Option 3"]
current_option = 0

def display_menu():
    print(f"Current selection: {menu[current_option]}")

def rotate_menu(change):
    global current_option
    current_option = (current_option + change) % len(menu)
    display_menu()

try:
    while True:
        clkState = GPIO.input(clk)
        dtState = GPIO.input(dt)

        if clkState != clkLastState:
            if dtState != clkState:
                rotate_menu(1)   # Scroll down
            else:
                rotate_menu(-1)   # Scroll up

            clkLastState = clkState
        time.sleep(0.01)
```

8.8 Using a Keypad

A **keypad** is a matrix of buttons arranged in rows and columns. It is commonly used in devices like security systems, calculators, and phone dials. When you press a button on the keypad, it triggers a specific combination of a row and a column, allowing you to detect which button was pressed.

Why Does This Matter?

Using a keypad with a Raspberry Pi allows you to create interactive input systems for projects like passcode entry, menu navigation, or any other project that requires multiple button inputs. Keypads are particularly useful in projects that require user interaction with numbers or text.

Using a Keypad

Step 1: Gather Components

You'll need the following components:

- 1 x **Raspberry Pi** (any model with GPIO pins)
- 1 x **4x4 keypad** (or **4x3 keypad**)
- Jumper wires (Male to Female)
- **Breadboard** (optional, for easier connections)

Step 2: Understand How a Keypad Works

A **keypad** is a matrix of buttons connected in rows and columns. When you press a button, it connects a specific row to a specific column, and by reading the state of the rows and columns, you can determine which button was pressed.

For example, in a **4x4 keypad**:

- There are **4 rows** and **4 columns**.
- Each button press corresponds to one row and one column being connected.

You will need to read the state of the rows and columns using the Raspberry Pi's GPIO pins to detect which button was pressed.

Step 3: Wiring the Keypad to the Raspberry Pi

1. **Identify GPIO Pins**: Use a **GPIO pinout diagram** like pinout.xyz to identify the GPIO pins on your Raspberry Pi. We will use **8 GPIO pins** to interface with the 4x4 keypad (4 for the rows and 4 for the columns).
2. **Wiring Instructions**:
   o **Connect the row pins of the keypad**: Connect the **4 row pins** of the keypad to **GPIO2 (Pin 3), GPIO3 (Pin 5), GPIO4 (Pin 7), and GPIO17 (Pin 11)**.
   o **Connect the column pins of the keypad**: Connect the **4 column pins** of the keypad to **GPIO27 (Pin 13), GPIO22 (Pin 15), GPIO10 (Pin 19), and GPIO9 (Pin 21)**.

Here's a summary of the connections:

- **Row 1 → GPIO2 (Pin 3)**.
- **Row 2 → GPIO3 (Pin 5)**.
- **Row 3 → GPIO4 (Pin 7)**.
- **Row 4 → GPIO17 (Pin 11)**.
- **Column 1 → GPIO27 (Pin 13)**.
- **Column 2 → GPIO22 (Pin 15)**.
- **Column 3 → GPIO10 (Pin 19)**.
- **Column 4 → GPIO9 (Pin 21)**.

Step 4: Install the Required Libraries

You will need the **RPi.GPIO** library to read the GPIO pins, and you can also use the **Keypad** library for Raspberry Pi to simplify working with the keypad.

Install the RPi.GPIO Library: In the terminal, install the **RPi.GPIO** library if it's not already installed:

```
sudo apt-get install python3-rpi.gpio
```

Install the Keypad Python Library: You can install the **keypad_matrix** library to make working with the keypad easier:

```
sudo pip3 install keypad_matrix
```

Step 5: Write the Python Script to Read Keypad Input

Now that everything is wired up, let's write a Python script to detect button presses on the keypad.

Create a Python Script: Open a text editor (like Nano or Thonny) and create a new Python file:

```
nano keypad_input.py
```

Python Code to Detect Keypad Input: Here's a basic Python script to read input from the keypad:

```python
import RPi.GPIO as GPIO
from keypad_matrix import Keypad
import time
# Define the GPIO pins connected to the rows and columns of the keypad
ROW_PINS = [2, 3, 4, 17]    # GPIO pins connected to the row pins of
the keypad
COL_PINS = [27, 22, 10, 9]  # GPIO pins connected to the column pins of
the keypad
# Define the keypad layout
KEYPAD_LAYOUT = [
    ["1", "2", "3", "A"],
    ["4", "5", "6", "B"],
    ["7", "8", "9", "C"],
    ["*", "0", "#", "D"]
]

# Initialize the keypad
keypad = Keypad(KEYPAD_LAYOUT, ROW_PINS, COL_PINS, GPIO)

try:
    while True:
        # Check if a key is pressed
        key = keypad.get_key()
        if key:
            print(f"Key pressed: {key}")
        time.sleep(0.1)
except KeyboardInterrupt:
    GPIO.cleanup()  # Clean up GPIO when the script is stopped
```

Run the Script: Save the file and run it in the terminal:

```
python3 keypad_input.py
```

What happens? When you press a button on the keypad, the script will print the corresponding key to the terminal.

Step 6: Customize the Keypad Behavior

You can customize the behavior of the keypad to trigger specific actions based on which key is pressed.

Use the Keypad for Passcode Entry: You can modify the script to store a sequence of keypresses and check if they match a passcode:

```python
passcode = "1234"
entered_code = ""

try:
    while True:
        key = keypad.get_key()
        if key:
            entered_code += key
            print(f"Entered: {entered_code}")

            if len(entered_code) == 4:  # Once 4 digits are entered,
check passcode
                if entered_code == passcode:
                    print("Passcode correct!")
                else:
                    print("Incorrect passcode.")
                entered_code = ""   # Reset entered code

        time.sleep(0.1)
```

Trigger Different Actions Based on Keypresses: You can assign specific actions to different keys on the keypad, such as turning on an LED or starting a motor:

```python
def perform_action(key):
    if key == "1":
        print("Action 1 triggered!")
    elif key == "2":
        print("Action 2 triggered!")
    elif key == "A":
        print("Action A triggered!")
```

```
try:
    while True:
        key = keypad.get_key()
        if key:
            print(f"Key pressed: {key}")
            perform_action(key)

        time.sleep(0.1)
```

8.9 Giving the Raspberry Pi a Shutdown Button

A **shutdown button** is a physical button connected to the
Raspberry Pi that, when pressed, safely shuts down the Pi. This
ensures that the operating system closes all open processes and
files properly, preventing corruption of the microSD card or loss of
data. This is particularly useful for projects where the Raspberry Pi
is running headless (without a monitor) or in situations where
powering it off safely is essential.

Why Does This Matter?

Shutting down the Raspberry Pi safely is important to avoid
damaging the operating system or corrupting your microSD card.
Without a proper shutdown, data can be lost or files can become
corrupted. Having a dedicated shutdown button allows you to easily
and safely power off your Raspberry Pi with a single press.

Adding a Shutdown Button

Step 1: Gather Components

You'll need the following components:

- 1 x **Raspberry Pi** (any model with GPIO pins)
- 1 x **Momentary push button** (normally open)
- 1 x **10kΩ resistor** (for pull-down resistance)
- Jumper wires (Male to Female)
- **Breadboard** (optional, for easier connections)

Step 2: Understand the Shutdown Button Circuit

The shutdown button will be connected to a **GPIO pin** on the Raspberry Pi, and when pressed, it will trigger a Python script to safely shut down the Pi. A **pull-down resistor** ensures that the GPIO pin reads **LOW** when the button is not pressed.

- **Button not pressed**: GPIO pin reads **LOW** (0V).
- **Button pressed**: GPIO pin reads **HIGH** (3.3V), triggering the shutdown.

Step 3: Wiring the Shutdown Button to the Raspberry Pi

1. **Identify GPIO Pins**: Use a **GPIO pinout diagram** like pinout.xyz to identify the GPIO pins on your Raspberry Pi. We'll use **GPIO3 (Pin 5)** to trigger the shutdown, which is a special pin on the Raspberry Pi that can also be used to wake the Pi from halt mode.
2. **Wiring Instructions**:
   - **One leg of the push button**: Connect to **GPIO3 (Pin 5)**.
   - **Other leg of the push button**: Connect to **GND (Pin 6)**.
   - **10kΩ pull-down resistor**: Connect between **GPIO3 (Pin 5) and GND (Pin 6)**.

Here's a summary of the connections:

- **GPIO3 (Pin 5) → One leg of the push button**.

- **GND (Pin 6) → Other leg of the push button and one side of the 10kΩ resistor**.

This setup ensures that when the button is **not pressed**, the GPIO pin reads **LOW** (0V), and when the button is **pressed**, the GPIO pin reads **HIGH** (3.3V).

Step 4: Write the Python Script for the Shutdown Button

Create a Python Script: You'll need to create a Python script that monitors the state of the button and issues a shutdown command when the button is pressed.

Open a terminal and create a new Python file:

```
sudo nano /home/pi/shutdown_button.py
```

Python Code to Shut Down the Raspberry Pi: Here's a simple Python script that listens for the button press and shuts down the Raspberry Pi safely:

```python
import RPi.GPIO as GPIO
import time
import os

# Set up GPIO mode
GPIO.setmode(GPIO.BCM)

# Define the GPIO pin for the button
shutdown_button = 3  # GPIO3 (Pin 5)

# Set up the GPIO pin as an input with a pull-down resistor
GPIO.setup(shutdown_button, GPIO.IN, pull_up_down=GPIO.PUD_DOWN)

try:
    while True:
        # Check if the button is pressed
        if GPIO.input(shutdown_button) == GPIO.HIGH:
            print("Shutdown button pressed. Shutting down...")
            time.sleep(1)  # Debounce the button press
            os.system("sudo shutdown -h now")  # Issue shutdown command

        time.sleep(0.1)  # Poll every 100ms to check button state

except KeyboardInterrupt:
    GPIO.cleanup()  # Clean up GPIO when the script is stopped
```

1. **Save and Exit**: Press CTRL + X, then Y, and Enter to save the script and exit the editor.

Step 5: Make the Python Script Run at Startup

To make the shutdown button work automatically every time the Raspberry Pi starts, you need to configure it to run the script on boot.

Edit the rc.local File: Open the `rc.local` file to add the script:

```
sudo nano /etc/rc.local
```

Add the Python Script: Add the following line just above the `exit 0` line:

```
sudo python3 /home/pi/shutdown_button.py &
```

1. This will run the Python script in the background at startup.
2. **Save and Exit**: Press `CTRL + X`, then `Y`, and `Enter` to save the file and exit.

Step 6: Test the Shutdown Button

Reboot the Raspberry Pi: Reboot your Raspberry Pi to make sure the script is running:

```
sudo reboot
```

1. **Test the Shutdown Button**: Once the Pi has rebooted, press the shutdown button. The Raspberry Pi should safely shut down after you press the button. You can monitor the console or an LED to see when the Pi powers off.

Chapter 9: Using Sensors with Raspberry Pi

9.1 Using Resistive Sensors

What's a Resistive Sensor?

A resistive sensor is a device that changes its resistance when something happens—like when you press on it or when the temperature changes. This change in resistance lets us measure things like pressure, temperature, or even touch!

Why Should You Care?

By using resistive sensors, your Raspberry Pi can "sense" changes in the real world! For example, you can make it detect how hard you're pressing something or how hot it is, and then trigger actions like turning on a light or fan.

Using Resistive Sensors with Raspberry Pi

Step 1: What You'll Need

- **Raspberry Pi** (any model will do)
- **Resistive Sensor** (like a Force Sensor or Temperature Sensor)
- **10kΩ Resistor** (this helps with reading the sensor)
- **MCP3008** (an ADC chip that helps read analog sensors)
- **Jumper wires** (to connect everything)
- **Breadboard** (optional, makes it easier to connect wires)

Step 2: How Resistive Sensors Work

A resistive sensor changes its resistance based on what it's measuring (like pressure or temperature). The Raspberry Pi can't read these changes directly, so we use something called a **voltage divider** and an **Analog-to-Digital Converter (ADC)** like the MCP3008 to convert these changes into something the Pi can understand.

3.1 Connect the Sensor with a Voltage Divider

A voltage divider helps us measure changes in the sensor's resistance:

- **One side of the sensor** goes to **3.3V** on your Raspberry Pi.
- **The other side of the sensor** connects to **one end of the 10kΩ resistor** and also to **Channel 0 (CH0)** on the MCP3008.
- **The other end of the 10kΩ resistor** goes to **GND** on the Raspberry Pi.

3.2 Connecting the MCP3008 to Raspberry Pi

The MCP3008 helps convert the analog signal from the sensor to digital data that the Raspberry Pi can understand:

- **MCP3008 VDD**: Connect to 3.3V on the Raspberry Pi.
- **MCP3008 VREF**: Connect to 3.3V (this sets the reference voltage).
- **AGND and DGND**: Both go to GND.
- **CLK (Pin 13)**: Connect to **GPIO11 (Pin 23)** on the Raspberry Pi.
- **DOUT (Pin 12)**: Connect to **GPIO9 (Pin 21)**.
- **DIN (Pin 11)**: Connect to **GPIO10 (Pin 19)**.
- **CS/SHDN (Pin 10)**: Connect to **GPIO8 (Pin 24)**.

Step 4: Installing the Software You'll Need

Your Raspberry Pi needs a bit of software to read data from the MCP3008:

1. **Open the terminal** on your Raspberry Pi.

Install the **spidev** library to communicate with the sensor:

```
sudo apt-get update
sudo apt-get install python3-spidev
```

Step 5: Creating Your Python Script

5.1 Open the Terminal

To create your Python script, open the terminal.

5.2 Write the Script

Type this command to create the script:

```
nano resistive_sensor.py
```

Now, paste this easy Python code to read your sensor

```python
import spidev
import time

# Set up SPI (communication with the MCP3008)
spi = spidev.SpiDev()
spi.open(0, 0)
spi.max_speed_hz = 1350000

# Function to read data from the sensor (from channel 0 on MCP3008)
def read_channel(channel):
    adc = spi.xfer2([1, (8 + channel) << 4, 0])
    data = ((adc[1] & 3) << 8) + adc[2]
    return data

# Convert the data to voltage
def convert_to_voltage(data):
    return (data * 3.3) / 1023  # 3.3 is the Pi's voltage

# Main loop to keep reading sensor data
try:
    while True:
        sensor_data = read_channel(0)
        voltage = convert_to_voltage(sensor_data)
        print(f"Sensor reading: {sensor_data}, Voltage:
{voltage:.2f}V")
        time.sleep(0.5)
except KeyboardInterrupt:
    spi.close()
```

5.3 Save the Script

- Press `Ctrl + X` to exit Nano.
- Press `Y` to confirm saving.
- Hit `Enter` to save the file.

Step 6: Running Your Python Script

6.1 Run the Script

Now, let's run the script you just created:

```
python3 resistive_sensor.py
```

6.2 See the Sensor Readings

When you run the script, you'll see the sensor data and voltage readings appear in the terminal. If you press on a force sensor, the numbers should change:

```
Sensor reading: 512, Voltage: 1.65V
```

Step 7: Customize the Script (Optional)

Want to do more with your sensor? You can make it trigger actions like turning on an LED when a certain pressure is detected.

Here's a simple script to turn on an LED when the sensor detects enough pressure:

```
import RPi.GPIO as GPIO

led_pin = 18
GPIO.setmode(GPIO.BCM)
GPIO.setup(led_pin, GPIO.OUT)

threshold = 500  # Change this based on your sensor

try:
```

```
    while True:
        sensor_data = read_channel(0)
        if sensor_data > threshold:
            GPIO.output(led_pin, GPIO.HIGH)  # Turn on LED
        else:
            GPIO.output(led_pin, GPIO.LOW)   # Turn off LED
        time.sleep(0.5)

except KeyboardInterrupt:
    GPIO.cleanup()
    spi.close()
```

Mistakes to Avoid

1. **Wrong Wiring**: Double-check that your sensor and MCP3008 are connected properly.

No Data?: Make sure SPI is enabled on your Raspberry Pi. Use this command to enable it:

```
sudo raspi-config
```

2. Then go to **Interfacing Options** > **SPI** and enable it.

Troubleshooting Tips

- **No Readings?**: Check the wiring again. Make sure the sensor and ADC are properly powered.
- **Script Not Running?**: Ensure you have the spidev library installed and SPI is enabled on your Pi.

9.2 Measuring Light

A light sensor measures the brightness of the light in its surroundings. One popular light sensor for beginners is the **Photoresistor (LDR)**, which changes its resistance based on the light intensity. The brighter the light, the lower its resistance, and vice versa.

Why Measure Light?

By measuring light, you can create projects like automatic night lights, brightness-adjusting screens, or even a plant monitor that alerts you if your plants aren't getting enough sunlight!

Measuring Light with a Raspberry Pi

Step 1: Gather Your Components

To measure light with your Raspberry Pi, you'll need:

- **Raspberry Pi** (any model with GPIO pins)
- **Photoresistor (LDR)** (to detect light levels)
- **10kΩ Resistor** (for a voltage divider circuit)
- **MCP3008** (ADC to convert the analog signal to digital)
- **Jumper wires** (Male to Female)
- **Breadboard** (optional, for easier wiring)

Step 2: How a Photoresistor (LDR) Works

A **Photoresistor** changes its resistance depending on how much light it detects:

- **Bright light** → low resistance

- **Low light** → high resistance

Since the Raspberry Pi cannot read analog signals directly, we will use the **MCP3008** Analog-to-Digital Converter (ADC) to convert the changing resistance into digital data that the Raspberry Pi can read.

3.1 Build the Voltage Divider Circuit

To read the light sensor's resistance, you need to set up a **voltage divider**:

- **One leg of the Photoresistor (LDR)** goes to **3.3V** on your Raspberry Pi.
- **The other leg of the LDR** goes to **one side of the 10kΩ resistor** and **Channel 0 (CH0)** on the MCP3008.
- **The other leg of the 10kΩ resistor** goes to **GND** (ground).

3.2 Wire the MCP3008 to the Raspberry Pi

Now, connect the MCP3008 to convert the light sensor's analog signal to digital:

- **VDD**: Connect to **3.3V** on the Raspberry Pi.
- **VREF**: Connect to **3.3V** (reference voltage).
- **AGND and DGND**: Connect to **GND**.
- **CLK (Pin 13)**: Connect to **GPIO11 (Pin 23)**.
- **DOUT (Pin 12)**: Connect to **GPIO9 (Pin 21)**.
- **DIN (Pin 11)**: Connect to **GPIO10 (Pin 19)**.
- **CS/SHDN (Pin 10)**: Connect to **GPIO8 (Pin 24)**.

Step 4: Installing the Required Software

To communicate with the MCP3008 and read the light sensor values, you'll need the **spidev** library:

1. Open the terminal on your Raspberry Pi.

Install **spidev**:

```
sudo apt-get update
sudo apt-get install python3-spidev
```

Step 5: Create the Python Script to Measure Light

5.1 Open the Terminal

To create the script, open a terminal window on your Raspberry Pi.

5.2 Write the Python Script

Use **Nano** to create a new Python script:

```
nano light_sensor.py
```

Now, write the following Python code to read data from the light sensor:

```python
import spidev
import time
# Set up SPI communication with MCP3008
spi = spidev.SpiDev()
spi.open(0, 0)
spi.max_speed_hz = 1350000

# Function to read data from the MCP3008 channel (0-7)
def read_channel(channel):
    adc = spi.xfer2([1, (8 + channel) << 4, 0])
    data = ((adc[1] & 3) << 8) + adc[2]
    return data

# Convert the data to a voltage level
def convert_to_voltage(data):
    return (data * 3.3) / 1023

# Main loop to read the light sensor data
try:
    while True:
        # Read from channel 0 (where the LDR is connected)
        light_level = read_channel(0)
        voltage = convert_to_voltage(light_level)
        print(f"Light level: {light_level}, Voltage: {voltage:.2f}V")
        time.sleep(0.5)

except KeyboardInterrupt:
    spi.close()
```

5.3 Save the Script

- Press `Ctrl + X` to exit Nano.
- Press `Y` to confirm saving.
- Hit `Enter` to save the file.

Step 6: Running the Python Script

6.1 Run the Script

In the terminal, run the Python script you just created

```
python3 light_sensor.py
```

6.2 Watch the Light Readings

The light levels and voltage will be printed in the terminal as the script runs. If you move the sensor into a bright or dark area, the readings will change:

```
Light level: 650, Voltage: 2.10V
```

Step 7: Customize the Script for Fun Projects

Want to do something cool with your light sensor? How about turning on an LED when it gets too dark?

Here's an updated script that turns on an LED when the light drops below a certain level:

```python
import RPi.GPIO as GPIO
led_pin = 18
GPIO.setmode(GPIO.BCM)
GPIO.setup(led_pin, GPIO.OUT)

dark_threshold = 400  # You can adjust this value based on your
environment

try:
    while True:
```

```
        light_level = read_channel(0)
        if light_level < dark_threshold:
            GPIO.output(led_pin, GPIO.HIGH)   # Turn on LED
        else:
            GPIO.output(led_pin, GPIO.LOW)    # Turn off LED
        time.sleep(0.5)

except KeyboardInterrupt:
    GPIO.cleanup()
    spi.close()
```

Common Mistakes

1. **Incorrect Wiring**: Double-check the connections between the light sensor, MCP3008, and Raspberry Pi.

No Data?: Make sure SPI is enabled on your Raspberry Pi. You can enable it with this command:

```
sudo raspi-config
```

2. Go to **Interfacing Options** > **SPI** and enable it.

Troubleshooting Tips

- **Unstable Readings?**: If the light readings are fluctuating too much, try shielding the sensor from ambient light or using a stronger pull-down resistor.
- **No Readings?**: Make sure all the connections are secure and that SPI is enabled.

9.3 Measuring Temperature with a Thermistor

A thermistor is a special resistor that changes its resistance based on temperature. There are two types of thermistors:

- **NTC (Negative Temperature Coefficient)**: Resistance decreases as the temperature rises.

- **PTC (Positive Temperature Coefficient)**: Resistance increases as the temperature rises.

For most projects, **NTC thermistors** are commonly used.

Why Measure Temperature?
By measuring temperature, you can build fun and useful projects like temperature-controlled fans, room temperature monitors, or even an alert system for when things get too hot or cold!

Measuring Temperature with a Thermistor and Raspberry Pi

Step 1: Gather Your Components

You'll need:

- **Raspberry Pi** (any model with GPIO pins)
- **NTC Thermistor** (commonly 10kΩ)
- **10kΩ Resistor** (for a voltage divider circuit)
- **MCP3008** (ADC for converting analog signals to digital)
- **Jumper wires** (Male to Female)
- **Breadboard** (optional, for easier wiring)

Step 2: Understanding the Thermistor

A **thermistor** changes its resistance depending on the temperature:

- **High temperature** → low resistance.

- **Low temperature** → high resistance.

To read this resistance change with your Raspberry Pi, you'll use a **voltage divider** circuit and an **MCP3008** Analog-to-Digital Converter (ADC) to convert the sensor's analog signal to digital data that the Pi can process.

Step 3: Setting Up the Circuit

3.1 Build the Voltage Divider Circuit

We use a voltage divider to measure the thermistor's changing resistance:

- **One leg of the thermistor** goes to **3.3V** on your Raspberry Pi.
- **The other leg of the thermistor** connects to **one side of the 10kΩ resistor** and **Channel 0 (CH0)** on the MCP3008.
- **The other side of the 10kΩ resistor** goes to **GND** (ground).

3.2 Connect the MCP3008 to the Raspberry Pi

To read the analog signal from the thermistor, wire the MCP3008 ADC:

- **VDD**: Connect to **3.3V** on the Raspberry Pi.
- **VREF**: Connect to **3.3V** (reference voltage).
- **AGND and DGND**: Connect to **GND**.
- **CLK (Pin 13)**: Connect to **GPIO11 (Pin 23)**.
- **DOUT (Pin 12)**: Connect to **GPIO9 (Pin 21)**.
- **DIN (Pin 11)**: Connect to **GPIO10 (Pin 19)**.
- **CS/SHDN (Pin 10)**: Connect to **GPIO8 (Pin 24)**.

Step 4: Installing Required Software

You'll need to install the **spidev** library to communicate with the MCP3008 and read the thermistor's data:

1. Open the terminal on your Raspberry Pi.

Install **spidev**:

```
sudo apt-get update
sudo apt-get install python3-spidev
```

Step 5: Create the Python Script to Read Temperature

5.1 Open the Terminal

Open a terminal on your Raspberry Pi.

5.2 Write the Python Script

Use **Nano** to create a Python script:

nano thermistor_temperature.py

Now, write the following Python code to read the temperature data from the thermistor:

```python
import spidev
import time
import math  # For thermistor temperature calculation

# Set up SPI communication with MCP3008
spi = spidev.SpiDev()
spi.open(0, 0)
spi.max_speed_hz = 1350000

# Thermistor setup values
R_thermistor_nominal = 10000  # Resistance at 25 degrees Celsius
temp_nominal = 25  # Temperature for nominal resistance (in Celsius)
b_coefficient = 3950  # B coefficient of the thermistor
R_series = 10000  # Value of the series resistor (in ohms)

# Function to read data from the MCP3008 channel (0-7)
def read_channel(channel):
    adc = spi.xfer2([1, (8 + channel) << 4, 0])
    data = ((adc[1] & 3) << 8) + adc[2]
    return data

# Convert the ADC data to temperature in Celsius
def convert_to_temperature(adc_value):
    # Convert ADC value to resistance
    voltage = (adc_value * 3.3) / 1023
    R_thermistor = R_series * (3.3 / voltage - 1)

    # Calculate temperature using the Steinhart-Hart equation
    steinhart = R_thermistor / R_thermistor_nominal  # (R/R0)
    steinhart = math.log(steinhart)  # ln(R/R0)
    steinhart /= b_coefficient  # 1/B * ln(R/R0)
    steinhart += 1.0 / (temp_nominal + 273.15)  # + (1/T0)
    steinhart = 1.0 / steinhart  # Invert
    steinhart -= 273.15  # Convert to Celsius
```

```
        return steinhart

# Main loop to read and print temperature data
try:
    while True:
        # Read from channel 0 (where the thermistor is connected)
        adc_value = read_channel(0)
        temperature = convert_to_temperature(adc_value)
        print(f"Temperature: {temperature:.2f} °C")
        time.sleep(1)

except KeyboardInterrupt:
    spi.close()
```

5.3 Save the Script

- Press `Ctrl + X` to exit Nano.

- Press `Y` to confirm saving.
- Hit `Enter` to save the file.

Step 6: Running the Python Script

6.1 Run the Script

To run the script, type:

```
python3 thermistor_temperature.py
```

6.2 Observe the Temperature Data

As the script runs, you'll see temperature readings displayed in the terminal. The temperature will update every second, and you'll see something like this:

```
Temperature: 23.45 °C
```

Move the thermistor into a warmer or cooler area, and the temperature readings should change accordingly.

Step 7: Customize the Script for Fun Projects

Want to take it further? How about using the thermistor to control a fan when the temperature gets too high?

Here's an example that turns on an LED if the temperature rises above 30°C:

```python
import RPi.GPIO as GPIO
led_pin = 18
GPIO.setmode(GPIO.BCM)
GPIO.setup(led_pin, GPIO.OUT)

# Threshold temperature to trigger the LED
temp_threshold = 30.0  # Celsius

try:
    while True:
        adc_value = read_channel(0)
        temperature = convert_to_temperature(adc_value)
        print(f"Temperature: {temperature:.2f} °C")

        if temperature > temp_threshold:
            GPIO.output(led_pin, GPIO.HIGH)  # Turn on LED
        else:
            GPIO.output(led_pin, GPIO.LOW)   # Turn off LED

        time.sleep(1)

except KeyboardInterrupt:
    GPIO.cleanup()
    spi.close()
```

Common Mistakes

1. **Incorrect Wiring**: Double-check the connections between the thermistor, MCP3008, and Raspberry Pi.

No Readings?: Ensure SPI is enabled on your Raspberry Pi. You can enable it by running this command:

```
sudo raspi-config
```

2. Then, go to **Interfacing Options > SPI** and enable it.

- **Temperature Fluctuations?**: If your temperature readings are unstable, try improving the connections or shielding the sensor from airflow.
- **No Temperature Reading?**: Make sure all wires are securely connected, and the script is set up correctly.

Expansion Ideas

Once you've mastered reading temperature with a thermistor, try adding more features:

- **Data Logging**: Track temperature changes over time and log the data.
- **Temperature-Controlled Devices**: Use temperature to control fans, heaters, or other appliances.
- **Multiple Sensors**: Use other MCP3008 channels to add more sensors for multi-room monitoring.

Tip: Start simple by just reading the temperature, and once you're comfortable, expand to controlling devices like LEDs, fans, or alarms based on the temperature!

9.4 Detecting Methane

A methane sensor (often referred to as a **gas sensor** or **MQ-4 sensor**) detects methane (CH4) in the air. These sensors work by changing their resistance based on the concentration of methane gas, which you can measure with a Raspberry Pi to detect gas leaks or monitor air quality.

Why Detect Methane?

Methane is a flammable gas that can be hazardous in high concentrations. By detecting methane, you can build safety systems, such as gas leak detectors, or monitor methane levels in the environment.

Detecting Methane with a Raspberry Pi

Step 1: Gather Your Components

You will need:

- **Raspberry Pi** (any model with GPIO pins)
- **MQ-4 Methane Gas Sensor**
- **10kΩ Resistor** (for a voltage divider circuit)
- **MCP3008** (ADC to convert the sensor's analog signal into digital data)
- **Jumper wires** (Male to Female)
- **Breadboard** (optional, for easier connections)

Step 2: Understanding the MQ-4 Methane Sensor

The **MQ-4 sensor** has a built-in heating element that helps it detect methane gas. The sensor's resistance changes based on the concentration of methane:

- **Higher methane concentration** → lower resistance.

- **Lower methane concentration** → higher resistance.

To measure this change, we use a **voltage divider** circuit and an **MCP3008** Analog-to-Digital Converter (ADC) to read the sensor's analog signal with the Raspberry Pi.

3.1 Connect the Methane Sensor

Here's how to wire the MQ-4 sensor:

- **VCC pin** on the MQ-4: Connect to **3.3V** on the Raspberry Pi.
- **GND pin** on the MQ-4: Connect to **GND** on the Raspberry Pi.
- **A0 pin** (analog output) on the MQ-4: Connect to **Channel 0 (CH0)** on the MCP3008.

3.2 Build the Voltage Divider Circuit

We need a voltage divider to measure the sensor's resistance:

- **One leg of the 10kΩ resistor** connects to **GND** on the Raspberry Pi.
- **The other leg of the 10kΩ resistor** connects to **CH0** on the MCP3008 and the **A0 pin** on the sensor.

3.3 Connect the MCP3008 to the Raspberry Pi

To read the analog data from the MQ-4 sensor, wire the MCP3008 as follows:

- **VDD**: Connect to **3.3V** on the Raspberry Pi.
- **VREF**: Connect to **3.3V** (reference voltage).
- **AGND and DGND**: Connect to **GND**.
- **CLK (Pin 13)**: Connect to **GPIO11 (Pin 23)**.
- **DOUT (Pin 12)**: Connect to **GPIO9 (Pin 21)**.
- **DIN (Pin 11)**: Connect to **GPIO10 (Pin 19)**.
- **CS/SHDN (Pin 10)**: Connect to **GPIO8 (Pin 24)**.

You'll need to install the **spidev** library to communicate with the MCP3008 and read the methane sensor data:

1. Open the terminal on your Raspberry Pi.

Install **spidev**:

```
sudo apt-get update
sudo apt-get install python3-spidev
```

Step 5: Create the Python Script to Read Methane Levels

5.1 Open the Terminal

Open the terminal on your Raspberry Pi.

5.2 Write the Python Script

Create a Python script using Nano:

```
nano methane_sensor.py
```

Now, write or paste the following Python code to read the methane gas data from the MQ-4 sensor:

```python
import spidev
import time
# Set up SPI communication with MCP3008
spi = spidev.SpiDev()
spi.open(0, 0)
spi.max_speed_hz = 1350000
# Function to read data from the MCP3008 channel (0-7)
def read_channel(channel):
    adc = spi.xfer2([1, (8 + channel) << 4, 0])
    data = ((adc[1] & 3) << 8) + adc[2]
    return data
# Convert the ADC value to a voltage
def convert_to_voltage(adc_value):
    return (adc_value * 3.3) / 1023

# Main loop to read methane sensor data
try:
    while True:
        # Read from channel 0 (where the MQ-4 sensor is connected)
        methane_level = read_channel(0)
        voltage = convert_to_voltage(methane_level)
        print(f"Methane level: {methane_level}, Voltage:
{voltage:.2f}V")
        time.sleep(1)

except KeyboardInterrupt:
    spi.close()
```

5.3 Save the Script

- Press `Ctrl + X` to exit Nano.
- Press `Y` to confirm saving.
- Hit `Enter` to save the file.

Step 6: Running the Python Script

6.1 Run the Script

In the terminal, run the script:

```
python3 methane_sensor.py
```

6.2 Watch the Methane Readings

As the script runs, the methane levels and corresponding voltage will be printed to the terminal. If methane is detected, you should see the sensor values change:

```
Methane level: 450, Voltage: 1.50V
```

Blowing air or gas near the sensor should cause the readings to change.

Step 7: Customize the Script for Projects

You can extend this project to trigger an alert or activate a fan when methane levels rise above a safe threshold. Here's an example script that turns on an LED if methane levels exceed a set threshold:

```
import RPi.GPIO as GPIO
led_pin = 18
GPIO.setmode(GPIO.BCM)
GPIO.setup(led_pin, GPIO.OUT)

# Set a threshold for methane levels
methane_threshold = 400
```

```
try:
    while True:
        methane_level = read_channel(0)
        if methane_level > methane_threshold:
            GPIO.output(led_pin, GPIO.HIGH)  # Turn on LED (alert)
        else:
            GPIO.output(led_pin, GPIO.LOW)   # Turn off LED
        time.sleep(1)

except KeyboardInterrupt:
    GPIO.cleanup()
    spi.close()
```

Common Mistakes

1. **Incorrect Wiring**: Double-check that the MQ-4 sensor, MCP3008, and Raspberry Pi are wired correctly.

No Readings?: Ensure SPI is enabled on your Raspberry Pi by running this command:

```
sudo raspi-config
```

2. Go to **Interfacing Options** > **SPI** and enable it.

Troubleshooting Tips

- **Unstable Readings?**: Methane sensor readings can fluctuate, especially if there's air movement. Try shielding the sensor from drafts.
- **No Response to Gas?**: Ensure the sensor has been powered on for a few minutes (the sensor's heater needs time to warm up).

Once you're comfortable with the basic methane detection, you can expand your project:

- **Data Logging**: Record methane levels over time for environmental monitoring.
- **Multiple Gas Sensors**: Add other gas sensors (e.g., carbon monoxide, hydrogen) to your Raspberry Pi using additional channels on the MCP3008.
- **Methane-Activated Devices**: Use the sensor data to activate fans, alarms, or other safety devices.

Tip: Start with simple detection—just measuring the methane levels. Once you get comfortable with the sensor, you can add features like alerts, logs, or automated responses!

9.5 Measuring Voltage

Measuring voltage is determining how much electrical potential exists between two points in a circuit. A Raspberry Pi can measure voltage using an **Analog-to-Digital Converter (ADC)**, like the **MCP3008**, because the Pi itself doesn't have analog input pins.

Why Measure Voltage?
Measuring voltage allows you to monitor battery levels, check power supplies, or measure sensor outputs in your electronics projects.

Measuring Voltage with a Raspberry Pi

Step 1: Gather Your Components

To measure voltage with your Raspberry Pi, you will need:

- **Raspberry Pi** (any model with GPIO pins)
- **MCP3008** (Analog-to-Digital Converter)
- **Voltage source** (a battery or other voltage source to measure)
- **Jumper wires** (Male to Female)
- **Breadboard** (optional, for easier connections)

Step 2: How Voltage Measurement Works

The Raspberry Pi cannot directly measure voltage since it only reads digital signals. By using an **MCP3008** ADC, we can convert the voltage from the source into a digital value that the Raspberry Pi can process.

For this project, we'll measure a voltage between **0V and 3.3V**, which is safe for the Raspberry Pi's GPIO pins.

Step 3: Wiring the MCP3008 and Voltage Source

3.1 Connect the MCP3008 to the Raspberry Pi

The MCP3008 reads analog signals (like voltage) and sends digital data to the Raspberry Pi:

- **VDD**: Connect to **3.3V** on the Raspberry Pi.
- **VREF**: Connect to **3.3V** (this is the reference voltage).
- **AGND and DGND**: Connect both to **GND** on the Raspberry Pi.
- **CLK (Pin 13)**: Connect to **GPIO11 (Pin 23)**.
- **DOUT (Pin 12)**: Connect to **GPIO9 (Pin 21)**.
- **DIN (Pin 11)**: Connect to **GPIO10 (Pin 19)**.
- **CS/SHDN (Pin 10)**: Connect to **GPIO8 (Pin 24)**.

3.2 Connect the Voltage Source to the MCP3008

The voltage you want to measure will be connected to **Channel 0 (CH0)** of the MCP3008:

- **Positive terminal** of the voltage source: Connect to **CH0** on the MCP3008.
- **Negative terminal** (or ground) of the voltage source: Connect to **GND**.

Step 4: Installing Required Software

To communicate with the MCP3008, you need the **spidev** library:

1. Open the terminal on your Raspberry Pi.

Install the library:

```
sudo apt-get update
sudo apt-get install python3-spidev
```

Step 5: Create the Python Script to Measure Voltage

5.1 Open the Terminal

Open the terminal on your Raspberry Pi.

5.2 Write the Python Script

Create a new Python script using Nano:

```
nano voltage_measure.py
```

Now, write the following Python code to read the voltage:

```python
import spidev
import time

# Set up SPI communication with MCP3008
spi = spidev.SpiDev()
```

```
spi.open(0, 0)
spi.max_speed_hz = 1350000

# Function to read data from the MCP3008 channel (0-7)
def read_channel(channel):
    adc = spi.xfer2([1, (8 + channel) << 4, 0])
    data = ((adc[1] & 3) << 8) + adc[2]
    return data

# Convert the ADC data to a voltage value
def convert_to_voltage(adc_value):
    return (adc_value * 3.3) / 1023

# Main loop to read and print voltage
try:
    while True:
        # Read from channel 0 (where the voltage source is connected)
        adc_value = read_channel(0)
        voltage = convert_to_voltage(adc_value)
        print(f"Measured Voltage: {voltage:.2f}V")
        time.sleep(1)

except KeyboardInterrupt:
    spi.close()
```

5.3 Save the Script

- Press Ctrl + X to exit Nano.
- Press Y to confirm saving.
- Hit Enter to save the file.

Step 6: Running the Python Script

6.1 Run the Script

To run the Python script, type the following command in the terminal:

```
python3 voltage_measure.py
```

6.2 Observe the Voltage Readings

As the script runs, you'll see voltage values printed to the terminal:

```
Measured Voltage: 2.45V
```

If you connect different voltage sources, the reading will change accordingly.

Step 7: Customize the Script for Projects

You can modify the script to monitor voltage levels in real-time. For example, you could trigger an alert if the voltage drops below a certain value (useful for battery monitoring):

```python
import RPi.GPIO as GPIO

alert_pin = 18  # Pin connected to an LED or buzzer
GPIO.setmode(GPIO.BCM)
GPIO.setup(alert_pin, GPIO.OUT)

low_voltage_threshold = 2.0  # Set your own threshold

try:
    while True:
        adc_value = read_channel(0)
        voltage = convert_to_voltage(adc_value)
        print(f"Measured Voltage: {voltage:.2f}V")

        if voltage < low_voltage_threshold:
            GPIO.output(alert_pin, GPIO.HIGH)   # Turn on LED/buzzer
        else:
            GPIO.output(alert_pin, GPIO.LOW)    # Turn off LED/buzzer

        time.sleep(1)

except KeyboardInterrupt:
    GPIO.cleanup()
    spi.close()
```

Common Mistakes

1. **Incorrect Wiring**: Double-check the connections between the voltage source, MCP3008, and Raspberry Pi.

No Readings?: Make sure the SPI interface is enabled on your Raspberry Pi by running:

```
sudo raspi-config
```

2. Then go to **Interfacing Options** > **SPI** and enable it.

Troubleshooting Tips

- **Voltage Not Displaying Correctly?**: Ensure the voltage source is within the 0-3.3V range. Higher voltages may damage the Raspberry Pi or MCP3008.
- **Fluctuating Readings?**: If the voltage readings are unstable, try checking your wiring or using shorter jumper wires to reduce interference.

Expansion Ideas

Once you're comfortable measuring basic voltages, try these advanced ideas:

- **Battery Monitoring**: Measure and track battery voltage levels over time to monitor power consumption.
- **Multi-Channel Monitoring**: Use other MCP3008 channels to measure multiple voltages at once.
- **Logging Voltage Data**: Store the voltage readings in a file to log data over time for analysis.

Tip: Start by measuring a known voltage, like from a battery, before moving on to more complex circuits or systems. Keep experimenting, and you'll soon be comfortable monitoring different voltage sources!

9.6 Measuring Temperature with an ADC

An **Analog-to-Digital Converter (ADC)** takes analog signals (like temperature readings from a sensor) and converts them into digital data that the Raspberry Pi can understand. One commonly used ADC is the **MCP3008**.

Why Measure Temperature with an ADC?
By using an ADC and a temperature sensor, you can easily monitor environmental conditions with your Raspberry Pi. This is great for building projects like weather stations, smart thermostats, or temperature alarms.

Measuring Temperature with an ADC and Raspberry Pi

Step 1: Gather Your Components

You will need:

- **Raspberry Pi** (any model with GPIO pins)
- **MCP3008** (Analog-to-Digital Converter)
- **Temperature sensor** (such as a **NTC thermistor** or an **LM35**)
- **10kΩ Resistor** (for a voltage divider if using a thermistor)
- **Jumper wires** (Male to Female)
- **Breadboard** (optional, for easier connections)

Step 2: How the ADC and Temperature Sensor Work

The temperature sensor changes its output based on the temperature:

- **Thermistor**: Resistance changes with temperature.
- **LM35**: Outputs a voltage directly proportional to the temperature.

The ADC converts the temperature sensor's analog output into digital data that the Raspberry Pi can process.

Step 3: Setting Up the Circuit

3.1 Connect the MCP3008 to the Raspberry Pi

The MCP3008 will convert the sensor's analog signal to a digital value:

- **VDD**: Connect to **3.3V** on the Raspberry Pi.
- **VREF**: Connect to **3.3V** (reference voltage).
- **AGND and DGND**: Connect both to **GND** on the Raspberry Pi.
- **CLK (Pin 13)**: Connect to **GPIO11 (Pin 23)**.
- **DOUT (Pin 12)**: Connect to **GPIO9 (Pin 21)**.
- **DIN (Pin 11)**: Connect to **GPIO10 (Pin 19)**.
- **CS/SHDN (Pin 10)**: Connect to **GPIO8 (Pin 24)**.

3.2 Connect the Temperature Sensor

If using a **thermistor**:

- **One leg of the thermistor** goes to **3.3V**.
- **Other leg** connects to **Channel 0 (CH0)** on the MCP3008 and **one side of a 10kΩ resistor**.
- **Other side of the 10kΩ resistor** connects to **GND**.

If using an **LM35**:

- **VCC pin**: Connect to **3.3V**.
- **GND pin**: Connect to **GND**.
- **Output pin**: Connect to **CH0** on the MCP3008.

Step 4: Install Required Software

To communicate with the MCP3008, you'll need to install the **spidev** library:

    1.   Open the terminal on your Raspberry Pi.

Install the library:

```
sudo apt-get update
sudo apt-get install python3-spidev
```

Step 5: Create the Python Script to Measure Temperature

5.1 Open the Terminal

On your Raspberry Pi, open a terminal.

5.2 Write the Python Script

Create a Python script using **Nano**:

```
nano temp_measure.py
```

Paste this Python code, which reads the temperature from the sensor:

```python
import spidev
import time
import math   # For thermistor calculation if using one

# Set up SPI communication with MCP3008
spi = spidev.SpiDev()
spi.open(0, 0)
spi.max_speed_hz = 1350000

# Function to read data from MCP3008 channel (0-7)
def read_channel(channel):
    adc = spi.xfer2([1, (8 + channel) << 4, 0])
    data = ((adc[1] & 3) << 8) + adc[2]
    return data

# Convert ADC value to voltage
```

```python
def convert_to_voltage(adc_value):
    return (adc_value * 3.3) / 1023

# Thermistor-specific temperature calculation (Steinhart-Hart equation)
def thermistor_temperature(adc_value):
    R_thermistor_nominal = 10000  # Resistance at 25°C
    temp_nominal = 25  # Nominal temperature (Celsius)
    b_coefficient = 3950  # B coefficient of thermistor
    R_series = 10000  # Series resistor value (10kΩ)

    # Convert ADC value to resistance
    voltage = convert_to_voltage(adc_value)
    R_thermistor = R_series * (3.3 / voltage - 1)

    # Apply Steinhart-Hart equation to find temperature in Celsius
    steinhart = R_thermistor / R_thermistor_nominal  # (R/R0)
    steinhart = math.log(steinhart)  # ln(R/R0)
    steinhart /= b_coefficient  # 1/B * ln(R/R0)
    steinhart += 1.0 / (temp_nominal + 273.15)  # + (1/T0)
    steinhart = 1.0 / steinhart  # Invert
    steinhart -= 273.15  # Convert to Celsius

    return steinhart

# Main loop to read temperature from thermistor or LM35
try:
    while True:
        adc_value = read_channel(0)
        if using_thermistor:  # Set this based on your sensor
            temperature = thermistor_temperature(adc_value)
        else:  # LM35 outputs voltage directly proportional to
temperature
            voltage = convert_to_voltage(adc_value)
            temperature = voltage * 100  # LM35 gives 10mV/°C

        print(f"Temperature: {temperature:.2f} °C")
        time.sleep(1)

except KeyboardInterrupt:
    spi.close()
```

5.3 Save the Script

- Press Ctrl + X to exit Nano.
- Press Y to confirm saving.
- Hit Enter to save the file.

Step 6: Running the Python Script

6.1 Run the Script

Run the script by typing:

```
python3 temp_measure.py
```

6.2 Watch the Temperature Readings

As the script runs, the temperature will be displayed in the terminal, updating every second:

```
Temperature: 22.45 °C
```

Move the sensor to a warmer or cooler place to see the readings change.

Step 7: Customize the Script for Projects

Want to add some functionality? You can trigger an action when the temperature reaches a certain threshold. For example, turning on an LED when it gets too hot:

```python
import RPi.GPIO as GPIO
led_pin = 18  # LED connected to GPIO 18
GPIO.setmode(GPIO.BCM)
GPIO.setup(led_pin, GPIO.OUT)
temp_threshold = 30  # Temperature threshold in Celsius

try:
    while True:
        adc_value = read_channel(0)
        temperature = thermistor_temperature(adc_value)  # Or LM35
calculation
        print(f"Temperature: {temperature:.2f} °C")

        if temperature > temp_threshold:
            GPIO.output(led_pin, GPIO.HIGH)  # Turn on LED
        else:
            GPIO.output(led_pin, GPIO.LOW)   # Turn off LED

        time.sleep(1)

except KeyboardInterrupt:
    GPIO.cleanup()
    spi.close()
```

Common Mistakes

1. **Incorrect Wiring**: Ensure the temperature sensor, MCP3008, and Raspberry Pi are connected correctly.

No Readings?: Check if SPI is enabled on your Raspberry Pi. You can enable it by running:

```
sudo raspi-config
```

2. Go to **Interfacing Options** > **SPI** and enable it.

Troubleshooting Tips

- **Fluctuating Readings?**: If the temperature readings are unstable, double-check the wiring or use shorter jumper wires to reduce interference.
- **No Data?**: Ensure the sensor and MCP3008 are correctly powered and connected to the right GPIO pins.

Expansion Ideas

Once you've mastered temperature measurement, try adding these features:

- **Data Logging**: Record temperature data over time for environmental monitoring.
- **Temperature-Controlled Devices**: Use temperature readings to control devices like fans or heaters.
- **Multi-Sensor Projects**: Use other channels on the MCP3008 to add more sensors, such as additional temperature sensors in different rooms.

Tip: Start simple by measuring the temperature with one sensor, then gradually add features like triggers and logging. Keep experimenting, and you'll get more comfortable with sensor-based projects!

9.7 Measuring the Raspberry Pi CPU Temperature

Why Measure the CPU Temperature?

The Raspberry Pi's CPU can get hot, especially when running heavy tasks. Monitoring the CPU temperature helps you ensure your Pi runs efficiently and prevent overheating issues. If the CPU gets too hot, it might throttle its performance or even shut down to prevent damage.

Good News: You don't need any external sensors for this— Raspberry Pi has a built-in way to measure its CPU temperature!

Measuring the Raspberry Pi CPU Temperature

Step 1: Use a Simple Terminal Command

The easiest way to check the CPU temperature is to run a command directly from the terminal.

1. Open the **Terminal** on your Raspberry Pi.

Type the following command to check the current CPU temperature:
`vcgencmd measure_temp`

This will return a result like:

`temp=45.2'C`

This tells you the CPU temperature in degrees Celsius.

Step 2: Create a Python Script to Continuously Monitor CPU Temperature

If you want to continuously monitor the CPU temperature or log it for later analysis, you can create a simple Python script.

2.1 Open the Terminal

Open the terminal to create a Python script.

2.2 Create a Python Script

Type the following command to create a new Python script using **Nano**:

```
nano cpu_temp.py
```

2.3 Write the Python Code

Now, type or paste this code into the editor to read and display the CPU temperature:

```python
import os
import time

# Function to read CPU temperature
def get_cpu_temp():
    temp = os.popen("vcgencmd measure_temp").readline()
    return temp.replace("temp=", "").strip()

# Main loop to read and print CPU temperature
try:
    while True:
        cpu_temp = get_cpu_temp()
        print(f"CPU Temperature: {cpu_temp}")
        time.sleep(2)  # Wait for 2 seconds before the next reading

except KeyboardInterrupt:
    print("Program stopped.")
```

2.4 Save the Script

To save the script:

- Press Ctrl + X to exit Nano.
- Press Y to confirm saving.

- Press Enter to save the file with the name **cpu_temp.py**.

Step 3: Run the Python Script

3.1 Run the Script

In the terminal, type the following command to run your script:

```
python3 cpu_temp.py
```

3.2 Observe the Temperature

You'll see the CPU temperature printed in the terminal every 2 seconds:

```
CPU Temperature: 45.2'C
```

To stop the program, press Ctrl + C.

Step 4: Customize the Script

Want to take it a step further? You can add functionality like triggering an alert or taking action when the CPU temperature gets too high. For example, turning on an LED when the temperature exceeds 70°C:

4.1 Example: Turn on an LED if the CPU Is Too Hot

Add the following code to your Python script to control an LED based on the CPU temperature:

```
import os
import time
import RPi.GPIO as GPIO

# Set up the GPIO pin for the LED
led_pin = 18
GPIO.setmode(GPIO.BCM)
GPIO.setup(led_pin, GPIO.OUT)

# Function to read CPU temperature
```

```
def get_cpu_temp():
    temp = os.popen("vcgencmd measure_temp").readline()
    return float(temp.replace("temp=", "").replace("'C", "").strip())

# Main loop to read CPU temperature and control the LED
try:
    while True:
        cpu_temp = get_cpu_temp()
        print(f"CPU Temperature: {cpu_temp}°C")

        if cpu_temp > 70:   # Turn on LED if temperature is above 70°C
            GPIO.output(led_pin, GPIO.HIGH)
        else:   # Turn off LED if temperature is below 70°C
            GPIO.output(led_pin, GPIO.LOW)

        time.sleep(2)

except KeyboardInterrupt:
    GPIO.cleanup()   # Clean up GPIO when the program is interrupted
```

Common Mistakes

1. **Script Not Running**: Make sure you are using Python 3. Run the script with `python3` instead of `python`.
2. **Incorrect GPIO Pin Setup**: If you use the GPIO pin for an LED, double-check the wiring and ensure the correct pin is specified in the code.

Troubleshooting Tips

- **Temperature Seems Too High**: If the CPU temperature is consistently above 70°C, consider adding a cooling solution like a heatsink or fan.
- **Script Not Working?**: Ensure that the `vcgencmd` command works by running it directly in the terminal. If it does, check for any typos in the Python code.

Once you've mastered basic CPU temperature monitoring, try adding more features:

- **Log Data**: Store CPU temperature readings in a file to monitor temperature changes over time.
- **Auto-Shutdown**: Create a script that shuts down the Raspberry Pi if the CPU temperature gets too high to prevent damage.

Tip: Start by reading the CPU temperature from the terminal. Once you're comfortable, move on to creating a Python script to monitor it automatically, and then add fun features like alerts or cooling control!

9.8 Measuring Temperature Using a Digital Sensor

A digital temperature sensor, like the **DS18B20**, directly provides temperature readings in a digital format, which the Raspberry Pi can read without needing an **Analog-to-Digital Converter (ADC)**. This makes it easier to measure temperature accurately with minimal wiring.

Why Use a Digital Sensor?
Digital sensors like the DS18B20 are precise, easy to set up, and don't require complex circuits, making them ideal for beginners. You can use them in projects like weather stations, thermostats, or even to monitor the temperature of your Raspberry Pi!

Measuring Temperature with a Digital Sensor and Raspberry Pi

Step 1: Gather Your Components

You will need:

- **Raspberry Pi** (any model with GPIO pins)
- **DS18B20 digital temperature sensor**
- **4.7kΩ Resistor** (for pull-up resistance)
- **Jumper wires** (Male to Female)
- **Breadboard** (optional, for easier wiring)

Step 2: Wiring the DS18B20 Sensor to the Raspberry Pi

2.1 Connect the DS18B20 Sensor

The DS18B20 has three pins: **VCC**, **GND**, and **Data**.

- **VCC** (Power): Connect to **3.3V** on the Raspberry Pi.
- **GND**: Connect to **GND** on the Raspberry Pi.
- **Data**: Connect to **GPIO4 (Pin 7)** on the Raspberry Pi.

2.2 Add the 4.7kΩ Resistor

Place the **4.7kΩ resistor** between the **Data** pin and the **3.3V** pin. This acts as a **pull-up resistor**, ensuring the sensor works properly.

Step 3: Enable the 1-Wire Interface on the Raspberry Pi

The DS18B20 uses the **1-Wire protocol**, which you need to enable.

1. Open the terminal on your Raspberry Pi.

Run the following command to enable the 1-Wire interface:

```
sudo raspi-config
```

2. Go to **Interfacing Options** > **1-Wire** > **Enable**.

Reboot your Raspberry Pi:

```
sudo reboot
```

Step 4: Verify the Sensor Connection

Once your Pi reboots, open the terminal and run:

```
ls /sys/bus/w1/devices/
```

1. You should see a folder that starts with $28-$, followed by a long ID number. This confirms that your sensor is connected and recognized.

Step 5: Read Temperature from the DS18B20

To read the temperature from the sensor:

Navigate to the sensor's directory:

```
cd /sys/bus/w1/devices/28-xxxx/   # Replace 'xxxx' with your sensor's ID
```

Read the sensor data:

```
cat w1_slave
```

This will display two lines of output. The temperature is shown at the end of the second line as a string like $t=23450$. This means the temperature is **23.45°C**.

Step 6: Create a Python Script to Continuously Monitor Temperature

If you want to monitor the temperature automatically and display it, you can write a Python script.

6.1 Open the Terminal

Open the terminal to create the Python script.

6.2 Create a Python Script

Type the following command to create a Python script using **Nano**:

```
nano ds18b20_temp.py
```

6.3 Write the Python Code

Now, type or paste this code into the script to read the temperature from the DS18B20 sensor:

```python
import os
import glob
import time

# Initialize the 1-Wire interface
os.system('modprobe w1-gpio')
os.system('modprobe w1-therm')

# Get the sensor directory
base_dir = '/sys/bus/w1/devices/'
device_folder = glob.glob(base_dir + '28*')[0]    # Detect the sensor
device_file = device_folder + '/w1_slave'

# Function to read raw temperature data from sensor
def read_temp_raw():
    with open(device_file, 'r') as f:
        lines = f.readlines()
    return lines

# Function to convert raw data to temperature in Celsius
def read_temp():
    lines = read_temp_raw()
    while lines[0].strip()[-3:] != 'YES':
        time.sleep(0.2)
```

```
        lines = read_temp_raw()
    equals_pos = lines[1].find('t=')
    if equals_pos != -1:
        temp_string = lines[1][equals_pos+2:]
        temp_c = float(temp_string) / 1000.0
        return temp_c

# Main loop to read and print the temperature
try:
    while True:
        temp = read_temp()
        print(f"Temperature: {temp:.2f}°C")
        time.sleep(2)   # Wait 2 seconds between readings

except KeyboardInterrupt:
    print("Program stopped.")
```

6.4 Save the Script

To save the script:

- Press Ctrl + X to exit Nano.
- Press Y to confirm saving.
- Press Enter to save the file with the name
  ds18b20_temp.py.

Step 7: Run the Python Script

7.1 Run the Script
To run the script, type:

```
python3 ds18b20_temp.py
```

7.2 Watch the Temperature Readings
You'll see the temperature readings printed every 2 seconds:

```
Temperature: 23.45°C
```

To stop the program, press Ctrl + C.

Step 8: Customize the Script

You can easily modify the script to add features like triggering an alert or turning on a fan if the temperature exceeds a certain value.

8.1 Example: Turn on an LED if the Temperature Is Too High

Add the following code to your script to turn on an LED if the temperature exceeds 30°C:

```python
import RPi.GPIO as GPIO

# Set up GPIO pin for LED
led_pin = 18
GPIO.setmode(GPIO.BCM)
GPIO.setup(led_pin, GPIO.OUT)

# Main loop to read temperature and control LED
try:
    while True:
        temp = read_temp()
        print(f"Temperature: {temp:.2f}°C")

        if temp > 30.0:
            GPIO.output(led_pin, GPIO.HIGH)  # Turn on LED
        else:
            GPIO.output(led_pin, GPIO.LOW)   # Turn off LED

        time.sleep(2)

except KeyboardInterrupt:
    GPIO.cleanup()
```

Common Mistakes

1. **Sensor Not Recognized**: If the sensor folder doesn't appear under /sys/bus/w1/devices/, double-check your wiring and ensure the 1-Wire interface is enabled.
2. **No Readings**: Make sure the pull-up resistor is connected between the data pin and 3.3V.

Troubleshooting Tips

- **Incorrect Temperature**: Make sure the sensor is wired correctly and the pull-up resistor is in place.
- **No Data?**: Ensure the 1-Wire interface is enabled in `raspi-config`.

Expansion Ideas

Once you're comfortable with basic temperature measurement, try adding more features:

- **Data Logging**: Save temperature data over time to analyze environmental changes.
- **Multiple Sensors**: You can connect several DS18B20 sensors to the same data pin and measure temperatures in multiple locations.
- **Temperature-Controlled Devices**: Use temperature data to control fans, heaters, or alarms.

Tip: Start by reading temperature from one sensor. Once you've mastered the basics, you can expand your project by adding more sensors or triggering devices based on temperature changes!

9.9 Sensing a Magnet with a Reed Switch

A **reed switch** is a magnetic switch that opens and closes when exposed to a magnetic field. When a magnet is nearby, the switch closes (completes the circuit); when the magnet is removed, the switch opens. This makes it useful for detecting the presence of a magnet in projects like door sensors, alarms, or proximity detection.

Why Use a Reed Switch?

Reed switches are simple, reliable, and can detect the presence or absence of a magnet. They're great for building projects like magnetic door sensors or even creating interactive toys that respond to magnets.

Sensing a Magnet with a Reed Switch and Raspberry Pi

Step 1: Gather Your Components

You will need:

- **Raspberry Pi** (any model with GPIO pins)
- **Reed switch** (any normally open type)
- **Magnet** (to trigger the reed switch)
- **10kΩ Resistor** (for pull-down resistance)
- **Jumper wires** (Male to Female)
- **Breadboard** (optional, for easier wiring)

Step 2: Wiring the Reed Switch to the Raspberry Pi

2.1 Connect the Reed Switch

- **One leg of the reed switch**: Connect to **GPIO17 (Pin 11)** on the Raspberry Pi.
- **Other leg of the reed switch**: Connect to **GND** on the Raspberry Pi.

2.2 Add a 10kΩ Pull-Down Resistor

Place a **10kΩ resistor** between the **GPIO17** pin and **GND**. This ensures the GPIO pin reads **LOW** when the reed switch is open.

Step 3: Write the Python Script to Detect the Magnet

3.1 Open the Terminal

On your Raspberry Pi, open the terminal.

3.2 Create the Python Script

Use **Nano** to create a new Python script:

nano reed_switch.py

3.3 Write the Python Code

Paste this code to detect when the reed switch is activated by the magnet

```
import RPi.GPIO as GPIO
import time

# Set up the GPIO pin for the reed switch
reed_pin = 17
GPIO.setmode(GPIO.BCM)
GPIO.setup(reed_pin, GPIO.IN, pull_up_down=GPIO.PUD_DOWN)

# Main loop to detect the magnet
try:
    while True:
        if GPIO.input(reed_pin) == GPIO.HIGH:
            print("Magnet detected!")
        else:
            print("No magnet detected.")
        time.sleep(0.5)   # Check every 0.5 seconds

except KeyboardInterrupt:
    GPIO.cleanup()
```

3.4 Save the Script

- Press Ctrl + X to exit Nano.
- Press Y to confirm saving.
- Press Enter to save the file as **reed_switch.py**.

Step 4: Run the Python Script

4.1 Run the Script

To run the script, type:

```
python3 reed_switch.py
```

4.2 Test the Reed Switch

Move the magnet near the reed switch. When the magnet is close enough, you'll see a message like:

```
Magnet detected!
```

When you move the magnet away, the script will print

```
No magnet detected.
```

Step 5: Customize the Script

You can modify the script to trigger actions, like turning on an LED or sounding a buzzer when the magnet is detected.

5.1 Example: Turn on an LED When a Magnet Is Detected

Here's how you can modify the script to turn on an LED when the magnet closes the reed switch:

```python
# Set up an LED on GPIO18
led_pin = 18
GPIO.setup(led_pin, GPIO.OUT)
# Main loop to detect magnet and control LED
try:
    while True:
        if GPIO.input(reed_pin) == GPIO.HIGH:
            print("Magnet detected!")
            GPIO.output(led_pin, GPIO.HIGH)  # Turn on LED
        else:
            print("No magnet detected.")
            GPIO.output(led_pin, GPIO.LOW)  # Turn off LED
        time.sleep(0.5)

except KeyboardInterrupt:
    GPIO.cleanup()
```

Common Mistakes

1. **Incorrect Wiring**: Make sure the reed switch is connected to the correct GPIO pin and GND, with the pull-down resistor properly connected.
2. **No Detection**: If the script doesn't detect the magnet, ensure the magnet is strong enough to close the reed switch and is positioned correctly.

Troubleshooting Tips

- **No Response from the Reed Switch**: Double-check the wiring, especially the pull-down resistor. Ensure the reed switch and magnet are aligned properly.
- **Unstable Readings**: If the readings are unstable, try using a debounce mechanism in the code to avoid false triggers from switch bounce.

Expansion Ideas

Once you're comfortable using a reed switch, try adding more functionality to your project:

- **Magnetic Door Sensor**: Use the reed switch to detect when a door or window is opened.
- **Multiple Switches**: Connect several reed switches to different GPIO pins for multi-point detection.
- **Activate Devices**: Use the reed switch to trigger devices like lights, alarms, or motors when a magnet is detected.

Tip: Start with a simple project where you detect the magnet with a reed switch. Once you've got the basics down, you can add more features like activating devices or building security systems that respond to magnets!

9.10 Measuring Distance Using Ultrasound

An ultrasonic sensor (like the **HC-SR04**) uses sound waves to measure distance. It sends out an ultrasonic pulse and measures the time it takes for the pulse to bounce back after hitting an object. By knowing the speed of sound, you can calculate the distance to the object.

Why Measure Distance?
Measuring distance with ultrasound is perfect for projects like obstacle detection, automated parking systems, or even distance-based alarms.

Measuring Distance with an Ultrasonic Sensor and Raspberry Pi

Step 1: Gather Your Components

You will need:

- **Raspberry Pi** (any model with GPIO pins)
- **HC-SR04 Ultrasonic Distance Sensor**
- **330Ω Resistor** (to protect the GPIO pins)
- **470Ω Resistor** (to create a voltage divider for the Echo pin)
- **Jumper wires** (Male to Female)
- **Breadboard** (optional, for easier wiring)

Step 2: Wiring the HC-SR04 Ultrasonic Sensor to the Raspberry Pi

The HC-SR04 has four pins: **VCC**, **Trig**, **Echo**, and **GND**.

2.1 Connect the HC-SR04 Sensor

- **VCC (5V)**: Connect to the **5V pin (Pin 2)** on the Raspberry Pi.
- **GND**: Connect to **GND (Pin 6)** on the Raspberry Pi.
- **Trig**: Connect to **GPIO23 (Pin 16)** on the Raspberry Pi.
- **Echo**: Connect to **GPIO24 (Pin 18)** on the Raspberry Pi, using a **voltage divider**.

2.2 Build a Voltage Divider for the Echo Pin

The HC-SR04 uses 5V for the Echo pin, but the Raspberry Pi's GPIO pins expect 3.3V. To protect the Pi, we'll use two resistors (330Ω and 470Ω) to create a voltage divider:

- Connect the **Echo pin** to one end of the **330Ω resistor**.
- Connect the other end of the **330Ω resistor** to **GPIO24 (Pin 18)**.
- Connect the **470Ω resistor** between **GPIO24** and **GND**.

This setup safely steps down the voltage from 5V to around 3.3V for the Echo pin.

Step 3: Create the Python Script to Measure Distance

3.1 Open the Terminal

Open the terminal on your Raspberry Pi to create a Python script.

3.2 Create a Python Script

Type the following command to create a new Python script using **Nano**:

```
nano ultrasonic_distance.py
```

3.3 Write the Python Code

Now, paste the following Python code to measure distance using the HC-SR04 sensor:

```python
import RPi.GPIO as GPIO
import time

# Set up GPIO pins
GPIO.setmode(GPIO.BCM)
TRIG = 23  # GPIO pin for Trig
ECHO = 24  # GPIO pin for Echo

# Set up Trig as output and Echo as input
GPIO.setup(TRIG, GPIO.OUT)
GPIO.setup(ECHO, GPIO.IN)

# Function to measure distance
def measure_distance():
    # Send a 10µs pulse to trigger the sensor
    GPIO.output(TRIG, True)
    time.sleep(0.00001)  # 10µs pulse
    GPIO.output(TRIG, False)

    # Wait for Echo to go HIGH (start of pulse)
    while GPIO.input(ECHO) == 0:
        pulse_start = time.time()

    # Wait for Echo to go LOW (end of pulse)
    while GPIO.input(ECHO) == 1:
        pulse_end = time.time()

    # Calculate pulse duration
    pulse_duration = pulse_end - pulse_start

    # Calculate distance (speed of sound is 34300 cm/s)
    distance = pulse_duration * 17150  # Divide by 2 (go and back)

    return round(distance, 2)  # Return distance in cm

# Main loop to continuously measure distance
try:
    while True:
        dist = measure_distance()
        print(f"Distance: {dist} cm")
        time.sleep(1)  # Wait 1 second before the next measurement

except KeyboardInterrupt:
    GPIO.cleanup()  # Clean up GPIO pins when the script is interrupted
```

3.4 Save the Script

To save the script:

- Press `Ctrl + X` to exit Nano.
- Press `Y` to confirm saving.
- Press `Enter` to save the file as **ultrasonic_distance.py**.

Step 4: Run the Python Script

4.1 Run the Script

To run the script, type:

```
python3 ultrasonic_distance.py
```

4.2 Watch the Distance Readings

As the script runs, you'll see the measured distance printed in the terminal every second:

```
Distance: 56.34 cm
```

Move an object closer or farther from the sensor to see the readings change.

Step 5: Customize the Script

You can modify the script to trigger actions when the distance is within a certain range, such as turning on an LED or sounding an alarm if an object is too close.

5.1 Example: Trigger an LED When an Object Is Too Close

Here's how you can modify the script to turn on an LED if the measured distance is less than 20 cm:

```python
# Set up GPIO pin for an LED
led_pin = 18
GPIO.setup(led_pin, GPIO.OUT)

# Main loop to measure distance and control the LED
try:
    while True:
        dist = measure_distance()
        print(f"Distance: {dist} cm")

        if dist < 20:  # Turn on LED if object is closer than 20 cm
            GPIO.output(led_pin, GPIO.HIGH)
        else:
            GPIO.output(led_pin, GPIO.LOW)

        time.sleep(1)

except KeyboardInterrupt:
    GPIO.cleanup()
```

Common Mistakes

1. **Incorrect Wiring**: Double-check the wiring, especially the **voltage divider** for the Echo pin to avoid damaging the Raspberry Pi's GPIO.
2. **No Readings**: Ensure that the **Trig** and **Echo** pins are connected to the correct GPIO pins and that the sensor is powered.

Troubleshooting Tips

- **No Distance Reading?**: Check that the sensor is properly powered (5V and GND) and that the Trig and Echo pins are correctly wired.
- **Unstable Readings**: If the readings fluctuate, try reducing interference by shielding the sensor or using shorter jumper wires.

Once you've mastered basic distance measurement, try adding more features to your project:

- **Distance-Based Alarms**: Trigger an alarm or notification when an object comes within a certain distance.
- **Obstacle Avoidance**: Use multiple sensors for obstacle detection in robotics or automated systems.
- **Distance Logging**: Record distance readings over time to track object movement or proximity changes.

Tip: Start by measuring distance with the HC-SR04 sensor. Once you've got it working, you can add fun features like turning on LEDs, sounding alarms, or logging data based on distance!

Chapter 10: Using Displays with Raspberry Pi

10.1 Using a Four-Digit LED Display

A **four-digit LED display** allows you to show numbers or text by controlling four 7-segment displays, which can represent digits from 0 to 9. This is useful for displaying numbers like a countdown timer, score, temperature, or time.

Why Use a Four-Digit LED Display?
It's a simple and effective way to present data visually in your projects, such as showing the time, sensor readings, or any numeric output.

Step-by-Step Guide: Using a Four-Digit LED Display with Raspberry Pi

Step 1: Gather Your Components

You will need:

- **Raspberry Pi** (any model with GPIO pins)
- **TM1637 4-Digit LED Display Module** (a popular module for beginners)
- **Jumper wires** (Male to Female)
- **Breadboard** (optional, for easier wiring)

Step 2: Wiring the 4-Digit LED Display to the Raspberry Pi

The **TM1637** display module has four pins: **VCC**, **GND**, **DIO** (Data), and **CLK** (Clock).

2.1 Connect the TM1637 to the Raspberry Pi

- **VCC**: Connect to **3.3V (Pin 1)** on the Raspberry Pi.
- **GND**: Connect to **GND (Pin 6)** on the Raspberry Pi.
- **DIO (Data)**: Connect to **GPIO17 (Pin 11)** on the Raspberry Pi.
- **CLK (Clock)**: Connect to **GPIO27 (Pin 13)** on the Raspberry Pi.

Step 3: Install Required Software

To control the TM1637 display, you'll need a Python library. The **tm1637** Python library makes it easy to interface with the display.

1. Open the terminal on your Raspberry Pi.

Install the **tm1637** library using `pip`:

```
sudo pip3 install tm1637
```

Step 4: Create the Python Script to Display Numbers

4.1 Open the Terminal

Open the terminal to create a Python script.

4.2 Create the Python Script

Use **Nano** to create a new Python script:

```
nano display_numbers.py
```

4.3 Write the Python Code

Paste the following Python code to control the 4-digit LED display:

```python
import tm1637
import time
from machine import Pin

# Set up the display (CLK: GPIO27, DIO: GPIO17)
tm = tm1637.TM1637(clk=Pin(27), dio=Pin(17))

# Brightness level (0 to 7)
tm.brightness(1)

# Function to display a countdown
def countdown():
    for i in range(9999, -1, -1):
        tm.number(i)   # Display the current number
        time.sleep(0.5)   # Wait for 0.5 seconds

# Main loop to run the countdown
try:
    countdown()

except KeyboardInterrupt:
    tm.show('----')   # Clear display when interrupted
```

4.4 Save the Script

To save the script:

- Press `Ctrl + X` to exit Nano.
- Press `Y` to confirm saving.
- Press `Enter` to save the file as **display_numbers.py**.

Step 5: Run the Python Script

5.1 Run the Script

To run the script, type:

```
python3 display_numbers.py
```

5.2 Watch the Display

The 4-digit LED display will show a countdown from 9999, updating every 0.5 seconds. You can modify the countdown speed by changing the `time.sleep()` value.

Step 6: Customize the Script

You can modify the script to display different types of information, such as sensor data or even the current time.

6.1 Example: Display a Custom Message or Number

Here's how you can modify the script to show a specific number or word

```
# Display a custom number
tm.number(1234)

# Display individual characters or words
tm.write([0x6D, 0x4F, 0x3F, 0x00])  # Shows "LO" (letters are limited
on 7-segment displays)
```

Common Mistakes

1. **Incorrect Wiring**: Make sure the **DIO** and **CLK** pins are connected to the correct GPIO pins on the Raspberry Pi.
2. **No Display**: If the display doesn't light up, ensure it's connected to **3.3V** and **GND** properly, and check the wiring.

Troubleshooting Tips

- **No Numbers Showing?**: Double-check that the wiring matches the GPIO pins used in the script.
- **Flickering Display**: If the display flickers, try reducing the update frequency by increasing the delay in `time.sleep()`.

Expansion Ideas

Once you've mastered displaying numbers, try expanding your project:

- **Display Sensor Data**: Show real-time sensor readings (e.g., temperature or distance) on the display.
- **Clock or Timer**: Create a countdown timer or a digital clock using the 4-digit display.
- **Interactive Controls**: Add buttons to control what's displayed (e.g., increase or decrease a counter).

Tip: Start by displaying simple numbers, like a countdown, and once you're comfortable with that, you can move on to more advanced features like displaying sensor data or using the display in interactive projects!

10.2 Using an LCD with Raspberry Pi

An **LCD (Liquid Crystal Display)** is a screen that can display text or numbers, making it a great tool for showing information like sensor data, messages, or project status. A common type is the **16x2 LCD**, which can display two lines of text with 16 characters each.

Why Use an LCD?
An LCD makes it easy to display dynamic information, such as temperature readings, time, or custom messages. It's perfect for projects where you want real-time feedback without needing a computer screen.

Step-by-Step Guide: Using a 16x2 LCD with Raspberry Pi

Step 1: Gather Your Components

You will need:

- **Raspberry Pi** (any model with GPIO pins)
- **16x2 LCD display** (with an I2C backpack to simplify wiring)
- **Jumper wires** (Male to Female)
- **Breadboard** (optional, for easier wiring)

Step 2: Wiring the LCD to the Raspberry Pi

If your 16x2 LCD has an **I2C backpack**, it simplifies the connection to just four wires.

2.1 Connect the LCD

- **VCC**: Connect to **5V (Pin 2)** on the Raspberry Pi.
- **GND**: Connect to **GND (Pin 6)** on the Raspberry Pi.
- **SDA**: Connect to **GPIO2 (Pin 3)** on the Raspberry Pi.
- **SCL**: Connect to **GPIO3 (Pin 5)** on the Raspberry Pi.

Step 3: Enable I2C on the Raspberry Pi

Before using the LCD, you need to enable the **I2C interface** on the Raspberry Pi.

1.   Open the terminal on your Raspberry Pi.

Run the following command to open the configuration tool:
`sudo raspi-config`

2.   Go to **Interfacing Options** > **I2C** > **Enable**.

Reboot your Raspberry Pi:
`sudo reboot`

Step 4: Install the Required Software

To communicate with the LCD, you need to install a Python library.

Open the terminal and install the **smbus** and **I2C-tools** packages:

```
sudo apt-get install python3-smbus i2c-tools
```

Install the **Adafruit LCD library**:

```
sudo pip3 install adafruit-circuitpython-charlcd
```

Step 5: Create the Python Script to Display Text

5.1 Open the Terminal

Open the terminal on your Raspberry Pi.

5.2 Create the Python Script

Use **Nano** to create a new Python script:

```
nano lcd_display.py
```

5.3 Write the Python Code

Paste this code to display text on the LCD:

```python
import board
import busio
import adafruit_character_lcd.character_lcd_i2c as character_lcd

# LCD setup
lcd_columns = 16
lcd_rows = 2

# Initialize I2C bus and LCD object
i2c = busio.I2C(board.SCL, board.SDA)
lcd = character_lcd.Character_LCD_I2C(i2c, lcd_columns, lcd_rows)

# Display a message on the LCD
lcd.message = "Hello, World!\nWelcome to Pi!"

# Keep the message displayed for 5 seconds
time.sleep(5)

# Clear the display
lcd.clear()
```

5.4 Save the Script

To save the script:

- Press Ctrl + X to exit Nano.
- Press Y to confirm saving.
- Press Enter to save the file as **lcd_display.py**.

Step 6: Run the Python Script

6.1 Run the Script

To run the script, type:

```
python3 lcd_display.py
```

6.2 Watch the LCD

The LCD will display the message:

```
Hello, World!
Welcome to Pi!
```

Step 7: Customize the Script

You can modify the script to display different messages or dynamic data, such as sensor readings or real-time information.

7.1 Example: Display Sensor Data

If you have a temperature sensor connected, you can display the temperature on the LCD:

```
# Assume 'temperature' is the value from a
temperature sensor
temperature = 23.5
lcd.message = f"Temp: {temperature:.1f}C\nStay
Cool!"
```

Common Mistakes

1. **No Display**: If the LCD doesn't display anything, double-check the wiring and ensure that the I2C interface is enabled.

2. **Wrong Address**: Run `i2cdetect -y 1` in the terminal to check the I2C address of your LCD. If it's not **0x27**, update the code to match the correct address.

Troubleshooting Tips

- **Blank Screen**: If the screen is blank, make sure the **contrast** on the LCD is adjusted properly. Some modules have a small potentiometer that you can turn to adjust contrast.
- **No Text Displayed**: Ensure that the I2C pins (SDA and SCL) are correctly connected and that the LCD address is set correctly in the code.

Expansion Ideas

Once you're comfortable displaying simple messages, try adding more functionality to your project:

- **Display Sensor Data**: Show real-time sensor readings (e.g., temperature, humidity) on the LCD.
- **Interactive Display**: Use buttons to change the message or switch between different types of data.
- **Scrolling Text**: Implement scrolling text to display longer messages that don't fit on the screen.

Tip: Start by displaying simple messages like "Hello, World!" and once you've mastered that, you can move on to dynamic data like sensor readings or custom messages that update in real-time!

10.3 Using an OLED Display with Raspberry Pi

An **OLED (Organic Light-Emitting Diode) display** is a small, bright display perfect for showing text, numbers, or even simple graphics. It uses less power than traditional displays and offers sharp contrast, making it ideal for projects like clocks, sensor monitors, or mini dashboards.

Why Use an OLED Display?

OLEDs are great for displaying clear and bright information in your Raspberry Pi projects. They're perfect for building interactive displays, showing sensor data, or even creating a mini game interface.

Step-by-Step Guide: Using an OLED Display with Raspberry Pi

Step 1: Gather Your Components

You will need:

- **Raspberry Pi** (any model with GPIO pins)
- **0.96" I2C OLED Display** (common type, 128x64 pixels)
- **Jumper wires** (Male to Female)
- **Breadboard** (optional, for easier wiring)

Step 2: Wiring the OLED Display to the Raspberry Pi

The OLED display uses **I2C** communication, so it requires only four connections.

2.1 Connect the OLED

- **VCC**: Connect to **3.3V (Pin 1)** on the Raspberry Pi.
- **GND**: Connect to **GND (Pin 6)** on the Raspberry Pi.
- **SDA**: Connect to **GPIO2 (Pin 3)** on the Raspberry Pi.

- **SCL**: Connect to **GPIO3 (Pin 5)** on the Raspberry Pi.

Step 3: Enable I2C on the Raspberry Pi

Before using the OLED, you need to enable the **I2C interface** on the Raspberry Pi.

1. Open the terminal on your Raspberry Pi.

Run the following command to open the configuration tool:

```
sudo raspi-config
```

2. Go to **Interfacing Options** > **I2C** > **Enable**.

Reboot your Raspberry Pi:

```
sudo reboot
```

Step 4: Install Required Software

To control the OLED display, you'll need the **Python Imaging Library (Pillow)** and **Adafruit SSD1306** library.

Open the terminal and install the required libraries:

```
sudo apt-get update
sudo apt-get install python3-pip python3-pil python3-numpy
```

Install the **Adafruit SSD1306** and **Adafruit CircuitPython** libraries:

```
sudo pip3 install adafruit-circuitpython-ssd1306
```

Step 5: Create the Python Script to Display Text

5.1 Open the Terminal

Open the terminal on your Raspberry Pi.

5.2 Create a Python Script

Use **Nano** to create a new Python script:

```
nano oled_display.py
```

5.3 Write the Python Code

Paste this code to display text on the OLED:

```python
import board
import digitalio
import adafruit_ssd1306
from PIL import Image, ImageDraw, ImageFont

# OLED display setup (128x64 pixels)
i2c = board.I2C()
oled = adafruit_ssd1306.SSD1306_I2C(128, 64, i2c)

# Clear the display
oled.fill(0)
oled.show()

# Create blank image for drawing
image = Image.new("1", (oled.width, oled.height))

# Get drawing object to draw on the image
draw = ImageDraw.Draw(image)

# Load a font
font = ImageFont.load_default()

# Display message
draw.text((0, 0), "Hello, World!", font=font, fill=255)
draw.text((0, 20), "Welcome to Pi", font=font, fill=255)

# Display image on OLED
oled.image(image)
oled.show()
```

5.4 Save the Script

To save the script:

- Press `Ctrl + X` to exit Nano.
- Press `Y` to confirm saving.
- Press `Enter` to save the file as **oled_display.py**.

Step 6: Run the Python Script

6.1 Run the Script

To run the script, type

```
python3 oled_display.py
```

6.2 Watch the OLED Display

The OLED display will show:

```
Hello, World!
Welcome to Pi
```

Step 7: Customize the Script

You can modify the script to display different messages or sensor data.

7.1 Example: Display Sensor Data

If you have a temperature sensor connected, you can display the temperature on the OLED:

```
# Assume 'temperature' is the value from a
temperature sensor
```

```
temperature = 23.5
draw.text((0, 0), f"Temp: {temperature:.1f}C",
font=font, fill=255)
```

7.2 Example: Display Images

You can also display simple graphics, like icons or custom drawings, using the **PIL** library.

Common Mistakes

1. **No Display**: If the OLED doesn't display anything, double-check the wiring and ensure the I2C interface is enabled.
2. **Wrong Address**: Run `i2cdetect -y 1` to check the I2C address of your OLED. If it's not **0x3C**, update the script to match the correct address.

Troubleshooting Tips

- **Blank Screen**: If nothing appears on the screen, make sure the power (VCC) and ground (GND) connections are correct.
- **No I2C Response**: If `i2cdetect -y 1` doesn't show the OLED, check the SDA and SCL connections.

Expansion Ideas

Once you're comfortable displaying simple text, try adding more functionality:

- **Real-Time Data**: Display sensor readings (e.g., temperature, humidity) in real-time.

- **Interactive Display**: Use buttons to change what's displayed (e.g., switching between sensor data or a clock).
- **Graphics and Icons**: Display simple graphics like battery icons or custom logos.

Tip: Start by displaying simple messages like "Hello, World!" and once you've mastered that, you can move on to more advanced features like displaying sensor data, graphics, or creating interactive projects!